How Horses Learn

How Horses Learn

Which training methods work and why

DR DEBBIE MARSDEN BSc, PhD

J. A. Allen

© *Dr Debbie Marsden, 2005*
First published in Great Britain 2005

ISBN 0 85131 877 0

J.A. Allen
Clerkenwell House
Clerkenwell Green
London EC1R 0HT

J.A. Allen is an imprint of Robert Hale Limited

The right of Debbie Marsden to be identified as author
of this work has been asserted by her in accordance
with the Copyright, Designs and Patents Act 1988

A catalogue record for this book is available from the British Library

Design by Judy Linard
Edited by John Beaton
Colour separation by Tenon & Polert Colour Scanning Limited, Hong Kong
Printed in China by New Era Printing Co. Limited

Contents

Acknowledgements 7

1 The ABC of Learning 9

2 Rewards, Punishment and Motivation 31

3 Training and Time 79

4 The Learning Process 101

5 Learning to Respond 131

6 Learning Not to Respond and 'Un-learning' 153

7 Practical Re-training Techniques 169

8 Maximizing Your Horse's Learning Potential 187

Appendix 219

Index 221

Acknowledgements

I should first of all thank my parents for my first pony, a 13:2 Arab who at the age of four taught his eight-year-old 'owner' a great deal – mostly about what not to do – as well as my farrier grandfather who picked up the pieces more than once! I also owe more that I can ever say to Mrs Monica McClintock, Mrs Pat McTavish and Mr Billy Patton who gave me super horses to ride and taught me that there were many different ways of doing most things equestrian.

I was lucky enough to be introduced to the science of animal behaviour by the enthusiastic Professor Aubrey Manning and guided and encouraged with great skill and kindness through further studies by the late Professor David Wood-Gush. I hope he would approve of this contribution towards further understanding between horse and rider.

I have also learned a great deal over the years from my dear customers and their wonderful horses 'naughty' and otherwise, and am most grateful to all for their support and encouragement while scribbling away. Alison Morris and Cathleen Baldwin in particular deserve a special mention for doing their best to organise me throughout. I am indebted to the equestrian journalist Jo Sharples whose idea it was for my 'sound bite' explanations to be written down as a book available to all and a special thank-you is also due to John Beaton for his encouragement and useful comments throughout the inception and editorial processes and in particular for his grace and patience while awaiting final delivery of both manuscript and illustrations!

I am very grateful to all who helped with photos, and would like in particular to thank Cathleen Baldwin, Angie Black and Ellie, Mary Booth, Laura Fleming and Patsy, Nick Foot, Fiona Ingram and Noir, Ian MacDonald, Lindsay McFadzean, Dilys and Sandra Macmillan and Pyrrhus, Alison Morris and Merlin, Eveanne Nicholson and Dee, Karin Oberländer and Farina,

Frances Pearson, Katie Pearson and Rhona and Tilly, Justin Rose DWCF, Peter and Margaret Rothan, Michelle Rushen, Katy Telfer, Sophie Telfer and Tickles, Louise Turnbull and Ziggy, and Patricia Veall, Reiver and Zar.

Finally, I would like to dedicate this book to Ian, without whose filling of hay nets and faithful checking and feeding of horses it could not have been completed.

AUTHOR'S NOTE

Please note that some names and other history details have been changed in order to protect the anonymity of my clients whose cases were used in the examples given.

Chapter 1

The ABC of Learning

Learning for most of us begins with ABC and with horses it's just the same.

- A stands for Antecedents — This is what happens just before the horse does something.
- B stands for Behaviour — This is what the horse actually does.
- C stands for Consequences — This is what happens to the horse immediately afterwards.

Learning is the process by which particular or specific _Antecedents_, _Behaviour_ and _Consequences_ become linked with each other and remembered in that order by the horse. A, B, and C have to follow each other in that order for learning to work, just like the alphabet!

In order to get the best results when training your horse, it helps to understand some of the more important features of each part of this ABC of learning. Knowing which features allow an event to be recognized by your horse as an _Antecedent_ or as a _Consequence_ allows you to set these up more effectively to directly encourage and reward desirable _Behaviour_ when training. This knowledge is also necessary to help you unravel the mysteries of how a learned behaviour problem may have developed, by helping you recognize the specific elements of any situation which represent the _Antecedents_ and _Consequences_ for undesirable _Behaviour_. This is often the key to solving behaviour and performance problems. Being able to identify and use _Antecedents_ and _Consequences_ correctly is a vital part of understanding your horse's _Behaviour_, whether you want to train towards international level competition performances or build a relationship which will allow you to handle your horse with confidence and enjoy a quiet hack without near death experiences.

ANTECEDENTS

The _Antecedent_ is what happens just before a horse does something. In the context of a behaviour problem, the _Antecedent_ is the situation in which the problem occurs and particularly the specific event just before the problem behaviour begins. One of the most important features of _Antecedents_ to remember is that, while any situation or event which precedes the behaviour we are interested in will be made up of many elements, only one specific element will be particularly noticed by the horse and becomes the trigger or _stimulus_ for the ensuing learned behaviour. Whatever this is, to function as part of an _Antecedent_, it must be perceptible to the horse and important or easily discernible to the horse. Therefore in order to recognize and use _Antecedents_, we have to think about the world from the horse's point of view and be aware of differences in the physiology of perception between us and horses. The relative timing of any _Antecedent_ event and the action of the horse is also critical for any effective and lasting links to be made in the horse's mind between the _Antecedent_ and his _Behaviour_. The _Antecedent_ event must immediately precede the horse's actions without any interruptions for these to become linked and for learning to take place.

Specificity and Stimuli

An antecedent event consists of many possible elements, often occurring simultaneously and a horse will take particular notice of one of these. For example, where the _Antecedent_ is an event such as an apple falling from a tree, three different elements which may be noticed by a horse could be a small cracking sound, the rustle of leaves, or a flash of red streaking to the ground. Any of these elements could be the one which the horse last notices just before he does something such as leaping sideways.

To give a practical example, when clipping a horse, if he is burnt by the clipper head just after it gets clogged and tugs his hair, he will become frightened of the altered feel with more vibration from the struggling motor. He may react adversely thereafter to the vibrations and feel of the clippers, but not the noise, as the noise has been going on for some time without being of any particular importance to him. The noise is an insignificant element of the _Antecedent_ events here. Alternatively, if his skin is nicked as soon as the clippers touch him, he may become frightened of the sound of the clippers close to him and react adversely when anyone approaches him with clippers, as this is what happened just before the pain.

Thus, one specific element of the _Antecedent_ becomes the _stimulus_ or trigger for the behaviour – a fear response in this case – and it is important to isolate the specific trigger for that fear before trying to retrain the horse to tolerate clipping or any other procedure which has upset him.

Pinpointing the exact element of the _Antecedent_ events involved in any learned behaviour problem can be difficult and may require a lot of detective work in real life, as just about any aspect of the world around the horse could be the specific stimulus involved in a bit of learned behaviour. Previous experiences can also make an individual horse much more sensitive to particular stimuli than others.

An unusual early experience was at the root of the problem in one of my cases in which a racehorse called Bindra, which had previously done very well indeed, had occasionally frozen at the start of a race before continuing to complete the race in great style but of course no longer in with a chance! The owner Mr K was understandably very concerned about this, as after the third time, the Jockey Club were no longer going to allow this horse to race. The behaviour could have been very dangerous to the other riders and their horses and of course greatly upset the betting fraternity.

No pattern had been found to the races in which this had happened. The problem was not associated with the jockey, the course, the going, the weather, the kind of start, amount of travelling, time of day, feed or water provided etc. He had frozen twice in the same way when training. This horse had had every veterinary examination and physical check-up known to man and no obvious medical reason for the sudden 'freezing' was found. I was asked to investigate to see if this was a 'psychological' problem.

I noticed that Bindra had unusually immature social behaviour and that he seemed very cautious of horses around the yard with which he was not very familiar. In particular he seemed overly submissive towards chestnut horses, always moving out of their way.

After a great deal of checking, and reviewing as many of his races as were available on video, a pattern began to emerge. Bindra froze when a chestnut horse started on his right and cut across him in the first furlong. When the freezing episodes had occurred during training, a new and chestnut horse was out with him in his group. Bizarre as this detail seemed, it was critical to understanding Bindra's problem. He did not have the social skills necessary to tell the difference between a horse just cutting across him for convenience and one which was doing this to threaten him into social deference. Being a sensible and perhaps rather cautious chap, Bindra chose to err on the side of safety and wait politely until any strange chestnut horse was well out of his way before continuing! He was more afraid of making an equine social gaff than disobeying the jockey's frantic attempts to get him going.

It transpired that while a youngster, Bindra had been badly kicked by a chestnut horse. We can assume that on that occasion the chestnut horse regarded itself as his social superior and probably cut across him from his right. He should have noticed all the social signals this horse would have given him, and waited or moved away, but he didn't and this extreme experience left him very sensitive to the specific stimulus of a chestnut horse cutting in front of him from the right. Coupled with his naturally poor social skills, and a relatively low frequency of chestnut horses in the racehorse population this led to the presenting problem. We gave him a winter of 'nursery school', living loose housed with yearlings to let him develop his equine social skills with others at the same stage of social development, where gaffs would be tolerated and forgiven while the youngsters worked out how to treat each other. He than had further training , using *counter-conditioning* (see Chapter 7) to teach him that chestnut horses were actually quite nice! Mr K was delighted when the Jockey Club allowed Bindra to race again.

Particular experiences apart, the *stimulus* or trigger element of the <u>Antecedent</u> event might simply be the last one which comes to his attention just before a horse does something, or something very nice or very horrid happens to him, but it is more usually the one which is most likely to grab his attention, for example by being the most novel or noticeable feature of the ongoing events.

Novelty of any kind is always worth paying attention to in a gentle creature of habit such as the horse.

For example, I had a case where a pony called Blue created a major rift in the P family, by shying violently at a newspaper headline board every day. Mr P was very concerned that Miss P would be seriously hurt someday. The newsagent's shop was at a very busy junction with the main road they were turning into curving left, making a blind corner. Motorists ignoring the 'twenty's plenty' signs came dangerously close to finding a solid little Highland rump on their car bonnet. Mr P wanted to sell the pony. Mrs P was adamant that Blue was in every other way a super little pony and that he would get used to the newspaper stand if they went past it every day. This was the only route from their home and Blue's paddock to a local Country Park where he could be ridden safely. Miss P was also very keen to keep Blue as he was her first pony and she absolutely adored him.

I spoke to the newsagent, who was very understanding and keen to help as the P family and their friends and neighbours were also his customers. He kindly let us borrow a headline stand and we duly set off with that day's headline sheet to set up our *habituation* retraining programme (see Chapter 6). We duly placed the stand in his field for a while and then beside the tie-up point in their back garden where Blue was fed and groomed. After a long weekend of leading and riding Blue up and down his paddock and drive he duly began to ignore the stand and went quietly past it. Mrs P was very pleased.

However, much to her horror, as soon as Miss P took Blue down the road, he immediately shied at the newsagent's stand as usual. Mrs P was very disappointed and Miss P almost in tears with visions of Daddy putting Blue in the 'free to a good home' section of the paper the next day. I wondered whether we had mistaken the *stimulus* and perhaps we had missed something else nearby which was causing the problem.

I went back to investigate further. On observation it seemed to me that Blue really was peering intently at the headline board before his nifty piece of lateral work. Then I realised, the headlines were different! Of course Blue was not really reading, although no doubt Highland pony aficionados would probably tell you they could. However, any horse could easily distinguish between letter shapes and would realize that these were different each day! So we had to continue the retraining using lots of different headline sheets, (including *counter-conditioning* to a change of headline see Chapter 7). To speed things up, Miss P had great fun writing her own 'family' news headlines on the blanks the newsagent kindly provided, so this story had a happy ending after all.

Sounds which are short and sharp in duration, with high pitch and are repeated with increasing pitch and increasing frequency are those most likely to be noticed by a horse, as these kinds of sounds are very arousing to his natural instincts, being features of alarm calls and other important forms of vocal communication between horses. Interestingly, most people instinctively tap into this and make the sounds they use to get the horse's attention in a similar form. You will no doubt have heard (or made!) that tongue in cheek clicking noise made by a desperate rider trying to encourage forwards movement when schooling or even in a dressage test. Listen next time and you will hear that this increasing pitch and frequency is the kind of pattern in which these 'gee up' and attention seeking noises are made. This is also the reason why a 'clicker' noise is used in 'clicker training' (see Chapter 5). Similarly a horse's attention will also naturally be riveted to bright colours, shiny or flashing sights, like the eyes of a predator as it makes its initial leap. This is why most horses are more 'spooky' on a bright sunny and breezy day. Movement of any kind is very eye-catching to a horse for the same reason – even a tiny movement very far away, such as a wren flying out of a hedge a quarter of a mile along the road or a micro-dot sized sheep or a hill walker decked out in purple and yellow several miles away across the valley.

On the positive side, when riding and training your horse to respond to your aids in the desirable way, it can help that they are so responsive to the world around them, including the tiniest of changes in our breathing and balance. However, this also means that it is vital that the aids used are given in exactly the same clear and consistent manner each time and that different aids are clearly distinguishable from the horse's point of view. Not too many of us have the brain/body awareness and degree of control over our balance and body movements, especially the lower leg, hand and seat, that we would like. Many ridden evasions develop as the rider is unaware that they are accidentally altering their position or contact in a way which encourages the horse to produce the evasion. So when I am instructing, I spend a lot of time helping riders feel and become aware of the signals they are giving their horse. A tiny change in the way they ride is often all that is required to fix even quite dramatic evasions. This is why it is well worth having regular riding lessons and spending some of your riding time working on your own position and body movements, so that you have better awareness and control over the signals you are giving the horse.

Most of us use only a few different leg aids as signals to mean 'go', 'steady', 'bend' and 'move over' etc. For dressage above Elementary level, it is necessary to give a greater number of different signals quickly and easily. This is what spurs are for; enabling the rider to use their leg in a greater variety of ways, touching the horse in different areas, in order to give a greater number of more precise signals. Even top level riders strive to improve their riding skills by working to monitor and control their own body movements. This is why the famous Spanish riding school in Vienna has so many mirrors – they are not just there for admiring how the horses are moving! There is also usually an experienced instructor in the arena when these fabulous horses are being schooled to keep an eye on things and to make sure that even these most excellent riders remain balanced and are not accidentally giving the wrong signals as <u>A</u>ntecedent *stimuli* to their horses.

Perceptibility

Most importantly for any event to work as the *stimulus* element of an <u>A</u>ntecedent event, it has to be something which the horse can see or hear or feel. So the first thing that trainers need to remember about *stimuli* is that the only events that can be considered as *stimuli* are those which are perceptible to the horse. Horses have much better sight and hearing than us and are therefore much more sensitive to the world around them than we are. This can sometimes pose a problem, as your horse may notice something which you cannot hear or see. If this becomes the *stimulus* element of <u>A</u>ntecedent events, it may be very difficult for us to recognize. Anyone who has ever hacked out on a sharp horse along the road will be amazed at the degree of attention their horse pays to things which are quite harmless, very far away or sometimes not even perceptible to the unfortunate rider. I have come across many frustrated riders in this situation who are referred to me after they have asked their vet to check out their horse's eyesight! It may seem to an exhausted rider that their horse is seeing ghosts as they cannot see anything of interest which might be upsetting him – which is of course why we call this 'spooking'!

Horses have much more sensitive palettes than us and can detect tiny

Fig 1.1. This pony is acquiring a taste for the finer things in life!

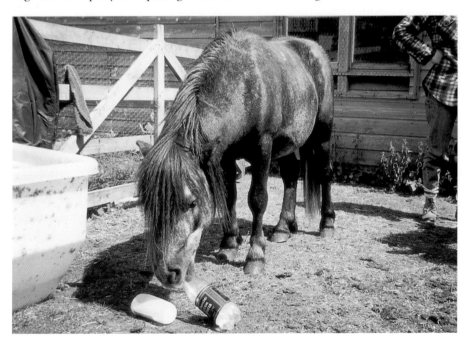

amounts of chemicals for example in water by the taste. We cannot make a machine which is as sensitive. Your horse may find enough nasty elements dissolving out of the air from evaporated urine in his water as to refuse to drink what seems to be perfectly clean and fresh water to us. These elements settle in automatic water drinkers and water buckets if they are filled up and left to stand in the recently mucked out stable all day. Most horses will tolerate this, some do not. Figure 1.1. shows a rather expensive solution, and it is generally much nicer for your horse if buckets are left to dry all day and filled just before he comes in. Often it is the taste not the hissing or 'squirty' noises which puts some horses off automatic drinkers. You can continue to enjoy the convenience of the automatic system and encourage these horses to use them by adding a strong and pleasant flavour such as few drops of peppermint or lemon oil, or tiny drops of almond or vanilla essence etc each day. This is also useful for horses who do not like drinking water away from home, as they are often reacting with understandable caution to a strange taste.

Horses can hear sounds of much lower and much higher frequency than us (up to 25 KHz). For comparison, most human speech varies between 2 and 4 KHz, and interestingly so do the sounds horses make, with a 'squeal' measuring around 4 KHz and a 'nicker' around 2 KHz. They are naturally very aroused by ground vibrations known as 'p' waves that we cannot feel. This helps them avoid unsafe ground and escape minor earth tremors, common in the areas in which it is thought horses evolved. This is partly why so many horses get jumpy with heavy vehicles and garden machinery. Your horse can probably hear a mouse tiptoeing through the grass 50m away. Most horses can discriminate between pitches differing by one seventh of a tone, between frequencies of ninety-six and one hundred beats per minute and loudness between sixty-nine and seventy decibels. Most horses can detect a difference in rhythm of one eighth the difference between two standard metronome settings. It's perhaps just as well most people and the average dressage judge can't!

Horses can also see further into the infra red spectrum than we can and have much better visual acuity than us in the green/yellow part of the spectrum. This is very important for a grazing animal to help them distinguish between poisonous and less nutritious plants and those it is good to eat. On the down side for the horse, they are not as good as people in judging distance and speed, as their eyes are arranged to maximize 'panoramic vigilance', because in the wild they are a target and very useful meal for many predators. We see the world a little differently, as human eyes are arranged to help measure distance and speed, as we evolved needing to hunt prey to eat. Predators (like us!) also need eyes which adjust quickly to changes in light when leaping out of the bushes, but this is much less useful to a browser and prey animal like the horse. Horses' eyes take approximately thirty times longer than ours to adjust to variations in light and dark, which is why most horses get a little jumpy in the shadows, particularly where light and shade alternate frequently as when walking along a woodland path or in some indoor schools. However, the 'upside' of this difference in physiology is that horses can generally see much better than us in poor light levels i.e. at dawn and dusk and those dull grey winter days.

You are probably familiar with the tragic tale of 'Clever Hans', a little horse who entertained audiences long ago by counting out the answers to sums posed by his trainer. Unfortunately for both, the trainer did not understand how Hans knew how many times to strike the floor with his hoof to give the answers, adamant that he was not giving Hans any signals at all as a clue to the correct number. However, Hans would not perform without his trainer being there. He was accused of witchcraft and both were killed. Later other horses were discovered who could perform similar tricks and studies in Russia found that they could only perform correctly if these horses had an audience who knew the answer. These horses were responding to subtle changes in the audience's breathing or body language as they approached the correct answer, and it was likely that 'Clever Hans' was also responding in a similar way to signals his trainer was not aware he was giving out. As horses are very highly sociable animals, it should not be surprising that they pick up tiny clues like this from us, and you should remember that communication between horse and trainer or rider is always a two way process. You may well have noticed that your horse behaves differently around you when you are feeling a bit low or under the weather – he is picking up on your body language clues about your mood. This can be beneficial and using this to improve your training is discussed further in Chapter 8.

In modern life, pinpointing the exact stimulus which triggers unwanted behaviour or provokes desirable behaviour can also be very difficult, but it is very important when training or problem solving and can often require quite a bit of detective work in itself.

A coloured Cob called Jigsaw perplexed his owner, Miss S, by very occasionally kicking his stable walls and pacing around his box in the morning to such an extent that he injured himself, finally to the point of needing stitches for a major hock wound. She could find no pattern to the days when this upset occurred and was concerned that the horse may be suffering some kind of sporadic fits, as in some forms of rare neuropathology. Her vet could find no physical signs of this when he examined the horse and he (and the insurance company) wanted to rule out a learned behaviour problem before committing the horse for further (very expensive!) tests, and so referred her to me.

I began to investigate, and indeed the days when the problem had appeared seemed indeed to be random, with exactly the same daily routine as on others where Jigsaw was his usual calm self. Feed and feeding time, turn-out, exercise, companions, weather, and all other aspects of husbandry and Jigsaw's life that we could think of were the same. Miss S kept a strict diary of each day in Jigsaw's life and even began creeping into the yard at 4 a.m. to keep watch and see if she could see or hear anything which might be upsetting Jigsaw. For ten days nothing happened and Jigsaw behaved beautifully. Then finally one morning he began to kick out at the back wall of his box, pacing and whirling around, sometimes crashing into the sides. The details described to me later were typical of frustration behaviour. Miss S distracted and settled Jigsaw, finally taking him out of the box to settle him. He seemed fine, alert and responsive, and rather keen on grabbing the pile of empty feed buckets left to dry from the night before. So, Miss S gave him (and the others) their morning feed back in his box where he now seemed fine. She was making her way in for her own breakfast rather dazed from all the excitement and half asleep, pondering on what on earth could have triggered this last episode, as she had heard and seen nothing that should have upset him. As she left the yard and crossed the lane to the house, she was nearly run over by the post van. Startled and to be honest as she later explained, really rather grumpy by now, she gave the postman 'a terrible row' and demanded to know 'What on earth he was doing there at such an ungodly hour?' i.e. 6.45 a.m. instead of the usual 8.00 a.m.. The unfortunate postman grovelled politely and explained that when there was no post for the farms to which her lane was one access route, it was easier for him to deliver her post before making his usual circuit in her area as this gave him a right turn into a very busy road before the rush hour. Usually, if these farms had post he continued, no doubt hoping to avoid this half crazed horsewoman making a formal complaint against him, he would have gone round the circuit, delivering to them via another road and returning past her house later with her post. She made some suitably indistinct grunt by way of acknowledgement and pottered off declining the handful of mail proffered through the van window and forcing the poor chap to get out and put it into the usual box.

Miss S recounted this sorry tale when I called later that day for a progress report, by which time she had begun to see how this encounter might have seemed from the postman's point of view and was wondering if she should call the depot to apologise. Slowly a light began to dawn. Around 8.00 a.m. was close to feeding time. Miss S came out of the house and began preparing the morning feeds around a quarter to eight. How often I wondered did the farms along the lane get no post. Could this coincide with the dates that Jigsaw had his 'tizzy fits'?

Several phone calls to the neighbours later, we had a plan. It turned out that the specific element of the morning pre feeding _Antecedent_ events that Jigsaw paid attention to was indeed the arrival of the postman. After a little experimentation, we discovered that Jigsaw could see the van coming along the main road from the window at the back of his box. There was a bright streak of red flashing in and out of the trees when the van was approximately ten minutes away. This was the stimulus that he had learned was associated with the imminent arrival of feed and on the few occasions when the post came at 6.45 a.m., Jigsaw duly expected to hear all the usual preparatory noises building up to his feed arriving shortly thereafter. When the expected preparations did not happen, he was understandably annoyed!

This theory fitted in with the nature of the problem behaviour, as kicking and pacing are often frustration related and can be caused by hormonal changes occurring in anticipation of a tasty feed. Armed with this knowledge, we were able to manage the problem in the first instance by feeding at 6.45 for a couple of weeks while an appropriate re-training programme was put into place to _extinguish_ this undesirable learned response (see Chapter 6).

Timing

It is often said that horses learn when they associate one thing with another happening at the same time. This is not strictly true, being a rather vague over-simplification. In order for the brain to make an accurate and clear link between any stimulus and subsequent actions, the _stimulus_ must be perceived by the horse just before the _Behaviour_ occurs. It is vital that the stimulus is perceived before and not at the same time as any action or _Consequence_. Many good trainers, who may not know much about learning theory, naturally give very clear signals in this way, thinking slowly, steadily and logically about what they are doing and what they are asking the horse to do.

The timing here is particularly critical and for learning to take place, the interval between any effective stimulus and the subsequent action needs to be less than about half a second. This is why some experienced riders are much more effective than novice riders, as with practice they have the physical skill and confidence to use the required aids in the correct sequence at the correct time. If you have to try to remember what your instructor or 'the book' said in the middle of a sequence of aids, the chances are you will lose fractions of seconds here, and end up applying the aid too late. So, before you try to train your horse you may first of all need to train yourself so that you can give the required signals at the right time (see more of this in Chapters 3 and 8).

Should anything interrupt the horse while his brain is processing the information from the stimulus and the feeling from his immediate actions, the link will be broken and he will not make the necessary association between the training stimulus and any desirable _Behaviour._ He may instead link the most noticeable aspect of the interruption to his subsequent activity and learn to respond to the wrong thing. Alternatively, the interruption, particularly if it is a common sight or sound with which the horse is very familiar, may cause a different reaction to that desired. He may link the original _stimulus_ with this undesirable activity thus developing a problem evasion. This is one reason why it helps to train in a peaceful and controlled environment where interruptions can be minimized (see Chapters 5 and 8).

While unscheduled _stimuli_ can be a nuisance, these can sometimes work for you.

> One of my clients momentarily lost her balance when working through some little grids in a jumping lesson. She listened to my instruction re feet forward and regained her balance immediately but not before shrieking a particular and common swear word! As the word fell on his ears within half a second before he took off for the next fence, her clever little horse linked this word with the bounce step the grid required him to do at this point. Ever since she has had a useful, if rather embarrassing, extra aid to getting out of trouble in tricky cross-country combinations!

Sometimes it just isn't practical to give an appropriate stimulus at the correct time, and there are a number of training techniques which work by linking a series of stimuli, such as _strings of stimuli_ or using a _bridging stimulus_, which is how 'Clicker Training' works. This is explained in Chapter 5 and more details on the importance and management of timing when training are given in Chapter 3.

BEHAVIOUR

Your horse's behaviour is the essential 'meat in the sandwich' of learning, the central part of the ABC of learning. He will respond to a _stimulus_ which is part of _Antecedent_ events and his _Behaviour_ or _response_ to this i.e. his immediate actions will result in either a pleasant or an unpleasant _Consequence_. Thus scientists often use the term _response_ when referring to a particular action or _Behaviour_, in the context of learning. You may have heard of the phrase '_stimulus-response_' when learning is discussed, and this is where it fits in to the whole learning process.

The most important aspect of your horse's _Behaviour_ in the context of learning is that he 'Does It Himself'.

DIY

It is your horse's _Behaviour_ and his own actions that matter here. For once it is not 'the thought that counts!' Some people think that animals can learn something just by watching others. This concept is called 'observational' learning. If horses could learn in this way, it would be very handy. For example, we would just have to take our horse to a Trec competition perhaps, and let him watch the top horses going through the obstacles or perhaps lengthening beautifully in a dressage test and save ourselves a lot of time and effort! Children do not learn to write by watching their teacher writing on the blackboard; they have to practise by tracing and actually trying to write the shapes of the letters themselves. It is exactly the same for your horse. Young horses do not learn to tolerate a rider on their back by watching other horses being ridden, they have to experience this for themselves before they get used to it. Scientists have studied the idea of

Fig 1.2. Unfortunately it is only the chestnut horse and not the grey which is learning to improve their trot work during this schooling session!

observational learning in horses and have never been able to prove that this occurs or demonstrates anything like it.

The idea that horses learn 'bad habits' such as crib-biting for example, by copying others is just not borne out in practice. This idea actually does a lot of damage as crib-biting is an inherited response to stress and isolating these horses by keeping them out of sight of the others is particularly upsetting to such a strongly social animal as the horse and only makes the crib-biting worse. The other horses do not copy this and start crib-biting in the same way – if they did we would find yards full of crib-biters all 'cribbing' in exactly the same way and we don't. The myth that 'cribbing' is copied probably comes from the slang meaning of this abbreviation. I believe that if 'observational learning' were possible in horses, our ancestors, many of whom relied for their lives on the obedience of their horses, would have worked this out. They would have built their stables around the school or manege, giving youngsters and 'problem' horses the best view! This does not happen and neither does 'observational' learning.

It is easy however to see how people could get the idea that this sort of thing does occur, but the apparent phenomenon of horses learning by copying each other can usually be explained in other ways.

I was giving a cross-country lesson one day to a couple of clients who often rode together as friends, Janice on Moo and Beverly on Catapult. Given those horse names, I was not anticipating an easy day but they both did very well over the training fences and quickly progressed to trying some of the smaller competition jumps around the course. There was one which looked deceptively easy but was placed on a very tricky line with a sloping take off on a slight curve, requiring the rider to place the horse very carefully. We had already practised 'holding a line' and they were keen to try this one. It was a good fence to test their newly acquired skills.

Moo who lived up to her name by generally holding back and requiring a lot of leg went first, with Beverly and Catapult looking on. Unfortunately for Janice, Moo dodged around the little log. After a brief discussion about what happened and a little extra placing of markers to help Janice 'ride the line', they made it over second time, actually in very good style care of some very determined leg work on Janice's part. Beverly set off with complacent abandon. Catapult also was well named as he was frightfully keen on his jumping and Beverley's main job with him was to steady him into a good rhythm and help him with early take-off points. However, much to Janice's quiet delight Catapult also dodged around the fence, at the same point in the same manner as Moo. Beverly was decidedly miffed but excused her horse by saying that he had just copied Moo and so it was really Moo's fault. I had to intervene, pointing out that the last thing he saw Moo do was actually jump it very well. I also reminded them that Moo had not learned to rush into fences and gallop off afterwards after watching Catapult do this at least twelve times in the past hour. Furthermore, Catapult had not learned to slow down and hesitate before each fence as he had seen Moo doing many times that afternoon.

I suggested that both riders had approached the fence without paying enough attention to the line we had discussed, as it seemed such an easy log. The course had been very cleverly designed to test the rider's ability to hold a line here with safety in mind as a run out at this point was of no more consequence than gaining faults. There were a number of reasons to do with the topography of the approach which encouraged both horses to evade in the same way, and the same riding techniques 'fixed' this evasion in both horses. I am happy to note here that both girls were still speaking to each other at the end of the lesson!

Whether the _Behaviour_ involved is a complex series of movements such as those needed to jump a fence or just a single step, the horse has to perform it himself in order for learning to occur.

I was once helping a friend get her foal used to travelling in a trailer, and we had reached the point of taking him out for short runs to nice exciting places. She was keen one day to use our training session to take him to wander around at a local show, where he would also get used to all the sights and sounds of this sort of thing (by the process of _habituation_ see Chapter 6). Everything had gone very well and we had had a lovely day out, with lots of admiring glances as it was a very cute little black foal. Fiona had led him easily up the ramp, but at the very top he had halted, and was having a last look around. He was quite a cheeky little character, and naturally a little reluctant to leave all the other horses for a lonely 'cave'. His attention was riveted on the fancy dress lap of honour, and while we waited for him to realize that this was actually very boring and that it would be much more fun to go and eat treats inside the trailer instead, two burly chaps came past with their prize-winning Clydesdale two-year-old. The colt was just dripping with ribbons, having won the in-hand Supreme Championship and they were in ebullient form themselves. They were also obviously very confident handlers and one of them leapt up the ramp, picked the wee foal up with one arm around his chest and the other around his rump and carried him into the trailer with a cheery 'There you go love' before we had time to do or say anything about it! We had to wait until we were sure he was well out of sight before we could take the foal out of the trailer and resume training, as we were sure he would think we were quite potty to let the foal back out again! However, there would have been no training benefit here. We needed the foal to decide to make the last step into the trailer himself, (a small step for a foal but a giant leap for our training programme), so that his brain could make the link between that action and the consequent reward. Thankfully, the fancy dress which had caught his attention was over, and this time he went in after just a few seconds' hesitation, so we were spared the embarrassment of trying to explain ourselves (and a little learning theory) to our jolly Glaswegian.

Patience here pays off, as it really is vital that the horse 'does it himself' and a great deal of the skill in training involves the setting up of an exercise (e.g. with poles or markers) or arranging fences (as in a grid) alongside handling and riding techniques all designed to encourage a horse to do something in the desirable way by himself. Successful trainers are very good at the practicalities of setting up the environment around a horse in this way; sometimes 'tricking' the horse into certain actions using his natural instincts (see more on this and *unconditioned stimuli* in Chapter 4). The horse has to make the necessary movements himself for the neural processing involved in learning to work properly (see more on brain and memory storage in Chapter 3).

CONSEQUENCES

If a horse does something which has a pleasant Consequence, he is more likely to do it again. If the action has an unpleasant Consequence, it is less likely to be repeated. For example, a horse which jumps into the next door field and has a lovely half hour munching long juicy grass will be more likely to try this again, whereas if he got caught up and injured by the fence, he will be less likely to try to jump it again. Indeed he may be put off jumping anything or obstacles like that fence (by the process called *generalization* see Chapter 5). This tendency, to repeat actions which have a good Consequence and not to repeat those with a bad Consequence, is a key element of learning, based on how a horse's brain works and the way in which information is processed. This also explains why it is often 'third time lucky' as the third time the horse does an action with a pleasant _Consequence_ is actually the first repeat of a predictably positive experience.

First experiences here are of particular importance. The timing of a _Consequence_ in relation to _Behaviour_ is just as critical as with _Antecedents_. Furthermore, the extent of the _Consequence_ of any action is also important, as a very bad or traumatic experience will generally only have to occur once for learning to take place, whereas lesser aversive experiences may require more repeats before your horse learns not to do the action associated with these. Consistency is vital, as it is very confusing and indeed stressful for a horse if an action sometimes has a pleasant _Consequence_, sometimes has an unpleasant _Consequence_ or sometimes is of no _Consequence_ at all.

First experiences

Due to the arousing effect of novelty, learning is particularly facilitated when a horse attempts anything for the first time. The _Consequences_ of this first experience are particularly important, and it is true that 'first impressions count'.

For example, if a young horse's first experience of an apple was a nice one, getting a lovely sweet juicy taste when he bit into the apple, he would be much more likely to approach and quickly bite into the next apple he saw. However, if the apple he bit into at first was a rotten one with a wasp inside and he got a nasty sting instead of the sweet juicy taste, the poor horse would be less likely to even approach, never mind bite into the next apple he saw. Indeed he might even run away next time he notices an apple on the ground!

This is part of a horse's natural survival mechanisms, helping him avoid dangerous situations and making sure he is much less likely to repeat any action which resulted in an unpleasant _Consequence_. This can be a nuisance for us, if our horse inadvertently has a bad experience on his first encounter with something which we would like him to accept, such as traffic, or a vet or farrier for example. It is often worthwhile making the effort to ensure that the first visit from those who might later have to do something which the horse may find uncomfortable at the time, but is necessary for his health and longer term comfort, is a social one i.e. when they are perhaps passing or at the yard to deal with another horse they give your horse a pat and a treat. This pleasant first encounter will make it much easier to get your horse used to any later professional visits (see more about the learning process of _habituation_ and the training system promoted as 'imprinting' in Chapter 6).

Because of the importance of the first experience here, it is best if you can make sure that your horse's first experience of activities where problems often arise is a good one e.g. perhaps by seeking professional assistance with backing, starting jumping, or loading and travelling etc. and even simply asking someone whose horse is obedient and familiar with the area to accompany you on your first hack from a new yard.

If the worst happens and your horse inadvertently has had a really bad experience, the good news is that all learning is reversible and with properly qualified professional advice and assistance and enough time and effort, you should be able to help your horse get over it (see Chapters 7 and 8).

Timing

Just as for _Antecedents_, the timing of a _Consequence_ in relation to any _Behaviour_ is critical if the horse is to make the required link between his actions and the _Consequence_ of these. The _Consequence_ must be perceived by the horse within approximately half a second of his _Behaviour_ for learning to take place.

Furthermore, it is vital that the horse perceives the _Consequence_ as a direct result of his own _Behaviour_. This is a common point at which misunderstandings between horse and owner occur in training. For example, if a horse moves obediently to the back of the box when asked, but then moves towards his owner while she fumbles in her pocket for a reward treat, she is actually teaching him that backing up is of no _Consequence_ but coming up to her and nudging her pocket is the action with the pleasant _Consequence_. It is better to have the treat handy and throw it to the back of the box just after asking him to back up. Alternatively, a rider who becomes unbalanced when jumping and momentarily 'jabs' the horse in the mouth will be inadvertently giving her horse an unpleasant _Consequence_, making him less likely to jump and bascule properly next time, and leading to those awkward cat leaps as he tries to jump avoiding a 'jab' in the mouth.

I recently witnessed an unfortunate child struggling to get a smug little strawberry roan into canter during a lesson at a Pony Club rally. Eventually 'wee Jennie' gave up and turned into the centre, pale and exhausted. A tight-lipped Mum dashed across, much to the young instructor's chagrin and stood there, jerking the rein, tugging Jennie's sleeve and giving both her and Rowan a row. She issued a screed of instructions on the use of the legs and stick, and was probably dying to smack the pony with the crop herself! At this point it was too late for the pony (or child) to learn to associate the shouting and jerks with not going into canter. Indeed the pony had had the pleasant _Consequence_ of earning a momentary rest off the track by finally walking instead of cantering and now associated the unpleasant situation as a _Consequence_ of the approach of Mrs J. With Jennie now in tears they retired to their lorry and, even though Rowan had been quite naughty in the lesson, I felt sorry for the pony when Mrs J screamed at her again after Rowan quite logically shied away from Mrs J when she tried to put a steadying hand on the rein, as the pony had just learned to associate this action with _Consequent_ pain.

Similarly there is no point threatening to do terrible things to your horse when you get him home after some misdemeanour out hacking or while at a competition, or keeping a horse which has proved difficult to catch from the field in his stable with no feed as a 'punishment'. Such unpleasant _Consequences_ occur too late to be associated with the undesirable behaviour and will not be perceived by the horse as a direct _Consequence_ of his own actions. They therefore do not help to teach the horse to do what is wanted. In fact they usually serve to teach the horse to be scared of the handler or something else.

Apparently effective delayed or 'late' punishments usually have another explanation. For example, you may be familiar with the spectacle of the experienced show jumper who turns his horse roughly away from a fence after a refusal and rides off taking both reins into one hand and administers a sharp blow with the stick while still riding away from the fence. The rider then usually turns back towards the fence with a lot of impulsion, on the correct line and riding strongly. The horse usually makes it over the fence this second time. These riders believe that the blow with the stick 'teaches the horse a lesson' and that this 'punishment', several seconds after the refusal and while the poor horse is doing exactly what the rider subsequently asked for, is what encourages them to jump better next time. Actually, what is happening is that the horse stopped because the line or impulsion and stride were wrong or the nature of the fence surprised him the first time. This has all been corrected by the rider on the second approach. The blow with the stick is actually of no _Consequence_ here, having no effect other than perhaps helping the rider get rid of his frustration at incurring his faults.

Generally, it is very difficult to apply any punishment or unpleasant _Consequence_ at the correct time for this to be an effective aid to training, and for this technical reason as well as the more obvious safety and welfare reasons, it is usually much better to simply ignore 'bad' _Behaviour_ and reward good when training your horse (see also Chapters 2 and 8).

Extent, repetitions and schedules of reinforcement

The technical term for a reward or pleasant _Consequence_ in the context of learning is *positive reinforcement,* and a punishment or unpleasant *Consequence* is referred to as *negative reinforcement.* In order for training to be most effective *Antecedents, Behaviour* and *Consequences* need to be repeated and the number and pattern of repeats is called a *schedule of reinforcement.* These are explained fully in Chapter 3, but are mentioned here as this is where the extent or nature of a *Consequence* becomes important in the development of a problem and begins to affect training.

Generally, greater *Consequences* need fewer repeats, or a simple *fixed schedule of reinforcement,* for learning to take place, while *Behaviour* with relatively little *Consequence* requires many more repeats, or a complex and *variable schedule of reinforcement,* to become part of a learned *Behaviour* pattern.

This is why one very traumatic event is often all that is required for a horse to learn never to do whatever he perceived caused a particularly painful or frightening *Consequence* again. Horses injured in road traffic accidents generally do not need to repeat the experience to become very frightened of traffic, even if they have previously had a lot of experience being ridden along that road without any incidents or aversive *Consequences.* Similarly a particularly wonderful *Consequence* may be enough for a horse to learn that it is definitely worth his while to do something again.

More training and repeats or perhaps a different *schedule of reinforcement* is required when the *Consequence* is relatively less important from the horse's point of view. For example a food reward is not so valued by the horse if he is not hungry, so if using a treat as a reward when training you need to train before the horse is fed and also maybe an hour or so after he has come out of the field (and kept without a haynet!), or use a different schedule of reinforcement (see Chapter 3). It is also very time consuming to try to tempt a horse who is tricky to catch with treats if he is in lush pasture. Here, you can speed up training by using an alternative 'better' *Consequence,* which can be difficult to arrange, especially in a busy livery yard on a lovely summer's day, or again, using an alternative schedule of reinforcement (see Chapter 3).

While a nuisance in some ways, this aspect of 'How Horses Learn' also explains how many quite subtle ridden evasions can develop, even though the pleasant *Consequence* is really a very minor one, such as a transient reduction in pressure on the mouth or a tiny change in pressure on the back muscles. Providing that there are enough repeats, the horse will learn that the *Behaviour* resulting in this is worthwhile. For example, this is how riding school ponies learn to tug children out of the saddle. You might think that this would be too much effort for the pony just to get a transient break from inexperienced hands or inconsistent pressure on his back, but as this behaviour has a repeatedly beneficial consequence every few strides, this common evasion is quickly learned. The children need to be taught to let the reins slip and stay in the saddle, using their legs if they can (and grass reins if they can't) to encourage the pony who is smart enough to keep his head down here to pick it up and walk on.

The details of how different schedules of reinforcement can be used to improve training are explained in Chapter 3.

Consistency

It is particularly important that the _Consequences_ a horse perceives as a direct result of any _Behaviour_ are always the same. Inconsistency here is one of the most common causes of the handling and performance problems that I am asked to deal with. Studies have shown that if an animal is uncertain whether any action is likely to have a nice or a nasty _Consequence_, they are much more stressed than if they know it will have a nasty _Consequence_. This is perhaps a surprising result, but emphasizes the importance of consistency not only when training, but at all times around your horse.

For this reason all 'Advance–Retreat' methods and some of the 'Natural Horsemanship' methods of training can be very confusing and stressful for a horse. These methods 'work' by a mixture of _classical_ and _operant conditioning_ using punishment (see Chapters 3, 4 and 5), chipping away the confidence of a bossy horse, as he gets no clue as to what is wanted until he has been punished for doing the wrong thing. The system used means that the handler reacts to the horse in unpredictable ways, sometimes being 'nice' sometimes being 'nasty'. The horse cannot predict whether his handler wants him to stand, approach or will chase him away until it is too late and the sudden movements of the handler eventually exhaust him mentally, diminishing his confidence resulting in the desired but transient submission. The wariness in his behaviour towards a handler on the ground, interpreted as 'respect' by aficionados of these systems is actually uncertainty. This is not only unpleasant for the horse, but a safety risk as well, as an uncertain horse's reactions to the handler in times of stress will also be unpredictable. They can cause considerable stress in under-confident horses and for this amongst other reasons, promoters of these techniques usually select the horses used for demonstration and teaching purposes before any event, choosing only those who are misbehaving through social dominance and over-confidence.

Once again, it is easiest to be consistent if you simply ignore 'bad' _Behaviour_ and always reward 'good' (see Chapters 2 and 8). Even tiny rewards are effective if these are frequent enough. According to some of my clients this approach also works very well for toddlers, teenagers and husbands!

SUMMARY

This chapter can really be summarized very simply by 'ABC'. The sequence and timing with which these follow each other is vital for learning to take place. _Antecedents_, _Behaviour_ and _Consequences_ need to happen strictly in that order within half second of each other for the horse's brain to link these together for effective learning.

Antecedent events must contain a clear and specific stimulus, perceived by the horse just before his own actions or _Behaviour_ result in an immediate and consistent _Consequence_.

Simple or vague 'associations' are not enough to train effectively or to work out the underlying cause of behaviour problems. There must be a recognisable, strict and consistent pattern of ABC. Good trainers are people who are naturally strict and consistent, and this perhaps explains the pedantic and bossy stereotype of army sergeants and Pony Club ladies! Good training really is like army drill or traditional ballet choreography, with great attention to detail required at every stage with impeccable timing.

While early experience and associations between odd antecedents and unusual consequences forms the basis for many individual differences and little foibles, all effective methods of training horses work on the same fundamental principles. Horses' brains have not changed much over the last few thousand years, and the way in which any horse develops a problem or learns to behave is exactly the same as every other horse, and indeed most animals and people!

There will always be 'variations on the theme' marketed as 'new' or 'alternative' training methods, but at the end of the day a horse is still a horse. The training methods used in the days of Xenophon and all those which are effective today are based on the same principles and work in exactly the same way. Just like modern magicians' tricks, which are really the same old tricks but given a modern flavour by updated props and language, any apparently 'new' system for training horses which actually works can always be explained by the same old principles of learning theory, _Antecedent_ ➤ _Behaviour_ (_stimulus response_) and _Behaviour_ ➤ _Consequence_ (_action-reward_).

So, while learning theory can be very complex, and there are a lot of important details to be considered as described above, in essence it really is as easy as ABC – _Antecedents_, _Behaviour_, and _Consequences_. So, just remember your ABC!

Chapter 2

Rewards, Punishment and Motivation

As described in Chapter 1, a *reward* is a pleasant consequence of any particular action, also known as 'positive reinforcement' in the context of learning; a *punishment* is an unpleasant consequence, also known as 'negative reinforcement'. As with all behavioural consequences, in order to be effective and for learning to take place, these need to be consistent and the timing has to be spot on i.e. the *reward* or *punishment* has to occur immediately after the behaviour concerned for your horse's brain to connect the two.

However, it is also particularly important to try to see things from the horse's point of view here. Many behaviour problems develop due to handlers and riders inadvertently *rewarding* 'bad' behaviour or accidentally *punishing* 'good' behaviour.

Take the irritating horse that bangs his stable door with a foreleg for example. This is usually done to get attention. Most people ignore this horse when he is quiet and turn to look or shout at him as soon as he bangs the door. People offer this angry yell as a *punishment*. However, from the horse's point of view, even unprintable words and the occasional chucking of grooming kit here constitutes attention. Any attention is better than none, and the yell is a *reward* from his point of view. The horse has got the reaction he wanted and this is why he stops banging the door for a few moments at this point. Ignoring him when he is quiet is actually *punishing* him for doing what is wanted. The trick to dealing with this sort of problem is to reverse the *rewarding* of banging and *punishing* of silence process by ignoring the door banging (e.g. pad the door with heavy duty coconut or rubber matting, or use a pole or breast bar from your trailer across the stable entrance instead of a solid door, wear earmuffs, turn the radio to full blast and walk away!) and to go over and pat this horse as soon as he is quiet even for a few seconds.

Sometimes we expect our horses to tolerate *punishment* for good behaviour. For example, we know that some unpleasant consequences to standing quietly are for their own good in the long run (e.g. some aspects of routine grooming, visits from the vet or farrier, or simply spraying with fly stuff etc). It can be very frustrating if your horse objects to all this sort of thing, as you know you are only trying to get him to allow you to do what is best for him. However, your horse does not know that this is being done for his own good. From his point of view he is being *punished* for standing still. Knowing this, you can train him to put up with any short term discomfort necessary for his long term welfare by linking this to a subsequent *reward* (see Chapter 5 on *strings of conditioned stimuli* and *bridging stimuli*). Experienced handlers and people who are naturally good with horses often do this instinctively, offering a kind word followed by pat or a treat immediately after the discomfort to 'settle' the horse. They are actually training the horse here by the process of *counter-conditioning*, whether they are aware of it or not, and this is explained in detail in Chapter 7. Shouting at the horse who has just kicked the vet and sent a vaccination syringe flying across the yard is ineffective, as he has already had his *reward* (avoiding the needle prick). This horse will only learn instead to become frightened of the shouting handler and pull away more at this point, just making the situation worse. So, in order to avoid misunderstandings which can lead to serious behaviour problems, it really is most important to think very carefully about *reward* and *punishment* from the horse's point of view.

I never advise the use of *punishment* when training horses. It can be technically very difficult to apply any *punishment* at the right time and in a manner in which the horse perceives any unpleasantness as a direct consequence of his own actions. There are also other obvious ethical, welfare and safety considerations here. Expert handlers and riders can use *punishment* effectively when training and many do. For example, most of the effective techniques used in the Parelli system and those promoted as 'Natural Horsemanship' are based on *punishment*, specifically using a horse's instinctive fear of sudden hissing sounds and hands or sticks waved in the horse's face near his eyes or making an unfit horse reverse quickly or whiz around in a very tight circle, which is physically stressful and can cause injury. This can help when the problem behaviour is due to simple naughtiness or social dominance, but will greatly upset a horse misbehaving due to genuine nervousness or the expectation of pain, making things much worse and in either of these cases is likely to cause a serious accident for both horse and handler. Every rider knows that there are times when appropriate use of a schooling whip to tickle the flanks can save a disobedient horse (and his rider!) from accident or injury, for example when the horse is swinging his hindquarters out into an oncoming vehicle or reversing into an electric fence, but it can be extremely dangerous all round for people to try to use *punishment* when training horses and I do not recommend it.

When I reach this point in a public talk on 'How Horses Learn', there is always someone in the audience with a story about someone they know who 'cured' a 'wicked' horse with a sharp blow with a shovel or some such extreme violence. I explain (patiently!) that there are always other safer and more humane ways of dealing with most problems. It is much safer and more effective in the long run to simply ignore 'bad' behaviour and *reward* the 'good'. This is the basis of most traditional behaviour modification programmes, including that popularized by the self help book *Don't Shoot the Dog* and the 'Positive Horse Magic' system promoted by Heather Simpson. It is also important to make sure that your horse is motivated to want the *reward* you have chosen to use, and this can often be manipulated quite easily by planning your training sessions to maximize this motivation, e.g. if using food by making sure he is not already full of treats, hay or grass!

Ignoring 'bad' behaviour and *rewarding* 'good' is often easier said than done. Great patience and considerable self preservation skills are required to ignore a half ton of horseflesh in the wrong place at the wrong time. It is sometimes impossible not to accidentally *reward* your horse for leaping around, for example by falling off or moving out of the way! Conversely, offering a *reward* at exactly the right moment can also prove difficult in practical terms, and unwitting errors in riding technique mean that it is relatively common for a novice rider to inadvertently *punish* their horse for moving forwards correctly, for example if their use of the reins inadvertently alters the contact or their balance is less than ideal.

There are probably as many different *rewards* and *punishments* as there are individual combinations of people and horses. The rest of this chapter describes some of the most common inadvertent *punishments* and accidental *rewards* that I have come across, which contribute to the development of behaviour problems, as well as some simple practical ways of *rewarding* your horse for desirable behaviour.

INADVERTENT PUNISHMENT

It is actually quite amazing that horses put up with us at all. It is often pointed out that most of the things we want our horses to do are contrary to their natural instincts. This is quite true, if you think about it for a moment. For example, often the first thing we do when we turn up is take our horse away from his companions. We expect him to cope with our weight on his back and worse, when schooling, we then want him to work harder with his weaker muscles. Afterwards we want him to stand still while we tickle his sensitive areas with brushes and scrub the sweaty bits with cold water. If I was a horse I might think twice about my side of this bargain!

The main ways in which people, in my experience, albeit with the best intentions in the world, inadvertently *punish* horses for 'good' behaviour fall into the following categories:

- Handling techniques
- Tack and equipment
- Riding surfaces
- Riding techniques
- Schooling methods
- Travelling
- Housing and pasture management
- Confidence

Handling techniques

Most experienced people do their best to handle their horse in a way which keeps the handler safe and the horse comfortable. Sometimes, however, it is easy to forget the physical differences between people and horses and this can lead to problems.

For example, we can easily turn into a stable doorway from a four foot (1.2m) wide corridor. Most horses and even ponies cannot. They are on average around nine feet (2.7m) long, and cannot flex their spine sideways much further back than their withers. Think pedestrian versus minibus! A horse trying to make such a turn will risk banging his pelvis or hocks against the wall or doorpost and will wriggle or rush to try to avoid hurting himself here. Similarly at gates, many horses just cannot make the 'handbrake turn' that the handler, keen to stop other horses rushing out, may ask for and end up rushing, 'hopping' and kicking to try to avoid slipping and falling over. A horse in this situation may become sufficiently unbalanced as to bump into

Fig 2.1. *Top:* Lifting a hind foot too high and/or too far away from his body is easy for the handler but very uncomfortable for the horse.

Fig 2.2. *Below:* Lifting a hind foot like this is hard work for the handler but much more comfortable for the horse.

the handler with his shoulder as he does his best to oblige. This can lead to major ground handling problems, as the horse is being inadvertently *punished* for trying to do what he is asked and will learn to behave in a socially dominant manner and push people around to avoid pain or discomfort.

Another common handling mistake that leads to *punishing* a horse for doing what you want is holding the hind leg too high or at an awkward angle for too long when picking up a foot. Horses who let you pick up a front foot but hop about, lean and pull away when you try to lift a hind foot are usually misbehaving through pain. They may simply be stiff or have a sore back or other hind limb lameness problems, and you should have your vet and a properly qualified physiotherapist check this out, particularly in the leg you can lift most easily. This is because they will be more stressed when the 'bad' leg is required to take all the weight of the hindquarters. Many people however inadvertently hurt their horse in the way the hind leg is held up for example by pulling this out at an awkward angle or lifting it too high or holding it up keeping all the joints flexed for too long (see Figure 2.1.). To keep your horse comfortable here, make sure you lift the leg so that you keep the point of buttock, hock and fetlock in a straight line underneath each other and do not lift the leg higher than absolutely necessary for you to bend over and pick out the hoof. For most horses this will be about the same height as the top of the fetlock on the other hind leg (see Figure 2.2.). Comparing the degree to which the handler has to bend and use their back in these two photographs shows the most likely reason for this common handling error!

You can make things easier for yourself here by picking out the foot in several short goes and not trying to pick out a well packed foot all at once. Riding or lungeing your horse to work off any stiffness immediately before he is shod may help your farrier here as well as your horse. If you know your horse is likely to be difficult or you are not sure whether or not he will stand quietly for the farrier, you should let the farrier know this when you book your visit. This helps to keep the farrier happy as he can then plan his day e.g. to leave your horse till last or allocate him more time and make sure he can bring along a capable apprentice should he have one to help. Naughty horses tend to make a particular fuss about lifting their front legs, and are better with their hind legs. A horse who still objects to the hind legs only being lifted, when this is done correctly may be misbehaving due to pain and should benefit from veterinary investigation, with subsequent saddle fit checking or physiotherapy as required.

Many horses can be naughty when being asked to rein back, move their hindquarters over or work on the lunge as this all involves extra physical exertion. Objecting violently to this kind of handling is also however a classic sign of some physical problems and your horse may therefore be inadvertently punished for doing what you have asked. With any major handling problems, you should involve your vet as soon as possible to treat or eliminate pain from a physical problem as the cause. A properly qualified horse behaviour consultant can differentiate misbehaviour due to pain and discomfort from disobedience or naughtiness, and teach you how to handle the latter safely (see Chapter 8 for details of what qualifications to look for and where to get the appropriate professional help).

Many people are aware of how they should be leading their horse ie from the shoulder, with the handler beside the horse's front leg pushing the horse in front of them, holding the lead rope at the clip end with the extra rope carefully held in the other hand passed to and fro across the palm so that it cannot wrap around that hand. This method not only keeps the handler in the safest possible place, it also keeps them in the most physically effective position to manoeuvre the horse and most importantly also keeps them where the horse will understand that the handler is the boss. However, many people become complacent and lapse into walking too far ahead of their

Fig 2.3a. The safest way to lead your horse when using a bridle

Fig 2.3b. The safest way to lead your horse when using a headcollar.

horse. If you are directly in front of your horse, not only are you highly likely to be run over or knocked sideways should anything spook your horse, you are also in a completely ineffective position in terms of basic control. Worse, a person in this position is acting like a subordinate, giving the horse the idea that he is the boss. It is also very confusing for a horse, if he is sometimes allowed to 'be the boss' in this way and then at other times expected to move away from the handler. This is how many social dominance relationship problems start in my experience, and how the handling system popularized as 'join up' creates this kind of problem. Horses lead from behind, with the boss horse pushing subordinates ahead of him. You will see this happening in your field as some of the top horses in the hierarchy push others away from the gate or take them off up the field by nudging or shoving them at their flanks. This keeps the boss horse safer, as others will fall into bad ground or be ambushed around the next corner etc before he is. So, if a horse is encouraged to follow a person around, he is being taught to act like the boss, pushing his person in front of him just like a herd leader would do with his subordinates. He will then be very confused and annoyed when this person then tries to tell him where to go!

Grooming

Traditionally, it was recommended to sponge the eyes, nose and dock daily and wash a gelding's sheath regularly. However, sponges can carry a lot of infection, and soap or other washing agents can irritate the eyes and be very damaging to the delicate skin around the sheath, and so it is best to only touch these parts of your horse when absolutely necessary. Similarly, you should be very careful when washing a mare's dock and ideally for all these procedures use only warm water with a pinch of salt to each pint and in so far as you can, leave them alone.

Many people unwittingly make small wounds much worse by trying to clean them too often or too vigorously with surgical scrub or antiseptic potions. It is very difficult to do this in a hygienic way with your horse leaping around as he objects quite justifiably to the stinging pain! Again, it is best to use only warm water with half a teaspoon of salt to every half pint. After a thorough clean when

Fig 2.4. Spending time grooming your horse is an excellent way of getting to know him.

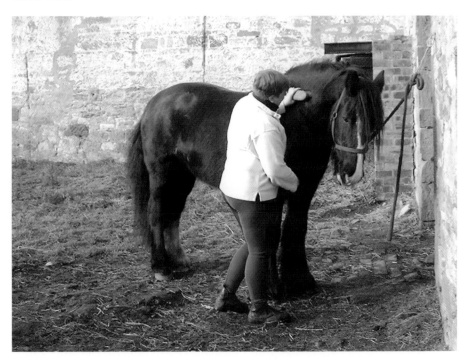

you first discover a small wound, it is usually best to treat it every other day, keeping it covered with a fly repelling wound cream in the summertime and a 'nappy rash' type of cream in the wintertime. If you are not sure how bad it is, if the skin is completely cut through, or you have a puncture wound, especially if this is near a joint, then you should seek veterinary help immediately as your horse may benefit from stitching or antibiotic treatment and your vet can check to see whether or nor the joint also needs treatment. If you are not sure about how to manage small wounds or indeed when assistance is necessary, ask your vet to give a talk on this to your riding club or livery yard. Some vets organize regular client evenings to advise and update their clients on all aspects of horse care and you should support and encourage these. Most vets will be happy to answer a quick question on this sort of thing when they attend to give your horse his annual vaccination and six monthly teeth check, and if you are concerned about anything in the feet, it is worth making sure you are present when the farrier attends your horse. You can learn a great deal about your horse from what the farrier can see in his feet and the way the old shoes are worn.

Some grooming brushes made with nylon bristles or other synthetic fibres can be very tickly and may even cause tiny electric shocks from static as they are stroked along the hair. Brushes made from natural materials reduce this irritating effect. Some horses like to be brushed slowly and gently, others prefer a quick firm stroke.

I have one regular rider who has a very tickly horse (aptly named Dancer) and she was always apologizing for the specks of mud on tummy and flanks when she arrived in the arena for her lesson. I did not mind, as the horse was sufficiently well groomed to have uncovered any small wounds and to be comfortable under her tack. I always reminded her that my lessons were not a turnout competition and that I would rather see a muddy horse working well than a spotless one all wound up! Poor Evelyn spent a fortune on the very best of 'real' bristle brushes, and tried every new and alternative grooming mitt or device she could find. One cold winter's day, after a very trying morning with children playing up and trailer brakes having seized, poor Evelyn arrived for her lesson very late and discovered much to her dismay that, with all the hassle, she had forgotten her grooming kit and had to prepare in haste as best she could. The only tool she could muster was an old metal curry comb she found rolling around the boot of the car. Much to her amazement, as she was delighted to recount at the start of the lesson, Dancer absolutely loved the feel of the curry comb, particularly when it was dragged firmly and quickly over her tummy, standing stock still save for bending round to mutually groom her beloved owner for finally scratching her tummy in the quick firm manner she had only dreamed of for years!

So, it is worth experimenting with different brushes and ways of grooming to find out which your horse will best tolerate or even enjoy.

It is also worth remembering that standing around to be groomed or waiting to dry off if brought in from grass can have a negative effect on your horse's ability to work well. He may get stiff, bored and if given a haynet to keep him amused while you get him ready, might even be too full to feel like any serious activity. You wouldn't want to stand around for an hour or more on a hard surface, filling up on a bulky meal before going jogging or starting circuits in the gym. Horses do not need to be dry to be ridden, as your numnah will protect the saddle and a quick wipe with a towel or sweat scraper will remove enough surplus moisture to enable you to tack up without worrying about the saddle – remember the numnah gets wet from sweat too when your horse is worked and this does not ruin your saddle! A dry and relatively clean numnah should be used each time you ride and those made of natural fibres especially real wool are best for absorbing sweat and moisture and minimizing discomfort to your horse.

It really is important to be aware of your horse's physical limits and individual likes and dislikes when working with him and to try to make sure that your routine handling procedures do not cause pain and are as pleasant as possible from your horse's point of view.

Tack and equipment

Uncomfortable tack and equipment is probably the single most common cause of discomfort and inadvertent *punishment* that I come across.

This may be because leisure horses now come in all shapes and sizes, and vary much more in body condition and fitness than did their working counterparts in days of old. There is also probably more choice of tack for horse owners now than ever before and it can be very confusing for anyone trying to kit out their first horse from the vast selection of equipment available in their local tack shop, advertised in magazines and offered for sale through catalogues and over the Internet.

A detailed discussion of choosing and fitting safe and appropriate tack is beyond the scope of this book and there are excellent books (such as the classic Elwyn Hartley Edwards *Bits and Bitting*) available on this topic. However, some of the most common ways in which horses may risk pain or injury and develop behaviour problems caused by inappropriate or poorly fitting tack in my experience are described below.

Saddles

Ideally, especially if you are relatively new to horse ownership, you should have your saddle checked for fit by a Society of Master Saddlers Qualified Saddle Fitter (SMS QSF). This is not the same as a Master Saddler who has shown competence in the skill of making saddles, but is someone who has been trained and passed the Society of Master Saddlers' specific exam in saddle fitting. Most tack shops have a Master Saddler on the premises but not all have a QSF. Difficulty tacking up and mounting, particularly if turning away from the handler, fidgeting, leaping sideways or collapsing when mounted, particularly with the tail clamped or tucked in, reluctance to trot, canter or jump, including bucking and changing leading leg frequently, refusing to move and violent rushing backwards and going hollow can all be signs of discomfort under saddle. In the absence of any physical problems causing a sore back, these signs are all typical of the behaviour problems I see in horses whose saddles do not fit them correctly. There are a great many pads sold to help adjust saddle fit but used incorrectly these can make any fitting problem worse. Most horses can change shape enough in three months to require the skilled assistance of a qualified saddle fitter to make the adjustments necessary to ensure continued good fit, so even if your saddle was perfect three months ago, changes in season, condition or work patterns and fitness can mean that professional help is required to maintain your horse's comfort.

There is a great range of saddlery now available to horse owners, and many new design concepts which offer a huge variety of options to keep horses comfortable and riders balanced. Faced with all these options and the intensive marketing strategies of some new concepts there is really no sensible alternative to seeking help from an independent and properly qualified Society of Master Saddlers Qualified Saddle Fitter, who can guide you through the vast range of saddlery now available and assist the responsible rider wishing to keep their horse comfortable and themselves safe (see Chapter 8 for more details here).

Numnahs

Most of us use a numnah or saddle blanket under the saddle. The job of a numnah is to keep the saddle clean and the horse comfortable by absorbing moisture and sweat as the horse is ridden. Numnahs made of synthetic materials are poor at this and may cause your horse discomfort, so it is best to use only pure wool or cotton numnahs and to wash these frequently with pure soap or hypo-allergenic detergents to avoid irritating your horse. Saddle fitters often make an analogy between numnahs and socks, explaining that if our shoes are uncomfortable or too tight, then putting on thick socks will not help and point out that, in the same way, using a thick numnah or all sorts of complicated pads under a less than perfectly fitting saddle will only exacerbate discomfort. It is best to use a thin numnah made or lined with pure wool or wicking cotton. Some types of numnah slip down and back as the horse moves and this can cause enough discomfort to lead to major problems, including difficulty mounting. You should make sure that your numnah is pulled well up into the gullet of the saddle when girthing up and check that it stays clear of your horse's withers throughout your ride. The best makes of numnah are shaped here to help them stay up away from your horse's withers and maximize his comfort.

Girths

The broader and smoother a girth, the less pressure it puts on your horse's tummy. Some girths carry all the pressure in reinforced bands or strips of stronger material in the centre, and these can be very uncomfortable. As with numnahs, synthetic materials are more likely to rub, although some kinds of synthetic girth have specially designed holes to help here. Girths narrowing at the elbow may help to accommodate horses with extravagant movement here, but this will increase pressure locally and is a common cause of girth galls. Girths made of natural, soft and absorbent materials will be the most comfortable. Some girths which spread the load by attaching to a running strap between the two girth and web straps are marketed as 'humane', but are in fact very dangerous. The reason we use two points of attachment for girths is a safety one, giving at least one secure point of attachment should a web or strap break. In these 'humane' girths, the rider will have a very loose saddle should either strap or web break and this could lead to a serious accident. Girths with elastic at only one end or indeed a lot of 'give' are a similar safety risk. Some new saddle designs aim to spread the load from the girth more evenly across the saddle than those using traditional web positions and this type of girthing arrangement should also help to reduce any discomfort from girths.

Please do be aware that your girth is vital to your safety, and that too much elasticity (aiming to increase horse comfort) can be a safety hazard for the rider, especially if used with saddles or numnahs fitted with airbags. A Society of Master Saddlers' qualified saddle fitter should be able to help you choose the best girthing arrangement for your saddle and horse.

Bridles

Most parts of a bridle (apart from the bit – see later) are easily adjustable and cause relatively little trouble in my experience. However, I commonly find nosebands which are set too high and rub the 'cheekbones' – the noseband should rest at least an inch or 3 cm below these – and browbands which are too short, pulling the headpiece forward to cut into the horse's very sensitive ears, particularly when the reins are tightened.

Not everyone puts their bridle on properly. You should stand with your back to your horse's chest and your right arm around his muzzle holding the bridle by the cheekpieces in your right hand and guide the bit in with your left hand while pulling the headpiece first of all over the ear nearest you, then the other one, taking care not to inadvertently catch your horse's eye or crumple his ear too much here.

Mr R spoke to me for hours over the phone about the difficulties he was having putting on his horse's bridle. Libby has been worked with by a great many different 'behaviourists' and the poor chap had spent a fortune on 'alternative' training courses trying to solve this horse's 'attitude' problem but to no avail. The most famous of the alternative trainers he used concluded that as his method hadn't worked, there must be something physically wrong hurting this horse's head on bridling. Mr R's vet could find no obvious signs of any physical problem, but, impressed by the sorry tale of persistent and apparently intractable difficulties endured, had packed Libby off to their local veterinary hospital for a complete set of head and spinal X rays just in case.

Mr R, although relieved in part that there was nothing seriously wrong with his horse, was really rather miffed to hear that no abnormalities at all could be found. Finally, having spent a great deal of money, he followed up on the hospital's suggestion to call me. I went along to assess this horse intrigued by the complex history. On arrival, I could see immediately a potential cause of bridling problems in the size difference between horse and owner. Mr R was an ex jockey less than five feet tall and Libby was well beyond 17.2 hh. I asked Mr R to let me see what Libby did when he tried to put her bridle on. To my great surprise, she obligingly put her head down and waited while Mr R approached bridling in a most unconventional manner. This may have worked for very fit and supple young Thoroughbreds of 15 hh, but was not at all effective with this older and much taller horse. He was all fingers and thumbs in his rush and after a moment or two, poor Libby was so exhausted she had to give up. This brought her head back up into the normal 'relaxed' position with her ears at the same

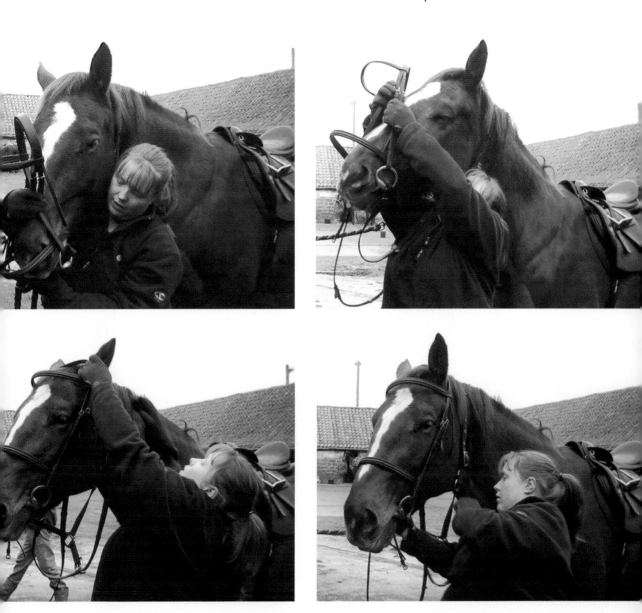

Fig 2.5. This series of pictures shows the best way of putting a bridle on safely

height as her withers. Needless to say, this was well out of Mr R's reach.

'There' he gasped in frustration! I struggled a little to find the most polite way of explaining that his stature as well as his bridling technique may be major factors causing this problem. I also explained that a horse has to actively use neck, shoulder and back muscles to put and keep their head down so that the ears come below the withers. These muscles have to work against the huge elastic strip of connective tissue and ligaments in the neck that keep the head off the ground without muscular effort when a horse is standing resting. As Libby's back was quite dipped and very light in muscle, this would be tiring for her. I demonstrated the traditional way of bridling described above, and encouraged Libby to keep her head down for as long as she could manage by placing a little hay on the floor. I also found a safe mounting block for Mr R to stand on while tacking this horse up. In less than a minute, a little common sense had 'solved' the insoluble problem. Mr R continued to use the mounting block and practise the correct technique and fed Libby's hay loose on the floor thereafter to help her stretch her back muscles and develop these.

We also had to deal with the root cause of Libby's weak back, involving a chartered physiotherapist and qualified saddle fitter in this case, but the experience taught me that even experienced people and some professionals can be unaware of simple practical difficulties which can lead to major problems.

Bits

Here, as with saddles, there is now a great range of 'new' bits available to horse owners. The traditional range itself is pretty huge, but all bit designs are ultimately variations on a few very simple themes. Look at the Etruscan

Fig 2.6. This Etruscan bit with independently moving sides is well over 2,000 years old!

bit (shown in Figure 2.6.), which was in use around 400BC. Does it remind you of the 'Myler' bits marketed today as 'new and humane'? Essentially the more complex a bit, the more difficult it is for the rider to communicate effectively with their horse. A complicated bit makes it harder for the rider to feel what their horse is doing with the contact and to send clear and consistent signals back. The old epithet that 'A bit is only as severe or as gentle as the hands at the other end of the reins' still remains very true. All bits move when the reins are used and a good bitting system will move in such a way as to gradually apply pressure progressively on each of the sensitive areas of the horse's mouth and head i.e. first making pressure in one area, then gradually adding pressure elsewhere, so that the horse has a degree of choice in when and how to respond, and the rider has options in the signals offered. Some modern bitting systems marketed as 'humane' are actually very cruel in that they apply pressure immediately on all the pressure points at once, effectively giving the horse no chance to listen and respond to a gentle request, and being so complex that the poor horse will only notice the rider's efforts as 'nothing' when on a loose rein (which is effectively leaving your horse on his own) or the equivalent of yelling 'stop!' as soon as the reins are used, as this is the only message that use of the reins here can communicate, as all the pressure points are hit hard at once.

Many people are tempted to reach for a different bit when they experience evasions at the head end, but this kind of problem usually reflects a need for a different approach in the way in which the rider uses their hands and upper body, and it is usually more beneficial to seek expert help first of all with riding technique. You should also have a veterinary surgeon check your horse's mouth in this instance, as pain from tooth problems is a very common cause of bit evasions, head tossing and rearing etc. A 'tooth man' or 'equine dentist' cannot diagnose or treat many of the physical disorders which can give rise to pain in the mouth and it is very important that you seek veterinary help first if you suspect a problem here. Your vet can eliminate (or diagnose and treat) any of these medical disorders or rasp the teeth himself safely and thoroughly using sedatives as required or recommend an appropriately qualified equine dental technician to do this work under his supervision.

Most horses should go perfectly well at riding club level in a simple snaffle, which is why these bits are the only kind allowed for competitions such as dressage for example. Some horses prefer an extra link in the middle (e.g. as in a French link or KK snaffle) or a loose ring to the fixed Eggbutt kind of snaffle. Some children's ponies require the additional brake power of a Kimblewick or Pelham type of bit which have extra leverage with their straight bar and sidepieces putting pressure on the poll and have the option of a curb chain pressing on the 'chin' groove. These arrangements use the physics of leverage to augment a child's little arms and light bodies. Apart from these classic variations on the theme, most other bitting arrangements are a poor substitute for skilful riding, and if tempted by the marketing claims of 'new' bitting systems, I would strongly advise any new horse owner to first seek help from a properly qualified riding instructor before inflicting complex contraptions on their poor horse's mouth. These will make the horse more uncomfortable and can only exacerbate confusion between horse and rider. A napping horse ridden in a gag is only likely to rear up and may fall over. Some modern bitting systems are sufficiently dangerous as to be likely to lead to a serious accident, causing the horse to hollow, rear or slip and fall on corners, should a novice rider suddenly tighten the reins.

Contrary to popular belief, the traditional 'bitless bridle' or modern American equivalent i.e. using some form of Hackamore arrangement is also very severe, and should only be used with great care and after receiving qualified instruction in its fitting and use.

Care also has to be taken when selecting a bit in terms of the quality of finish and materials used. Stainless steel from which the best metal bits are made comes in various degrees of quality both in steel used and fineness of finish. This is why two apparently similar bits may vary a lot in price. Choose the highest quality steel and tightest finish you can afford. Check the quality by holding all the moveable elements between the fingertips of one hand and make them move with the other hand, feeling for any wobble or gaps which could lead to the development of sharp edges and catch your horse's delicate lips causing sudden pain and which could lead to him rearing and falling over. Bits made of other metals, including the alloy marketed as 'sweet metal', will wear a lot faster than stainless steel and make a bitter taste in your horse's mouth. The ensuing salivation is often misinterpreted as a sign of a happy or relaxed horse. In the absence of chemical stimulation, it is true that a relaxed horse will salivate and you will see froth at the mouth, but when this is achieved by using metals like copper or iron or 'sweet metal' alloys that cause a chemical reaction in the mouth from which the horse has to protect himself by producing heaps of saliva, you have only a fake or artificial version of the desired sign of relaxation. Try sucking a piece of copper or iron and see how it compares with the taste of stainless steel! Another common element of some modern bits is the use of different metals in the same bit i.e. a mouthpiece with rolls or strips of copper or 'sweet metal' inset. These are highly likely to eventually upset your horse, as different metals wear at different rates and you will inevitably get sharp edges between the different metals which will one day cut into your horse's tongue and lips. To avoid accidents here, it is best to use a bit made from only one type of metal or with a solid nylon or treated rubber mouthpiece for young horses.

While pound for pound a thinner bit puts more pressure on the bars of the mouth, a thicker bit may be uncomfortable for horses with thicker lips or bigger tongues, and most horses have an individual preference for a particular thickness of bit, so it may be worth experimenting if your horse seems uncomfortable in his mouth, particularly if he opens his mouth a lot. It is very cruel just to strap the mouth shut with a drop or flash noseband, as you will not have treated the source of his discomfort or reason for the evasion. A bit which is too long or too short or fitted too high or too low in the mouth will hurt and confuse a horse. Again, if you are not sure whether your bit is the correct size for your horse or if it is fitted correctly, you should seek professional help from a qualified saddler, riding instructor or loriner (see Chapter 8).

Headcollars

Most people use the traditional Newmarket style of headcollar, which is safe (with many 'easy break' points around the metal rings) and perfectly adequate for most well behaved horses. A leather one will break before your horse does under strain and does not melt in a fire like a nylon one, so these are ideal for travelling or whenever a horse is left tied up unsupervised. If you have problems leading your horse or handling him from the ground, you need to use a bridle and make sure you are leading correctly i.e. sending the horse in front of you from the safety zone beside his shoulder. There are an increasing number of American style rope halter types of headcollar available today and marketed as giving the handler better control. These are particularly dangerous, as they work in the short term by applying sudden and extreme pressure on all the delicate areas of your horse's head at once. This is very severe and will only further upset a misbehaving horse, eventually teaching him to rear and can lead to a serious accident. In a tug of war situation the average horse will beat the average person! Furthermore these halters are usually made of nylon, which will cause rope burns and will not break in any emergency for example if your horse catches it in something or gets away from you and stands on the rope or even worse, wraps it around his leg where he will trip and may fall breaking either the leg or his neck or even falling on top of the unfortunate person trying to

Fig 2.7. This traditional Newmarket style is the most humane and effective headcollar commonly used today.

recapture him! Many of these types of halter are sold with a very long lead rope which is attached directly to the nylon loops of the headcollar without a safety break. The length of this rope only increases the risk of this kind of accident should your horse break away from you. Likewise lead ropes with knots or thickened bits at the end represent a safety risk, helping the rope become entangled around a leg or giving the handler a major rope burn as it is pulled through their hand. Horses are managed on the ground by skill not strength, and it is better to make sure you are using a safe method of handling than trying a gadget claiming to give you better control.

Lungeing equipment
I once had a horse referred to me as 'completely unmanageable', only to find that the root cause of the sudden and dramatic decline in behaviour could be traced back to a very tiny error in the way in which a lungeing cavesson was fitted. A lungeing cavesson must be fitted correctly to be comfortable, and if you are not sure how it should fit, or how to use a lunge line and

bridle, do get a lungeing lesson from a qualified instructor. There is a great deal more to lungeing than letting your horse run rings around you, and it is much harder to do safely and effectively than it looks! Some of the cheaper brands of cavesson have the nose plate too loosely attached to the noseband and the end pieces swivel and dig in to the horse's nose when he takes a contact on the line. These can be modified with a padded Velcro strap or sewn into place. Many people are unsure how to fasten and use side reins safely and effectively, and if you are one of these, it really is vital to get some lessons and practice here. To keep your horse comfortable and yourself safe, do make sure you can fit and handle this equipment easily before you try to lunge your own horse by yourself.

Boots and Bandages

There are many situations, including lungeing, travelling and jumping or fast work when boots or bandages are required. However, it is vital that boots fit and are put on correctly to minimize the risk of rubbing or coming loose and tripping the horse up. Uneven or over-tight bandaging can cause injuries. All forms of wrapping up horses' legs heats them up, increasing the risk of tendon sheath injuries and may trap particles of sand or mud, all of which will make your horse very uncomfortable, so think very carefully about the pros and cons before choosing how and when to protect your horse. Again, if you are not sure how tight is too tight, get a lesson on bandaging from your instructor or see if a local veterinary nurse will come to your yard or riding club to give a group lesson and demo. These can be quite good fun, especially if you can persuade people to act as guinea pigs in the first instance by impersonating their own horse being 'difficult' here!

Rugs

The rugs available today made of lightweight breathable materials are wonderful aids to good stable management, mostly by allowing us to keep our horses outside grazing for as long as possible, particularly in the winter months.

However, many people forget that their horses are waterproof and have their own coats to protect them from the elements. You can make your horse very uncomfortable by clipping off their coat. This is usually only required to aid cooling in racehorses and can help make grooming a lot easier for children with very hairy ponies and in large yards where one groom has to look after a great many muddy and sweaty horses. In this latter case, clipping is done for the convenience of the staff, not the benefit of the horses. Even rugging up to 'replace' the coat leaves tummies bare and if I was a horse, I would object most strongly here! Most leisure riders do have the time available to wash sweat marks off after riding and to groom their own horse thoroughly. Remember that sweating is vital if your horse is working – when did you last go to the gym and get away without sweating? Would you prefer that the temperature in the gym was reduced so that you didn't sweat but needed to be well covered by a heavy cloak across your back to compensate for your bare tummy most of the time? I once inadvertently upset a neighbour who came to me, at the end of a very long day with a problem largely caused by her own making, by remarking tersely that 'that is what the fur is for'! Clipping is for the most part a fashion statement for leisure horses – if your horse does not sweat he is not working and he will not get any fitter. It is not in his interests to clip him so that he does not sweat out hacking or when schooling him.

A very good friend of mine spent several years studying the winter coats of horses and after making controlled rain showers over ponies with hoses in sheds and counting the numbers and lengths of hairs per square inch in various parts of the body, I was particularly impressed with the manner in

Fig 2.8a. *Left:* Horses' coats are designed to shed water most efficiently. This photograph shows how guard hairs form 'run off' channels and how the undercoat wicks water away just like a sweat rug.

Fig 2.8b. *Right:* This close up shows how the longer guard hairs form a roof tile pattern to allow rain to run off keeping the softer undercoat and skin dry.

Fig 2.9. This Highland pony's thick winter coat and fabulous mane help to keep him comfortable living out whatever the weather.

Fig 2.10. A good rug gives this little Arab the same freedom to indulge in a natural lifestyle even in the worst of Scotish weather.

which she was able to demonstrate how a horse's coat is designed to shed the rain most efficiently. If you look at your horse's back and rump in the rain, you will see how the coat hairs form a roof tile pattern and shed the water exactly as roofs do. I have another friend who has a Dales type cob which can stand knee deep in a river for ten minutes without getting the skin of his legs wet underneath his magnificent feathers!

While very elderly, injured or sick horses may appreciate rugging up in the summer months, most horses do not and with the exception of the anti-midge covers, which are super for horses with sweet itch and allergic to midge bites, most horses will not appreciate summer sheets and make their feelings quite clear when you come to put the rug on, while standing like angels to have their rugs taken off. Think about whether or not you would enjoy lying on the beach or doing the garden wearing a 'light weight' mackintosh over your summer clothes just in case it rains!

There is also another risk to covering your horse up at all times of the year, as they need sunlight on their skin to make the vitamin D needed for calcium metabolism and healthy bones and teeth just like we do. Sunlight with a rain rinse now and again is also very good for keeping the coat healthy. So, if your horse is rugged up most of the time he is out in the summertime, especially if you also put a neck hood on, you should make sure you are feeding enough vitamin D and calcium.

Some designs of rug need leg straps to keep the rug on. These can be very uncomfortable if not adjusted correctly and horrendous when they break. It is best to use a rug which is cut and designed to stay on without leg straps. Most of the white marks on horse's withers are caused by rugs rubbing and not previous saddles as many people think. Choose a rug design which fits your horse. It can really help here to ask to try on the rugs of stable companions which are a similar size and shape to your horse to check how they sit on your horse. Rugs which are cut to hang off the neck in front of the withers are least likely to rub here, and a loose fit at the front also minimizes shoulder rubs. Do not be tempted to replace a fillet string with bailer twine. This can rub badly, and cause terrible injuries if it becomes entangled around a leg. Most rugs are sold with a spare fillet string, and most rug manufacturing companies will send you a stack of these for the cost of postage and packing.

It is often very difficult to know whether or not it is time to rug up, and in the spring and autumn months difference of opinion between owners and yard staff is probably the biggest single cause of disputes I know of in livery yards. I have a very simple rule which helps me decide if it is time to rug up.

If I feel the need of gloves while going for a walk or pottering about the yard, then I reckon my horse will benefit from a rug. On days when I don't need gloves, I leave the rug off.

It is also very important that a rug is taken off and the horse underneath it checked properly at least once a day.

I did once see a horse with the most unusual problem of refusing to allow anyone to take his rug off, while being fine to have it put on again. It turned out that a few weeks previously this poor horse had been bitten through his rug. Being a very good rug made with 1200 denier ballistic nylon outer shell, this didn't tear, and the bite went unnoticed for a few days until Mrs B. brought the horse in to ride. The wound underneath had bled and oozed enough to be completely stuck to the rug lining, which the unfortunate owner only discovered when, as she was starting to take the rug off, Ally 'exploded' to cower at the back of the box, threatening to kick anyone approaching him while the partially removed rug tore the wound gradually and most painfully open again. It took weeks of very careful *systematic desensitization* (see Chapter 7) before Ally would stand quietly enough again for his rug to be removed safely.

So, it is vital to think very carefully about the effect on your horse's comfort of all that we routinely expect him to tolerate. All that some assassins had to do in 'ye days of olde' was to put a tiny thorn from the hedgerow into the saddle blanket of their victim's horse and wait for the inevitable fatal accident!

Keep it simple, and make sure you know the correct fitting and use of all the tack and equipment you use. If you are not sure, then seek properly qualified and accountable professional assistance (for details on what qualifications to look for and where to get help see Chapter 8).

Riding surfaces

We often forget that the surface we are asking our horses to ride on can be difficult going, sometimes to the point of becoming likely to cause injury. Many farmers diversifying into livery are completely unaware of the requirements for a safe and lasting school surface, and, initially under pressure from their new liveries, are tempted to 'do it themselves' with a few loads of cheap 'soft' sand and any old gravel from the back of a mate's lorry, using that boggy patch at the back of the shed that is not much use for anything else! The resulting surface may be too deep, have holes, soft patches, boggy patches, be prone to flooding, pack rock hard in dry weather and if put down without a proper membrane become a stone producing factory! This approach is quite simply a false economy, and there is no substitute for a well drained and compacted base, built up with graded layers of gravel under a good quality membrane topped off with a well compacted layer of the correct amount of the chosen surface, again made up of good quality materials. Even more unpleasant for your horse is an indoor arena with a sprinkling of sand or peat over a smooth concrete floor, as found in farm sheds which were previously used for grain drying, or dunes of the stuff. Both too much and too little sand can cause injury, or lead to an accident, should horses reach the floor and slip or strain something in the dunes. Regular and appropriate maintenance is also required to keep a surface rideable, especially where it gets a lot of use such as in a livery yard. I have been asked to teach in some schools which are just not safe and it is a miracle that the horses even got around the corners with out falling over, never mind having trouble 'maintaining an outline'.

If you are thinking of building your own arena, it is well worth doing a lot of homework and visiting as many different arenas in your area to see how they ride in a variety of weather conditions before deciding on what surface to go for and what professional assistance you need. You can get a lot of effective schooling done while hacking along lanes and fields and indeed this is often a better introduction to gymnastic schooling for young or unfit horses as the constant corners of an arena can make things very difficult and may only teach your horse that schooling is difficult, uncomfortable and a physical strain.

There are risks out hacking too of course, slippery or deep mud, unexpected holes, tussocks, drains, and even the road surface can be very difficult for your horse. Tarmac is slippery, road paint more so, and the slope at the sides of the road making a camber which is more pronounced on corners can seriously unbalance your horse. Trotting on a hard surface such as a tarmac road, can also be very uncomfortable for a horse and may predispose him to a variety of concussion related injuries, including laminitis. When using farm tracks or forestry roads, your horse may find better footing in the middle of the lane. Furthermore, keeping to the middle of these will also encourage landowners to continue to allow equestrian access, as the damage caused by a shod hoof (which breaks up the road by leaving tiny indents for rain to fill and crack the surface as this freezes and thaws) will be in the centre and not create potholes in the vehicle tracks.

Generally, most horses will find being asked to work repeatedly over any slippery, uneven, too hard, too deep or unstable surface most uncomfortable at best and a great strain or even painful at worst.

Riding techniques

All too often 'the spirit is willing but the flesh is weak'!

Most of us would not dream of attempting half of the things we did as teenagers when in our thirties and forties, but some optimists expect to hop back onto a horse after years of taking a break from riding and still be as supple, strong and balanced as they used to be. Riding really is an athletic sport, and it is best to be aware of your own fitness and tailor your riding to suit, while doing whatever else is required to help improve your fitness for riding at the same time. A few lessons from a qualified instructor can get you off to a good start again and you can learn a great deal about your own balance and position from a friend watching you. Sometimes a non-horsy friend can be more helpful than a horsy one, as a non-horsy person will just tell you exactly what they see, whereas a horsy friend may turn into the 'instructor from hell'! Photographs can sometimes give a misleading snap shot, making you either look very good or very bad depending on the exact second and angle at which they are taken, but having a friend video you riding or schooling is an excellent way of finding out what your body is actually doing when your brain tells it to sit straight and still and apply the aids in the classical manner! This is why traditionally schooling arenas had mirrors, as even top professional riders need to check what they are doing as well as how the horse is moving. Alternatively, if you have ridden the same horse for many years, you may have inadvertently developed habits in how you sit and ride that suit this horse and which may not suit your next horse. We all have our own foibles and weaknesses and even very experienced riders do need to be mindful of how their own particular riding habits affect their horse.

So, it is not an admission of failure to have regular lessons and indeed most top competition riders spend a lot of their budget on coaching. Working on your own riding technique need not cost a fortune however. For example, you can get together with others at your yard and form a coaching syndicate, taking turns to watch and video each other. It is very nice to have the tapes for posterity and you will be surprised how much you can improve yourself by making a few tiny adjustments to your position. You will also be very surprised at what a difference this will make to your horse. They are so sensitive to our body movements that they can feel the difference between us breathing in and out. So imagine how uncomfortable a tipping or squint rider will be and the relief your horse will feel when the rider becomes straight and balanced and moves in harmony with him. I have been instructing for nearly twenty years and still get a thrill when one of my riders 'gets' an adjustment and grins with joy when they feel the dramatic improvement in their horse.

Schooling methods

It is also important to use schooling exercises which are within your horse's current physical limits and to try to use 'self *rewarding*' types of exercise such as loops for example, with frequent changes of rein. It is very tempting when you get something nice to sit and enjoy it for a while, but this usually ends in tears, as the horse will only learn that doing what you ask him is jolly hard work. He will soon stop 'doing it right' if this means having to maintain his exertions for some time, effectively being punished for giving you the desired response. So, it is best to use short repeats of any strengthening manoeuvre such as transitions, leg yielding or shoulder-in, so that your horse is *rewarded* by a short rest – even a few steps or a change to a different bend is enough to constitute a *reward* here. Try a little gymnastic jumping (e.g. over small grids)

Fig 2.12. A gentle hack is an excellent and pleasant warm up for both horse and rider before a schooling session.

Fig 2.13.   Most people remember to 'warm up' but 'warming down' is also important, particularly after any unusual new or strenuous work – a paddle in the sea is a lovely way for both horses and riders to relax after a fun day out at the beach!

or hacking (e.g. for longer and including more hills) to help strengthen your horse for flatwork, and make your schooling work progressive – start with an easy exercise in walk around the track, then work on it in trot in straight lines before you try it on a circle. Then use a quarter of a circle initially with a straight few steps 'rest' in between quarters, gradually joining these up into half circles and eventually a whole circle etc. until after a few weeks your horse will be fit enough to work correctly for several consecutive circles and so on.

Travelling

Many horse transport vehicles are effectively a horse 'torture chamber'. There may be very limited ventilation, and a stuffy, humid atmosphere which is very irritating to the sensitive respiratory tract of a horse. Worse still if the vehicle is not kept spotlessly clean the atmosphere will include a lot of ammonia and other gases which will be even more unpleasant for your horse.

There may be not enough space for your horse to safely spread his legs to balance, or his head may be tied up too short to allow the movement necessary to help him use his back properly to assist with balance. A saddle on his back will make this much more difficult. A companion may be hogging the 'shared' head space and bracing his legs under the partition, at worst biting or stepping on your horse and at best preventing him putting his head or feet where they need to be to help him balance.

There may be not enough bedding to soak up any urine produced en route. Without at least four inches (10cm) of shavings, for example, the floor will get wet and become slippery. Rubber matting is quite lethal once wet – even a few droppings can be enough to cause your horse to slip and pull a muscle on a rubber floor as you go round a corner.

There may not be enough hay to last the trip. Use a small holed net or even a bag made from several such haynets inside each other, and make sure it is tied up securely where your horse can easily reach it and make certain it is not too high or above resting head height, where it may swing into his face and be very difficult to eat from.

Your horse may not be able to see where he is going, and be swung violently and unpredictably from side to side as you go around a corner or turn at a junction. It is illegal to have a person inside a trailer while it is travelling on the public highway, but anyone who has been in a trailer moving along a lane or in a field will tell you that it is almost impossible to stay on your feet without holding on to the breast bar, and even then that it is very difficult, so imagine how hard it is for your horse!

Some horses learn to manage in one side of the trailer, developing a travelling technique leaning one way only with their hooves wedged into the solid side and their body leaning on the partition. Should they have to travel on the other side for any reason, this can result in serious panic scrabbling, especially when trying to turn in one direction. These horses will happily go into the trailer again, but panic even when back in by themselves on their usual side, should the trailer move or begin to turn in the direction which unbalanced them. This can cause serious injury as well as a lot of damage to the trailer, but is fixable once the horse's physical difficulties are appreciated, with a careful *desensitization* programme (see Chapter 7).

A lorry has much less 'swing' than a trailer. This is why some horses travel much better in a lorry, as it is usually much easier for them to balance. There is also usually a lot more scope to adjust the space available to fit the horses being carried in a lorry. Many of the lightweight 'double' trailers available today are too narrow for two horses to travel comfortably and may also be over the legal weight limit for the average family car to tow with two horses on board. If you are not sure you can check with the Department of

Transport or any motoring organization such as the AA or RAC and the British Horse Society Safety Department may also be able to advise you. If you are taking only one horse for most of the time, it is best to remove the centre partition to give your horse as much space as possible. You must then get both a single span breast bar and a similar single span breaching bar from the manufacturer, which most companies now produce as an optional extra.

One girl who attended one of my courses on equine behaviour problems for vets remarked that she found dealing with trailer problems very easy – she just told people to buy a lorry! Most horses do travel a lot better and seem to prefer a lorry, but it is an expensive option with annual running costs approximating to half the cost of buying a trailer. However, these could be markedly reduced by buying and sharing a lorry between a group of people keeping their horses at the same yard, providing a sensible written agreement can be reached.

There have been quite a few studies carried out on the most comfortable way to transport horses, and the gist of many academic findings is that tail end in front of head end is usually less physical strain for a horse. Left to their own devices under carefully controlled experimental conditions, horses choose to wedge their tail into the front driver's side corner and stand at around thirty to forty degrees from this, so the traditional 'herringbone' design of many lorries is about spot on! Do not be tempted to try a 'new' system in your 'old' vehicle. You do have to travel your horse in the manner for which your trailer or lorry is designed and it is extremely dangerous to let your horse stand facing backwards in a trailer designed for forwards facing travel.

Many people focus on loading procedure when thinking about travelling problems and forget about what happens at the other end i.e. unloading procedure. Many horses find reversing down a slope in a straight line physically very difficult, and need to raise their head considerably to see what they are doing here. Front and side ramps can make unloading much easier and safer all round. Horses having to reverse should be allowed to take their time and to put their head up so that they can watch what they are doing.

Few horses will voluntarily venture up an unsteady ramp, and a small wedge of wood is ideal to make sure that your ramp is steady when parked on uneven or sloping ground. This also prevents damage to the hinges. Most horses also are naturally wary of hollow sounds underfoot, as in the wild this could signal danger from insecure footing, so padded ramps with coconut matting or other non slip covering can help muffle this.

Many trailers or lorries can appear like dark, stuffy, scary caves to your horse, and all his instincts will tell him not to go inside. To make your trailer or lorry appear light, airy, spacious and therefore as inviting as possible, open all windows, ramps and doors and widen the opening you wish your horse to go into as much as you can. Put the interior lights on and park with the sun shining into the box i.e. not behind it casting a shadow. Park on a slope if necessary to make the ramp less steep, and make sure it is solid and does not wobble by using a wedge. Research is currently being done to see whether bright coloured ramps are more attractive to horses than dark ones which might look like shadows or unsafe footing.

Last but by no means least, when thinking about how we inadvertently punish our horses for doing what we want, the single most common way this is done when travelling is by driving too fast and too unevenly i.e. accelerating too quickly or braking too abruptly. One study found that driving faster than fifteen miles an hour on typical 'B' class roads stressed horses in even the best designed lorries. You should drive your horse as smoothly as possible which usually means slowly and the maxim 'twenty's plenty' is a good one here. Choose a route minimizing distance required to travel along 'B' or lesser class roads and maximizing use of dual carriageway and motorways where it is much easier to drive smoothly, with fewer sharp corners and junctions. Too often people are running late because their horse has been difficult to load and then drive too fast, which results in the horse having a terrible journey and becoming less likely to load quietly next time, and so a vicious circle of problems arises.

If your horse objects to loading it is a good idea to take him for short trips, e.g. to a friend's place for a gentle hack or even round the block and out to his own field, so that travelling doesn't always end in strenuous exertion such as at a competition or the beach or worse in examination by a vet or a spell in hospital.

I find that the quality of the journey, largely depending on the quality of the driving, is usually much more of a factor in determining a horse's attitude to loading next time than the loading procedure used. Driving slowly and steadily is by far the best way to avoid *punishing* your horse for going into a vehicle which all his natural instincts told him would be dangerous!

Housing and pasture management

Horses are outdoor creatures and need a lot of space. There is a Chinese saying that 'Horses have hooves to carry them over frost and snow; hair to protect them from wind and cold. They eat greens and drink water. Palatial dwellings are of no use to them' (attributed to Chang Tzu c300 to 400 BC) according to a translation by H Giles in the British Museum. The stable management book written by Blackwood and Cadell in 1978 is quoted by the well known equine vet and welfare enthusiast Dr R N W Ellis in an article he wrote for the magazine *In Practice* in 1990 as saying that 'stabling' has been considered as 'no more than dungeons, built with little regard for the comfort and health of the horse'. This feeling is reiterated in an article on 'The Balance of Welfare' by R Hopes in a 1984 edition of the *Equine Veterinary Journal* (No 16) where he wrote 'with regard to not only modern housing, but also husbandry regimes in particular, the equine industry lags greatly behind on the subject of optimal requirements for housing, management and training'. So, it seems that over the years things have not improved much and writing now, I would have to say that these comments are still sadly also true today!

Many city fringe livery yards are very short of grazing and effectively have very limited turnout which is often poached and overcrowded. In this situation, turn out can become more of an ordeal than a pleasure, particularly

Fig 2.14. Giving your horse as much space as possible minimizes keeping costs and maximises his quality of life.

for horses who are at the lower end of the social hierarchy. Most horses will benefit from at least two acres each and this is very far from stocking densities seen in many livery yards.

The stable dimensions given in most stable management books are actually absolute minima i.e. they are recommending that the stable be no smaller than 12 feet x 12 feet or 4m x 4m. These are not ideal sizes, generally speaking the bigger the better. To give you an idea of industry standards here, the Home Office guidelines for horse stables i.e. for equines over 14.2 hh, say these must be no smaller than 4.3m x 4.6m, the BHS suggest pony boxes be at least 3m x 3.6m. Guidance given to vets inspecting riding establishments suggest following War Office recommendations that stables provide a minimum volume of $45m^3$ per horse with a minimum roof height of 3m. One study showed that horses actually use more space than this when lying down and standing up again in an unrestricted area, and so even boxes built to these standards 'cramp their style'.

I was asked for a second opinion on the 'state of mind' of a very successful competition horse who suddenly began to suffer severe bouts of azoturea (an illness also known as 'tying up' or rhabdomyolysis the main sign of which is severe muscle cramps). The referring vet could find no medical reason why this horse should suddenly develop this kind of problem in the middle of his career, and was keen to eliminate any kind of 'nerves' or behaviour problem before conducting further very expensive tests. Some of the details of George's previous behaviour indicated that he was a fairly confident, bossy type of horse. I asked the trainer for video tape of some other aspects of George's everyday behaviour and saw that he was at times very agitated in his box, although the first bout of azoturea had happened when he was at pasture.

It transpired that he had been kept in a lot since then just in case. As this was therefore to some extent to be expected, the owner Mrs H was not overly concerned about it. However, I investigated this agitation further and discovered that he became particularly upset when certain horses came into or left the yard. A greater than average interest in the movements of other horses and the equine 'social scene' is typical of bossy confident horses like George. They had all been there for at least a year, and there had been no other social changes that the trainer or owner could think of. The yard staff confirmed that they had not changed their turn out routine at all. However, George was showing all the signs of isolation anxiety and careful analysis of the video tape showed that George's agitation had developed into stereotypic behaviour which is a sign of extreme arousal. He would pace repeatedly along the wall, and had begun to weave when standing at the door of his box. When an anti-weave grill was shut across his door, this developed into a complex head-twisting stereotypy, illustrating how distressed he had become. I discovered that this had led to several further bouts of azoturea before I became involved.

Mrs H was by now also quite distressed and could think of nothing at all which had changed before the first bout of illness. She was concerned that the very expensive stable management she was paying for might be questioned and repeatedly emphasized her faith in the yard and how good they had been to her and George. 'They even moved him across into one of the biggest boxes when Santa left' she said. At last, the penny dropped. 'How long ago was that?' I enquired. 'Just before George's first episode of azoturea in the field,' she replied, followed by a gasp as she realised the implications of this! I looked very carefully at the old box to see how it differed from the bigger one from a horse's point of view. In the end the solution to the mystery was obvious. From the old and smaller box, the window looked out into the pasture. The new box was on the other side of the barn, and although it was bigger, you could not see any horses from it. Furthermore, it was at the end of its line and it transpired that the yard staff brought horses in and out in order according to what box they were in, so while from the staff's point of view, nothing had changed, it certainly had from where George was standing! This turned out to be by himself as the last one in the field and this was probably the precipitating factor for the first bout of azoturea. As a horse keen on his social life would have become very agitated at being left alone and dashing around madly calling for his mates could well have precipitated the first bout of azoturea. This was also what was upsetting him in the new box. There were times when he could not see his mates and worse, times when he could not see any other horses at all. This very disabling problem was easy to solve and George was returned to his 'room with a view'.

This example shows how important it is to think about the stable not only in terms of size but also from all aspects of your horse's life particulary the social scene which is very important to most horses. It has even been suggested that safety mirrors may help to calm horses which become distressed at times in their stable or which have to be isolated for medical reasons.

Studies have also shown that most modern stabling is severely under ventilated and even in 'top' yards getting three figure sums per week for livery, there are not enough air changes to maintain respiratory health. If your stable or American barn building feels noticeably warmer to you than the outside when you first go in, or you can smell that 'nice stabley smell', or you see dust on the cobwebs, then there is not enough ventilation.

Fig 2.15. Horses are naturally highly social animals and when given enough space choose to live together in small groups.

You can help to give your horse more fresh air in his stable by keeping the top door and all windows open all the time. More openings, particularly if on the opposite wall and higher up than the door will increase air flow. Insulating the roof will also help and keep the box cooler in the summer. You can reduce the dust in your stable by using plenty of good quality bedding and mucking out early enough to let it all settle before your horse goes back in. This also allows the floor to dry when your horse is out and reduces the humidity he is exposed to. When designing your stable, try to build in as much passive ventilation as possible, maximizing openings and roof heights. While a gale blowing through the central corridor of an American style barn may not be very nice for you, it will be a much appreciated breath of fresh air for your horse!

Confidence

Most people are aware of the dangers of overconfidence and attempting a fence or manoeuvre beyond them or their horse at any stage in their training. However, under confidence can also lead to problems where a rider approaches an exercise or jump with a lack of self belief or trust in their horse and can give the unfortunate horse some very mixed signals, leading

Fig 2.16. *Right*: Both partners in this youthful combination show their concern as they approach a drop fence just beyond their current scope when trying to match an older sibling.

Fig 2.17. *Below*: Choosing the smaller option allows a more confident approach by both pony and rider and helps to build their confidence and trust in each other.

to confusion. At best the rider is left behind when the horse goes, becomes unbalanced and hurts the horse, accidentally *punishing* him for actually being better than 'obedient' and doing the task presented without the usual guidance, encouragement or support of his rider. At worst, this can also lead to a refusal or fall and in either case an unpleasant consequence to 'good' behaviour for the horse.

Figure 2.16. shows a young combination both looking less than keen to try the drop fence this little girl's sister has just flown over on her pony. Peer pressure is a terrible thing! Figure 2.17. shows how much happier they are taking the option which they know they can both safely manage.

So, don't encourage anyone beyond their capabilities and make sure you are not pushed beyond your own limits yourself, even by an instructor. Only attempt what you believe both you and your horse are capable of and then ride positively, committing yourself fully to the task in hand and give your horse the guidance and encouragement he needs, to help him do his best for you.

ACCIDENTAL REWARDS

Unfortunately for our horses, this section is much shorter than the previous one on inadvertent *punishment*. Unwitting *rewards* for 'bad' or undesirable behaviour can however lead to serious behaviour problems and this is a major causal factor in many of the behaviour problems I am asked to deal with.

There are three main ways people commonly *reward* 'bad' behaviour by mistake or without knowing it in my experience. These are:

- Handling technique
- Riding technique
- Attention

Handling technique

Allowing your horse to follow you around, especially around the stable e.g. as when skipping out, is always perceived by the horse as you letting him push you around. He is being *rewarded* for behaving like a 'bossy' horse by your continued 'submission' as you keep moving away from him. This can lead to confusion in your relationship with your horse and serious social dominance related handling problems, so do tie your horse up, or even better take him out of the box to skip out or change rugs etc. It really is worth the extra hassle in the long run.

Ineffective ground handling, letting your horse get into a position from which he can easily pull away from you, and eat grass or go back to his companions, is another common cause of many of the problems that I see. Do make sure you are leading your horse correctly as described in the section above on handling in 'Inadvertent *Punishments*'. If you are having persistent trouble here, you can always ask a riding instructor to give you a lesson on 'ground handling'. It really is important when leading to stay beside your horse's shoulder and push his head in front of you while moving his hindquarters along or around you.

Many people struggle to hold a horse's leg up for any length of time, especially if the horse begins to fidget or lean. Again, a riding instructor can show you how to do this safely and effectively. If you are having difficulty here, it is better to pick the foot up several times for several short bouts of picking out than to try to hold it up for long enough to do this all at once.

Remember, horse handling is a game of skill, not strength, and it is much better not to let things go too far than end up with a 'tug of war' which your horse will always win.

Riding technique

It is sometimes very difficult not to fall off and leave your horse to his own devices! Some horses realize that a rider will give up when they get tired, and put up with a certain amount of discomfort for the *reward* of the subsequent rest when aids are applied ineffectively. It can help here to also learn the best time to give your aids and how to relate these to your horse's stride patterns, maximizing your effectiveness while minimizing your physical effort. Improving your skill level and fitness here is the best way not to accidentally *reward* your horse here.

Attention

Many of us cannot resist a certain look, posture or particular little 'party trick' in our horses. Looking cute is a great way of getting attention for being naughty and most horses have a huge repertoire of little poses they use to great effect here, usually reaping huge *rewards* in looks, laughs, indulgent 'admonishments' and treats.

Do your best to resist and ignore your horse when he is trying to be cute!

Fig 2.18. These three pictures illustrate some of the most common kinds of attention seeking 'cute' behaviour which develop by operant conditioning from instinctive responses to frustration and are best ignored!

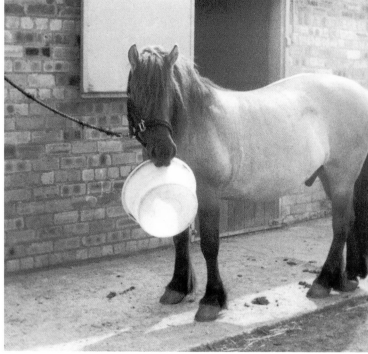

PRACTICAL REWARDS

These can be broadly divided into the following categories:
- Food
- Calming
- Relief from pressure
- Company

Food

Most horses are very highly motivated towards food, and a novel or particularly tasty treat usually makes an excellent *reward*. You can make these healthy and affordable. For example, use tiny pieces such as half a polo mint or one pony cube at a time. Cut carrot or apple or other fruits and vegetables which your horse likes into tiny pieces and keep them in a polythene bag. For horses needing to keep to a strict diet, take a few handfuls from the bucket feed when you have made up his usual ration and put this into a polythene bag to use later when training.

To avoid 'teaching bad habits' and your horse nudging or nipping for treats, do not leave these in your pocket or grooming kit when you are not training, and give them from the sternum, so that your horse has to tuck his head down and in to get the treat (see Figure 2.19. overleaf). This puts him in a socially subordinate posture and is also a nice warm-up stretch. You can also encourage your horse to bend his head and neck round e.g. to his elbow, knee or fetlock for a treat. As this is part of some of the exercises a physio-therapist would use to encourage mobility and suppleness, you are also doing a little physical training here as well as psychological. You can also throw treats into the stable or scatter these on pasture to manipulate your horse by *rewarding* him for moving to a particular spot, and so on.

You can seed your riding route with little treats placed on fence posts or even set up your own bright little pots (flowerpots or margarine tubs can be useful here) along the way to allow you to *reward* a nappy horse or one which is spooking out of naughtiness.

It is important that everyone involved with the horse knows the system being used and that they all use the same techniques as consistency is very important with *reward*s.

> Many years ago, in my student days, I was helping a friend retrain a young horse who had been involved in a 'near miss' road accident. Buckley had previously been well used to traffic but since being 'nudged' by a car when

hacking out locally one day, had understandably become very nervous on the road and panicked at the sound of approaching traffic. We had spent a few weekends getting him used to this and practising with our own vehicles in their yard and farm lanes (using calming words and pats as *rewards* and the training techniques known as *systematic desensitization* and *counter-conditioning* (see Chapter 7) until he was calm enough to accept a treat as a *reward*. Finally we were ready to try him on the road again.

My friend rode and I accompanied her on a bicycle, armed with a pocket full of treats. We quickly discovered that it was not very practical for the cycle rider to nip back and offer a treat immediately the rider heard a vehicle approaching. Mostly this was due to the lack of fitness of the cyclist, but in my defence, also partly due to the hilly terrain and twists and turns in the roads, which were also bounded by high beech hedges which muffled sounds at the cyclist's level. So, we swapped, keeping the treats in the rider's pocket and offering these from the rider's hand instead. Buckley quickly learned that when you heard traffic in the distance, if you stopped and turned your head to the right, you got a tasty piece of carrot. We were very pleased with ourselves and reported great results back home at dinner, telling my friend's husband that Buckley had got over his fright and was now fine to hack out again. Unfortunately for hubby, we omitted the exact details of our final session and the new reward system.

Keen to test our success, the poor chap went for a hack the following day. Buckley seemed settled, and was trotting nicely up a small incline, when they heard the faint sound of a large van in the distance. Hubby didn't quite trust our training programme and stories of success. He could see a lane a few hundred yards ahead and tried to trot on quickly to seek sanctuary there just in case. But good old Buckley, having been properly trained, stopped and turned his head and neck sharply right for the anticipated treat. Hubby was abruptly deposited over the left shoulder into the not so welcoming beech hedge! He managed to keep hold of the reins, and luckily the van slowed down and passed the disgruntled pair safely. Needless to say, my friend's husband was not best pleased with our efforts, and the memory of the look on his face when he returned to the yard was enough to remind me evermore of the importance of choosing *rewards* and the system of delivery very carefully, in particular to make sure that everyone who has anything to do with the horse is aware of the new training regime.

Food works best when your horse is hungry and also when he is calm and relaxed, so this is not the best *reward* to use when you are training your horse to get used to something of which he is particularly frightened. In this situation calming is usually much more effective in the first instance.

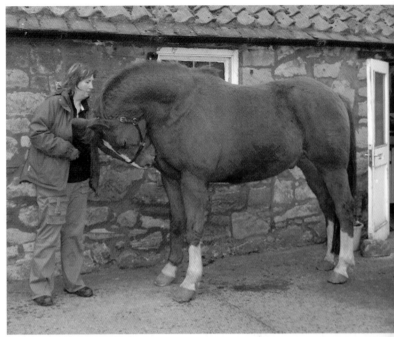

Fig 2.19a. and b. These two pictures show the best way to present a treat to your horse to avoid being mugged or nipped in the future!

Calming

When horses are very scared or nervous, speaking in a deep low pitched voice, using words with one or two syllables, soft consonants and long vowel sounds are naturally calming. Changing the pitch to a lower one as the vowels extend and decreasing the frequency i.e. slowing the sounds also mimics the vocalizations horses make to each other which have a calming or relaxing effect.

It has been shown that vigorous rubbing in the withers area and down the shoulder stimulates nodes of nerve cells which have the physical effect of lowering heart rate and so this should also feel calming to your horse. Just watch him grooming another horse by scratching with his teeth and look for the spots they use. This sort of mutual grooming is done at times of social tension and also reduces heart rate, so it should also feel relaxing. When you are riding you can press your knuckles firmly into your horse's neck on either side of his mane, to achieve the same effect, while still holding the reins securely. This has the added benefit of also providing an 'emergency brace' for the rider and is very useful should you anticipate your horse spooking or spinning round.

Relief from pressure

Most horses will instinctively move away from pressure from someone on the ground whom they respect and push back towards someone doing this that they don't respect. However, when ridden, all horses will instinctively move away from pressure from a rider's legs, seat and hands and this is how many ridden aids work. A little change in body position, balance or contact pressure with the leg or rein can set up a pressure which the horse will then move away from. It is vital that the rider's technique and feel here is good enough for them to realize when the horse has moved in the desired way and to be able to gently release this pressure to *reward* the correct response immediately. This skill is the basis of really good riding and many people who are 'naturally good horsemen' do this instinctively.

> I once had the benefit of a marvellous lesson from an Icelandic trainer who was himself a superb horseman. He had this 'give and take' reward system down to a fine art, and with very few words of English, merely saying 'more' or 'less' at the appropriate times, he taught me more about riding Icelandic horses in a few minutes than I had managed to learn over the previous couple of years. He made different wild hand gestures with each of these comments so I could pick up what was required at long range. By experiencing the 'feel' of when to give and when to take the reins, I began to 'get it' (by the process of *classical conditioning* see Chapter 4) and was then better able to *reward* my client's magnificent little horse more promptly for the desired activity, and was finally *rewarded* myself by some wonderful steps.

I was also very impressed that this trainer was also using learning theory instinctively in his lessons on the riders as well!

Company

Horses are highly social animals, and will find access to the right companion most *rewarding*. You can use this to encourage your horse past or over obstacles and with nappy horses arranging to meet up with a favoured companion around the corner just beyond where the napping start can be a very effective *reward*.

MOTIVATION

You will have noticed that this chapter concentrates heavily on *rewards*. This is because so do most horses! Most instinctive behaviour and all learned behaviour actually only happens if there is a *reward* at the end of it from the horse's point of view and activity which is *punished*, however inadvertently, will be unlikely to happen again. How many people do you know who would go to work every day if they did not need the money to pay their bills? Furthermore, horses, and indeed all animals including ourselves, require the desire for *reward* to motivate them into almost any kind of activity. These desires are prioritized from moment to moment and as soon as any one desire is satisfied, another desire becomes the most important and behaviour then changes towards satisfying that instead and so on. The technical term for this series of fluctuating desires is *motivation* and it is important to remember to think about this when choosing which *reward* to use in your training because *rewards* are only effective when your horse has the desire for that sort of thing. Most importantly, a horse will only regard food as a *reward* if he is hungry, and effective training treats usually have to be very tasty!

One of the nicest horse owners I have ever met was, at the time I met her, pinned to the corner of her stable beside the door by a particularly bossy mare, which greeted my approach with much lungeing and chomping of teeth over the stable door. Instead of my usual cheery 'How are you?' at the beginning of the consultation, I was moved to enquire tremulously from a safe distance 'Would you like a hand?' and steeled myself to rescue her, breaking many of the academic conventions of non interference while assessing the nature and extent of the problem.

'Oh no thank you' came the cheery reply, 'that's just her way of saying hello!'

I took a deep breath and embarked on what I thought would be one of my most challenging cases to date. Luckily, this horse lived on a farm where treats were considered to encourage bad habits and hardly ever got any, so I had a particularly effective 'weapon' on my side as it were. We began that day, using a treat to encourage Clara to turn her head towards Miss N while she tickled the mare's abdominal muscles to elicit a reflex making the mare step away on the command of 'over' (see Chapter 4 on the Learning Process).

To prevent Miss N being 'mugged' for treats in the future, we made sure these were always given only for a correct response and offered at the sternum so that the mare had to tuck her head right in to get them. We tacked up and, using the rider asking for halt as the final stimulus, taught this horse to stop immediately the handler stopped, with a *string of classical conditioned stimuli* (see Chapter 5 on Learning to Respond), ultimately giving her a treat, again at the sternum. Within five minutes this horse had worked out that doing what someone asks you results in a very tasty treat and is much more worthwhile than shoving people around! We had a lot of work to do to consolidate this attitude and maintain this good behaviour, but within a couple of weeks, this little horse was showing all the signs of the super mare she was going to become and I was dubbed forever 'the sweetie lady'!

Luckily for us *motivation* is cyclical and we can often plan ahead and train at times when the *motivation* for the *reward* we are using is high, as some time after eating, your horse will become hungry again (see more about this in Chapters 3 and 8). You can often manipulate motivation, e.g. by tempting your horse by letting him smell a particularly tasty or favourite treat, or moving companions around to create the desire to go in a particular direction.

This is how 'giving a lead' from another horse over a difficult jump or past a spooky point works. Your horse may not initially see the point in getting over the jump or past the flapping haylage wrappers, perhaps suggesting that you should spin around NOW and head for the relative safety and relaxation of the yard instead!

When the lead horse starts to go past the obstacle, your horse is suddenly faced with increasing isolation and being left behind. For such a strongly social animal as the horse, this creates a considerable desire to follow and catch up. As the lead horse gets further away, the desire to follow increases until it becomes stronger than the desire to be lazy or the fear of the obstacle. Your horse's behaviour will change to satisfy the newly prioritized motivation and he will now want to get on and catch up with his chum. The desire to catch up can be further increased should the lead horse disappear around a corner, step onto a softer surface, where his footsteps are less obvious, or he picks up speed e.g. trotting off!

It is essential to choose a *reward* your horse will be motivated to want at the time you are training and some practical ways of manipulating motivation and creating desires for easy to offer *rewards* are given in Chapters 3 and 8.

In terms of basic biology all animals are motivated by the same few essentials of survival. These are water, sex, food, freedom from fear or pain, physical comfort (i.e. not too wet, dry, hot or cold) and in social animals appropriate companions. Most horses will usually prioritize their desires in this order.

Fig 2.20a. *Left*: For most horses the right companions are very important for a quiet life.

Fig 2.20b. *Right*: The wrong companion can change an expected rewarding situation into inadvertent punishment and this sort of aggressive social behaviour can lead to serious injury.

> I have a colleague who enjoyed considerable competitive success with a stallion, often travelling him alongside mares in season and having no problems at all with any other mares at competitions. Very impressed with her equestrian skills, I was moved to enquire how she managed this, and waited eagerly for what I was sure would be some very useful tips in her answer. Much to my disappointment but our considerable amusement she remarked carelessly 'Oh he's just like my husband – more interested in food than sex – so we don't have any bother!'

So, it is important to get to know your own horse's individual likes and dislikes. Some horses for example go mad for beetroot but won't touch strawberries and vice versa. Using the wrong horse as a companion can turn an attempted *reward* into a *punishment* (see Figure 2.20.). We all have different tastes and preferences and it is well worth while experimenting to find the best sort of treat or *reward* for your own horse.

The end of this chapter brings us to the 'million dollar' question – 'how do you *reward* your horse within a half second of appropriate or desirable behaviour when he is out of reach or you are trying to teach him a complex manoeuvre or series of steps which last for longer than half a second'?

The answer s that this is done by training your horse that a special stimulus or signal is followed immediately by your *reward*. These signals are sometimes called *bridging stimuli* as they 'bridge' the gap between desired behaviour and final reward. You can build up a chain of these, teaching your horse that one signal leads to another and so on until the one linked with the final *reward* is reached. A 'chain' of signals might start with a call of 'good boy' and finish with you giving a treat, allowing you to cope with any situation you wish. How to build a 'chain of stimuli' to make training easier is explained in Chapter 5.

SUMMARY

Much of this chapter describes some very common ways in which, despite the best of intentions horses may be accidentally *rewarded* for 'bad' behaviour and inadvertently *punished* for doing what we asked them to. Although it can at times be very difficult in practice, you can encourage your horse to do his best for you by ignoring the 'bad' behaviour and doing your best to offer an immediate and appropriate *reward* when your horse does what you want.

Finally, as many of the case history examples given in this chapter show, it is very important to think about *rewards* and *punishment* from your horse's point of view. What seems to be 'nice' to us may sometimes be quite the opposite to your horse! Do your best to ignore 'bad' behaviour and reward 'good'.

Chapter 3

Training and Time

Chapters 1 and 2 have emphasized the importance of rewarding good behaviour immediately when training and how many behaviour problems develop from immediate punishment of desirable activity, regardless of how inadvertent this may be.

There is more 'bad news' here in that training takes time – a lot of time. No matter how it is done, training which will last, preventing the recurrence of problems in the future and facilitating maintenance of the desired response in times of stress or great excitement, requires careful planning and consolidation over time. There is no such thing as a 'quick fix'!

Fairly early on in my career, I was asked to see a horse with some serious travel problems and which the owner had never been able to load successfully. At the time, I was juggling lecturing and writing with this kind of consultancy work and had a three week waiting list. I was most apologetic to Miss T and relieved that she did not seem to mind the long wait. Indeed, 'I'm very busy myself at the moment' she said, and was quite specific that, not only was it not a problem for her to wait a few weeks for me to come and see her horse, but that the only date she could manage was about three weeks away.

I turned up on the appointed day to find the trailer all prepared for a journey as I had requested. I was most impressed by Miss T's attention to detail and the realism of the set up provided. I relaxed, thinking how easy it would be to work with such a patient and thoughtful person. About an hour later, when I had taken the history and found out why Mercury would not load, I was ready to explain the first steps in Mercury's training and to teach Miss T the initial reward system we were going to use. I was in the middle of explaining that I would be sending a full written report, describing the progressive series of training exercises we would be using to teach this genuinely frightened horse that being near the trailer was a good thing, when we were interrupted by the arrival of a very smart and extremely large horse lorry.

Miss T went pale and then very pink. 'Oh no!' she exclaimed 'They're early – they shouldn't be here until half past four.' Somewhat puzzled, I said soothingly, 'It doesn't matter – we can finish now and pick up from where we left off in the next session'. Imagine my surprise when a very frazzled Miss T blurted out 'But that's no use to me at all – we are moving today!' The lorry that had just arrived contained the people who had bought her house (and paddock) and the horses that they were expecting to be able to turn out that evening.

I discovered that, impressed by my reputation and having seen a few horsy 'handling demos', Miss T expected me to load Mercury immediately, thereby facilitating her move. This was why she had been 'very busy' over the last few weeks. She had no idea of the time and number of sessions that would have been required to teach her very nervous horse to load safely and quietly every time and really just wanted help in shifting him! I learned the hard way to be a little clearer about this on the phone when making the first appointment.

Some well known 'gurus' can put on a great show and appear to 'fix' problems in a few moments during exciting and often very entertaining demonstrations. These are not usually long term solutions however, and all too often I meet clients who have sent their horse away to be 're-schooled' at some considerable expense, only to be most disappointed to find that the problem recurs within a few weeks of bringing the horse home. This is because the 're-training' has not been consolidated and the 'good' behaviour seen initially is highly likely to have resulted in part from a change of environment and to be more of a response to confident, experienced handlers and riders than the results of effective training.

TIME AND TRIALS

Essentially, whether you are trying to teach your horse to do something new or to stop doing something, it is the number of attempts he makes during the time you spend training which count towards long term learning. The technical term for an attempt in training is a 'trial' and it is the number of trials which determine how long it takes for a horse to learn anything. For example, it may take the average horse fifteen trials to learn to come to the field gate to be caught when you call his name. If you only do this once every day, it will take him fifteen days to 'get' this. If you repeat the training five times every day, he will have 'got it' in just three days and so on. There is however, a limit here on the effectiveness of lots of trials in one day, as it takes time for learned behaviour to be consolidated into memory, and most trainers find using a few trials each day is more effective than packing as many trials as possible in one day. So, to some extent speed of learning and the overall number of trials required to teach your horse something can be manipulated by how and when you organize your training sessions.

A number of studies have looked at rates of learning in horses and how the number of trials and time between training sessions or pattern of sessions affects this. They show that different patterns of training work better for different forms of learning, and the optimum pattern of trials depends on what you are trying to teach your horse. Generally, around fifteen to twenty trials per session and training once a day seems to work well for most routine training and you can reduce the number of sessions required overall by leaving more time between training sessions to let your horse 'process' what he has just learned and commit this to memory. One study found that horses trained once a week learned in fewer sessions than horses trained daily and that those trained twice a week were somewhere in between. This beneficial effect of increasing the time left in between training sessions is sometimes called 'latent learning' and this is probably a reflection of the way in which the horse's brain processes information and the time required to transfer information between short and long term memory.

This allows you to get the maximum benefit from the *time* you spend training by carefully *planning* and structuring your training to take advantage of what is known about how your horse's *brain* and *memory* work. This includes organizing your reward system according to various *schedules of reinforcement* and the value of *repetition,* as well as knowing how to *measure progress* and predict exactly how long it will take for any particular piece of training to be completed.

PLANNING A TRAINING PROGRAMME

When planning your training, it is important to think about the practicalities of what is possible with the facilities you have, to book well ahead any extra facilities and any help you may need and to think carefully about what you can realistically achieve in the time you have available.

When should I train?

Planning is the key to choosing the best time for you to train your horse, whatever the task.

First of all think about whether or not a problem has to be worked on at any particular time of the year, such as clipping for example, which may be best worked on in the winter, when you might want your horse clipped. Think about what time of year the weather or day length may be most conducive to your training. For example, loading is often easier to work on in the summer in good weather and on bright days.

Think also about your own work and family commitments. Obviously, a sudden crisis could develop at home or work at any time, but ideally you should plan your training around any expected busy times and choose a time of year and days of the week that you can reasonably expect to be able to make the time required on a fairly regular basis. You will be much better able to focus on the task in hand if you are working in comfort at your own convenience.

You may need extra facilities to those which are usually available at your yard, and if you need to borrow equipment, hire a vehicle, use indoor areas or have help from other people, this needs to be booked in advance. If you have to lay out any expenses up front, for example when hiring a vehicle or school, and you need help, it is best to have a contingency 'back up' helper in mind and on standby, should your first choice helper be ill or otherwise unable to make it on the day. This prevents you being tempted to try to manage without the help you need which can be counterproductive.

Choose your training period so that you do not have anything else going on at the same time which could interfere with your training programme. For example, 'real' trips in the trailer in the middle of a *systematic desensitization* programme (see Chapter 7) will spoil weeks of careful training. If you are trying to teach your horse to stand for the farrier, you will get on much more quickly if your training sessions are not interspersed by stressful 'real' shoeing attempts. Here, it may be better initially to have the shoes removed, give up fast and road work for a couple of months or so and instead spend the shoeing budget on a few short 'training' visits from your farrier, weekly if possible! This allows him to keep an eye on the state of your horse's feet, trimming these if necessary, while showing you the various stages of the shoeing process that you can work on getting your horse used to each week.

I had one very good looking female client who was lucky enough to have a young local farrier who was persuaded (I'm not sure how!) to pop in and give her horse an apple over the field gate every time he was passing. He also very kindly lent her some old tools to tap her horse's feet gently with when she was picking out his feet and a piece of torn apron to wear when she fed him. This horse, which would previously not be caught if the farrier's van was in the yard, began to hover around the gate instead, and now whinnies as soon as he hears the farrier's van at the end of their lane! (See Chapter 7 for an explanation of the training techniques used in this case.)

You will find it easier to resist events which might spoil a training programme if you plan ahead to carry out your training at a time of year when you do not need to travel, or when there are no competitions nearby to tempt you.

One of the easiest cases I ever had to deal with was in a yard where I did a lot of regular teaching. The girl who had the box next door to that of my regular rider was a very capable horsewoman and a qualified instructor who had worked in a very well known equestrian centre for many years. Her horse Ben had had some serious injuries to a front leg in the past and suffered from very bad mud fever in this area. Her vet had suggested every known treatment for this and she had tried them all without success. It transpired that she was unable to apply ointments or even to wash and dry his front legs thoroughly as he would not let her touch them in the affected areas. Miss M had struggled to cope with this problem for two years and was aware that his behaviour was a direct result of anticipated pain.

As I went through the history, I began to get a sinking feeling, as the ways she had tried in the past to get him to tolerate her touching his 'no go areas' essentially covered all the effective training methods I was aware of! I noticed that Ben's legs were surprisingly clean considering, and commented on this. 'Oh I just crack on and blast him with the power hose when I have to – like for competitions or for you coming today!' Unfortunately for Ben, what she did not realize was that by periodically 'just cracking on' she was inadvertently spoiling all the good work she had done in the preceding weeks, and this was why her training had not had the desired results, even after two years. My advice in this case was very simple. All Miss M had to do to keep Ben's progress on track was to stop the periodic 'blasting' and continue to work through her training, progressively building up Ben's

> tolerance of her handling of his legs until he could stand for the complete wash and dry process. After two years of frustration, Miss M was delighted when after a couple of months of uninterrupted training, Ben was able to tolerate enough handling to allow her to apply the mud fever treatment her vet had recommended, the mud fever was cleared up and the following winter she was able to keep his legs clean and dry enough to prevent it recurring.

You should also plan to allow for a few sessions to teach your horse your reward system (see Chapter 5 on *strings of conditioned stimuli* and *bridging stimuli* etc), and build in some 'revision' time as well as some extra sessions to allow for the unexpected, such as bad weather, illness or injury. This should remove any temptation to rush a session or plough on irregardless when it would be safer and more effective in the long run just to cancel a session (see more in Chapter 8 on maximizing the effectiveness of your training).

Horses have their own daily or 'circadian' rhythms and usually split their twenty-four hours into alternating bouts of resting and grazing. Left to their own devices, they tend to spend a couple of hours being fairly active and pottering around grazing followed by a couple of hours standing 'dozing' in 'slow wave' or non paradoxical sleep, before having a stretch and setting off to spend a couple of hours grazing again and so on. You can take advantage of this by timing your training sessions according to the state of mind you would prefer in your horse. If you are teaching your horse to tolerate something scary or to stand or work quietly for example, you would be best to choose to train during the two hours he would be expected to be 'resting'. He is not likely to be particularly motivated by food at this point, and especially tasty treats may be required as rewards here. If, on the other hand, you are teaching him something which requires him to be alert and very active, including strenuous ridden work, then it is best to train during an active 'feeding' phase. Any food is likely to be a desirable reward at this time. You will get the best from your horse if you can fit your training in around his natural daily rhythms.

Luckily, unlike us, horses only need about fifteen to twenty minutes of 'deep' or REM sleep twice each day, and lie flat out requiring complete muscle relaxation for this, usually at some point between midnight and 2 a.m., and again in the middle of the day from around midday to 2 p.m.. It is unlikely that your ideal training regime will interfere with your horse's 'midnight sleep', but many people may be tempted to make use of a long lunch or a break in the middle of the day, for example when all the children are at school or nursery, to do a spot of training. If you are unlucky enough to get to your horse before he has had his 'midday sleep', you may find him less than co-operative! Horses also need to lie down for about thirty minutes twice a day for some of their non-paradoxical sleep, and this usually happens around 8 to 10 a.m. and again, some twelve hours later. The exact time your horse chooses for this is largely determined by day length and to a lesser extent the weather, diet and feeding times when he is stabled. Young horses will do this more often. You can save yourself a lot of hassle by asking around at the yard or spending a few mornings watching your horse to determine his routine at the time of year you are planning to train, so that you do not try to work with him when he is attempting to sleep!

How long will it take?

This is as difficult to answer as the question 'How long is a piece of string?' It is my experience that some horse and rider combinations will learn a simple ridden manoeuvre, such as shoulder-in, after half a dozen attempts in a single half hour training session. Other tasks, particularly those where you are trying to get a horse used to something he is frightened of, may take several months of careful training to achieve.

As emphasized above, the more frequently your horse attempts anything new, the sooner he will learn it. This means that, unfortunately, behaviour problems can develop rapidly and may escalate from an occasional annoyance to an unacceptable situation in a few days. However, this also means you can reduce the time it takes to teach your horse something new by getting him to try or experience it as frequently as possible, maximizing the number of 'trials' offered. For example, when working on a complex ridden manoeuvre such as a transition, you should pack as many of these into your schooling session as possible – try a transition at every marker! Generally, however, as a practical guideline, I find that most people can teach their horse a complex new task in a few training sessions spread out over a period of a couple of weeks, whereas two to three months may be required to completely 're-train' a horse who is genuinely frightened of the clippers, travelling or the farrier etc.

How often should I train and how long for?

You should set aside blocks of time specifically for training, and schedule these sessions to fit in with your own daily commitments and the yard routine. It is usually better in the long run to be pragmatic and schedule your training to fit in with the yard routine if your horse is kept at livery, as most livery yards do not have enough staff to cope with individual schedules, and in my experience, despite the best of efforts on the owner's part to minimize disruption to the yard, 'special requests' requiring deviation from the normal husbandry routine are rarely fully complied with for any length of time.

You may be limited by practicalities to training less often than you initially want to, but it is better to be realistic here and maybe have time for an extra session now and again than try to stick to an overly optimistic programme. Ambitious schedules usually lead to disappointment and loss of confidence to the point where you might actually be spoiling previous good work and make mistakes when you are tired or rushing to try to stick to an impossible schedule (see also Chapter 8 on Maximizing your Effectiveness as a Trainer).

You may also find your training sessions will be limited to the times when help or certain facilities are available. Think about your reward system and schedule sessions to fit in around feeding and turn-out times for example, especially when you are planning to use food as a reward. You might also like to try to train when the yard is quiet and there are fewer people around to interrupt you or fritter your precious training time away chatting!

Above all, do not imagine for one second that you can fit your training in around your daily routine while you 'do' the horse. Despite what your family or non-horsy friends might think, most people do not have a minute to spare when they are at the yard, and time spent training must be added on to the time you need to 'do' your horse.

Once the above has been taken into consideration, 'little and often' is the simplest answer to offer to the question of how often and for how long should training best be done. I find that for most people, working on a specific ridden task for twenty minutes a day and no more than half an hour on a handling problem is quite sufficient. I once had the great privilege of watching one of the best horse trainers I have ever seen working with her horses at the Circus Knie in Switzerland. The daily training session for these world famous performing horses only lasted an hour, and this is also enough for horses competing at international level to learn the skills required in most other equestrian disciplines. It is quality of training not quantity that matters for long term success and five minutes of 'good' and correct training is much better than several hours of incorrect training (again see Chapter 8 for more on Maximising the Effectiveness of your Training).

It's not all 'bad news' here. I mentioned earlier that you can reduce the number of trials needed and thereby the time it takes to teach your horse anything by how you organize your training sessions. The two most useful ways of doing this are by using different reward systems known as *schedules of reinforcement* and the ways in which long and short term *memory* work when planning your training.

SCHEDULES OF REINFORCEMENT

Do you remember chanting your multiplication tables or the correct spelling of a difficult word over and over again at school? In order for training to last in the long term, the ABC (remember the <u>A</u>ntecedents, <u>B</u>ehaviour and <u>C</u>onsequences described in Chapter 1) of your action-reward attempts or *trials,* needs to be repeated for the correct response or desirable activity and its link with the consequent reward to be committed to memory. The number and pattern in which rewards are given in repeated *trials* is called a *schedule of reinforcement.*

First of all, you need to consolidate the link between action and reward, e.g. by giving your horse a reward for every correct action within half a second of the desired behaviour. This reward system is called a *fixed ratio schedule of reinforcement*, and this is the simplest way to train your horse. Some re-training techniques work by gradually increasing the ratio of correct responses required per reward (see Chapter 7 on Practical Re-training Techniques). When you are giving one reward for one correct action, this is technically referred to as an F1 or FR1 schedule. If you change this to giving one reward for two, or five, or eight correct actions, you are using an F2, F5 or F8 schedule of reinforcement and so on. A simple *fixed ratio schedule of reinforcement* is how all good training begins, and how you initially teach your horse the reward system.

The extent of any *reward* or *punishment* affects the number of trials required for your horse to learn anything. For example, if the reward you are using is of relatively little consequence to your horse, such as the tiny reduction in pressure used in many ridden aids, you will need a lot of *repeats* for learning to take place and for the desired response to be incorporated into your horse's memory. This is why partners and children always complain they get nagged about little things! If the consequence of forgetting something is of no great importance to them, they are less likely to learn to remember it and you will have to remind them again and again. The smaller or less attractive your *reward*, the more *repeats* or 'trials' it will take for learning to take place. Behaviour with huge rewards will be learned in many fewer trials. Serious behaviour problems can be learned from just one episode where there were considerable consequences to any activity. For example, you may only need to fall off a genuinely spooking horse once for him to learn that this is a very good way of dislodging the rider and being free to dash back to the stables. Conversely, it usually takes only one serious *punishment*, however inadvert, to teach a horse to learn to be absolutely terrified of whatever caused this. This is how single traumatic accidents cause major behaviour problems, where the consequences to something are just so bad that your horse never wants to repeat that activity again.

You might think that the value or desirability of any particular *reward* at any particular time will always be the same (see Chapter 2 on Rewards, Punishment and Motivation). However, you can manipulate this value and make any particular reward more desirable by playing with the number of rewards given per 'correct' action or the length of time that the 'good' behaviour must last for to get a reward. Once your horse has learned by the simple *fixed ratio* system that any specific activity is rewarded, you can change the rules and require him to do it more times or for longer to get the reward. This makes the reward more valuable to the horse. If you have to work all week to earn a pound, it will mean much more to you than if you get one given to you for just getting out of bed each day! Studies have shown that, while increasing the work required per reward in this way helps to make it worth more, varying the number of times a horse must do the right thing in order to get a reward is the best way to maximize the value of any reward. This kind of reward system is known as a *variable ratio* schedule of reinforcement. If you vary the length of time your horse must maintain 'good' behaviour to get a reward, effectively increasing the interval between the initial 'correct response' and the reward now and again, you are using a reward system known as a *variable interval* schedule of reinforcement.

The practical upshot of this is that you can increase the value of any reward by giving it on a *variable ratio* or *variable interval* schedule of reinforcement. Increasing the value of the reward reduces the number of trials needed for learning to take place and committing the correct behaviour to memory, which speeds up the training process.

Apart from speeding up training, *variable ratio* and *variable interval* schedules of reinforcement can be useful practical aids, building on previous training, particularly handy for consolidating new learned responses and maintaining good behaviour. For example, when you have taught your horse to come to be caught when you call his name (see Chapter 4 on the Learning Process), you will initially have to give him a treat each time – a simple *fixed ratio* of reinforcement. If you then progress to only giving him a treat sometimes when he comes to you to be caught on command, you have put him onto a *variable* schedule of reinforcement, maintaining the response, using fewer treats and making the days when you have run out or forget to bring the packet of treats with you no problem.

Conversely, lack of awareness of the effect of varying reward ratio or interval on learning is often a factor in the development of a behaviour problem. For example, do you remember the door banging example mentioned at the beginning of Chapter 2 on Rewards, Punishment and Motivation? The best way to deal with this is to ignore the horse when he bangs the door and reward him with attention when he is quiet instead. Many people do their best to try to follow this advice, but may lapse eventually, usually when they are very busy, tired, trying to concentrate or speak to someone. The horse, annoyed by the lack of effect his previously reliable 'party piece' is having, initially tries longer or louder bangs to get the attention he wants until they give in and yell 'enough' or some other phrase at the horse as soon as he bangs the door. By sometimes rewarding him immediately for a single banging episode and then at other times rewarding him after several episodes or for banging the door for longer, they are inadvertently putting this horse onto a *variable* schedule of reinforcement, and making the occasional yell i.e. attention even more valuable to the horse than when they had him on a *fixed* schedule of reinforcement by yelling at him every time he banged the door. By increasing the value of the inadvertent reward that led to the development of this problem in the first place, they are actually training this horse more effectively to bang the door more often or for longer! This makes the problem worse, and so they are more likely to get frustrated and yell at this horse more often and so on – a vicious circle ensues.

So, behaviour with great rewards or particularly attractive consequences will need less *repetition* and fewer *trials*, for learning to take place, and a simple *fixed schedule of reinforcement* will usually be enough to keep training progressing at a rate that satisfies most people. Behaviour with relatively little consequence requires more *repetition* and a greater number of trials for learning to take place and here you can speed up the training process by using a more complex *variable schedule of reinforcement* to get the desirable response committed to *memory* and become part of a learned behaviour pattern.

BRAIN AND MEMORY

The extraordinarily complex way in which the brain works is only just beginning to be understood by scientists and there is a great deal remaining to be discovered. However, we can use a little of this knowledge to improve the efficiency of our training when working with horses.

Most people are aware that the average human brain is much larger per unit of body weight than that of the average horse. Our brains are around sixteen to twenty times bigger relative to body size than those of our horses. Many people reckon that we should therefore be around sixteen to twenty times 'cleverer' than our horses. Brain size is not a particularly reliable indicator of this however, and the idea that it is related proportionally to 'intelligence' has many flaws. People are good at being people and horses are good at being horses! Furthermore, most of the 'extra' weight in a human brain is because we have a greatly enlarged neocortical area of the cerebrum, compared with other animals. This part of the brain is not required for long term memory and if it is damaged or rendered inactive in any way, long term memory and ability to learn, by simple forms of *classical conditioning* for example (see Chapter 4 on the Learning Process), are not affected. While studies have shown that many other parts of the brain are also involved in learning and memory, and that the frontal cortex is involved particularly in short term memory and the acquisition of more complex learned behaviour, using *operant conditioning* for example (see Chapter 4), the consensus of most of these studies is that the area of the cerebellum called the *thalamus* is where most memory and complex learned behaviour seems to be stored long term. Relative to our body sizes, in people and horses the *thalamus* weighs about the same. If a weight for weight equivalence in learning ability is assumed, then our horses should be able to learn just as well as us and indeed have the same sort of capacity for long term memory. Horses can learn concepts such as 'the food is always in the biggest box' or the brightest box or 'if the food was in this box this time, it will be in the other box the next time,' and so on, as well as to discriminate between a number of objects varying in a particular way just we can and this is sometimes called '*discrimination learning*' or '*reversal set learning*'. These kinds of learning are often referred to '*conceptual learning*' because they show that horses can learn concepts and so 'think' about things in some ways just like us.

There is no evidence at all for any differences in rate of learning or 'intelligence' between breeds or types of horses. Indeed, there is a great deal of evidence to the contrary, and many studies, including a study looking at differences in temperament in horse types as varied as Thoroughbreds, Clydesdales and Icelandic horses, found that no breed effects could be distinguished and that rate of learning was very much an individual thing. The idea that you can judge a horse's intelligence by the shape of his muzzle is a modern 'old wives' tale'. Such beliefs are complete nonsense.

There are however, physical restrictions on rate of learning. Learning is limited by the rate at which your horse can sort out and transfer the relevant information his brain collects while training into his memory. You are probably aware of the saying that 'time flies when you are enjoying yourself' and have perhaps gone out for a relaxing hack on a sunny afternoon and been horrified to find, when you get back after you thought was an hour's ride, that it was actually two-and-a-half hours! Conversely, you may have also experienced seeing things 'in slow motion' during an accident perhaps when falling off. These are real effects on consciousness which result from physical constraints in how the brain works. For example, when you are very relaxed and happy, your brain reduces the amount of information about what is happening that is transferred into the areas used for conscious processing. This is a direct result of changes in the levels of some chemicals in the brain, including an increase in those which naturally help to create the 'happy' feeling. It is as though a brain high in 'happy' chemicals reckons it doesn't need to worry you about what is going on in the outside world because everything is fine, and so a lot less information is sent 'upstairs' to consciousness for processing. However, when things go badly wrong, and you are very stressed, as for example when falling off your horse, the hormones including adrenalin that help your body react more quickly to the ongoing disaster affect this processing system in the opposite way. They cause physical changes in brain chemicals that result in a great deal more information being sent 'upstairs' to consciousness for processing, the greater the stress the more information is sent off. It is as though the brain in this state recognizes that things are not going as they should and that it may have made a few 'wrong' decisions and so needs to assess more of the incoming information to work out what to do to fix things.

Your conscious perception of time passing is actually a count of the number of impulses passing through particular nerve cells at the 'gateway to consciousness' as it were. These special cells usually get a fairly constant number of impulses due to the steady stream of information which is usually on its way into consciousness for processing and this is how your brain measures time. There are fewer impulses passing these cells when you are happy, as less information has been sent off for processing. This part of your brain still counts them as if occurring at the standard rate and so you perceive time going quicker. On the other hand, when there is a rush on information processing, the very high count of impulses from all this information heading off into consciousness in any period of time makes you perceive 'time' slowing down and you 'notice' things one by one which would normally not be consciously perceived. This creates the 'world in slow motion' effect, which can be disconcerting but does help you (and your horse!) survive in disastrous situations.

There are two main 'storage areas' for memory in the brain, one for *short term memory* in the *frontal cortex* and one for *long term memory* in the *thalamus*. All sorts of things are initially stored in the *short term memory* and only the more important of these are transferred to the *long term memory* some time later. The storage and transfer processes takes time because they are based on physical movements and changes in brain chemicals known as *neurotransmitters* and *amino acids* which are parts of *protein* molecules. Electrical activity in a nerve cell causes chemical changes in the levels and movement of *amino acids* and *neurotransmitters* in and around it, which eventually leads to some nerve cells building the special *proteins* that seem to be the physical basis for *memory*. It is these *neurotransmitter* chemicals which make us feel sleepy or alert and changes in the levels of these is what makes you feel very tired or exhausted when studying or learning a lot, despite the fact that you are unfortunately not expending any more calories than when you are just sitting at your desk daydreaming! In this way the amounts of neurotransmitters and amino acids available in different parts of the brain at any time limits rate of learning.

Because the supply of the *neurotransmitters* and *amino acids* used to build *proteins* is limited, animal brains have evolved an intriguing processing system to prioritize the information to be stored, only keeping 'important' stuff. They 'throw out' a great deal of the 'usual' information that comes into the brain every day, store some in *short term memory* and prioritize the transfer of 'important' information to *long term memory*, from which it can be recovered later. When you are very tired, the partly processed information stored in your *short term memory* can be transferred to your consciousness much more quickly than it can be sent there directly, e.g. from your eyes or ears etc., due to the chaos caused by the backlog of unprocessed information your senses are sending to your brain all the time. This creates the bizarre sensation known as déjà vu or 'already seen', when you remember something, which cannot possibly have happened earlier, before you actually experience it consciously. Your brain did not have enough chemicals left to transfer the incoming information to both the area where brain activity is perceived as consciousness and the *short term memory* at the same time. As information in the *short term memory* can be sent on from there to the area for consciousness, the brain is set up to prioritize the *short term memory* when supplies of *neurotransmitters* are limited and sends information only to this, because it nearly always goes on from there to consciousness as well. A split second later, when *neurotransmitter* levels recover, the brain may then also be able to send the original information directly to consciousness as usual, and you experience something directly as if for the 'first time' after you remember it! This physical constraint on memory is also why neither you nor your horse may be able to remember details of events occurring shortly before or soon after any accident causing injury to the brain, as any loss of blood and oxygen simply physically inhibits the activities of the chemicals involved in the storage and transfer process around this time and these details do not make it from short term into *long term memory* in the usual way.

In these kinds of 'emergency' situations, the information is stored instead in other parts of the brain, in association with any irrelevant sights, sounds, smells that may also have been noticed co-incidentally around that time. The brain here is operating rather like a frantic secretary under great pressure to store an important report in the fireproof filing cabinet just before dashing out of the building herself in the event of a fire. She may just shove the pages into any old file that happens to be handy and open at the same time, and the pages of the important report may get separated in this way and end up stored all over the place in all sorts of other files. Here, these other files represent other areas of the brain and the pages of the report represent various little bits of the memory of the traumatic event. The fireproof cabinet is the long term memory. The place in the cabinet where our secretary would usually expect this report to be filed is empty, the important report seems lost. This is analogous to the memory loss which commonly surrounds very traumatic events, particularly those involving any head injury. Later on when going through these other unrelated files, our secretary will come across the isolated pages of the 'lost' report, and may eventually be able to piece it all together again and re-file it in its 'proper' place. This is analogous to how 'flashbacks' represent 'recovering' memory loss and how people may eventually be able to remember more details about any major trauma.

It is likely that horses' brains work in a similar way here, and this 'emergency' filing system may explain some seemingly bizarre aspects of horse behaviour following major accidents. For example, a horse sustaining a head injury in a lorry during a traffic accident may unexpectedly be initially quite happy to load and travel again, for weeks or even months, probably having no detailed memory of the events leading up to his injury, which are accessible to consciousness in the usual way (i.e. filed in the 'proper' place). However, he may subsequently 'freak out' when travelling for no apparent reason, most probably due to a 'flashback' perhaps hearing a similar vehicle going past to one which went past his lorry just before the accident happened. While in this way some aspects of how the brain works can cause problems, it also shows how efficiently the information processing system is designed to maximize information stored even when the chemicals required to do this with are very much in short supply, making the best of the physical constraints on how memory works.

These physical constraints on how information is processed are also why it is best to train in a quiet place without interruptions. Reducing the amount of 'irrelevant' incoming information requiring processing saves more *neurotransmitter* chemicals for transfer of information about your training to memory, thus helping your horse to learn more quickly.

Despite these physical constraints, however, the processing system by which our brains work is remarkably efficient and had a major advantage. Once 'important' information is stored in the physical structure of the proteins built in the areas deep in the brain used for *long term memory*, it is 'safe'. It can be accessed later and is not affected by subsequent damage to the superficial areas of the brain that created it in the first place. This does mean however that the brain has to prioritize the incoming information it is processing to find the 'important' stuff that is worthwhile committing to *long term memory* in this way.

There is also a 'fast track' process for the transfer of 'very important' information more rapidly into *long term memory,* and you can speed up your training by manipulating the way in which your training information is perceived by your horse's brain, particularly by making it seem 'very important'.

The brain regards anything new which happens frequently as 'very important' and sends this information along the 'fast track' system, 'filing' it in *long term memory* sooner, which is where *repetition* helps learning. Training using lots of simple repetitive trials makes your horse's brain pay particular attention to the nerve impulses involved and gives these a special priority in the processing queue. This means that the information they produce is therefore much more likely to be transferred to *long term memory* and so your training will last. You probably still remember your multiplication tables from school even though you may not have used them for many years!

The brain also regards anything very unusual or of major consequence as very important, and transfers information about this immediately to *long term memory*, particularly if that consequence is fear or pain related. This aids long term survival and is how one single very traumatic event can be enough to create a learned behaviour problem.

Most 'ordinary' information however can take much longer to get into *long term memory*. It has been shown that information gained from newly acquired 'routine' tasks, such as learning a path through a maze for example, can take up to three days to be transferred into *long term memory* under normal husbandry conditions in horses. One study found that horses learned in fewer sessions when these were three days apart rather than when training daily. These are particularly useful findings when planning a training programme.

For example, if your training sessions are difficult to arrange, and you need to book or spend money on special facilities or help, it is a 'waste' in terms of *long term memory* storage to organize these any more frequently than three days or even weekly. To maximize the long term effect of your training here you should organize sessions at least three days apart and ideally train weekly rather than daily. This is very 'good news' for career girls and working riders as it means that in this instance you have a good excuse for only training at the weekends!

However, if your training sessions are relatively easy to organize and do not require much extra effort or expenditure, it can be worthwhile training more frequently, particularly if you are trying to get your horse used to something he is genuinely scared of or teaching him something that you may need him to do in times of great stress – which includes any competitive performance as far as most of us are concerned! Stress and the emotions of excitement, fear, anger and anxiety also involve chemical changes in the brain, particularly the sub cortical part of the cerebrum involved in learning by *classical conditioning*. While *neurotransmitter* chemicals are busy stimulating and relaying these emotions in this part of the brain, they are unavailable for storing and retrieving learned information. This is why learning is hampered by fear or anxiety and simple things seem to be 'forgotten' at these times. The knowledge or learned behaviour pattern is still there, in the 'storeroom' of the memory as it were, but there are no 'porters' or *neurotransmitters* available to process or retrieve it. This apparent nuisance however helps with survival in the wild. For example, if you cannot manage to pay attention to fear or pain and remember something else at the same time, it is usually more important to be aware of fear or pain, so that you can assess the danger and risks involved in the situation you are in, than to learn something new or remember something learned previously, even though this may help.

Apart from the obvious fact of making sure your horse is as fear and pain free as possible when you are trying to work with him, you can reduce the detrimental effect of stress and emotions on your horse's learning ability by using more frequent trials in your training sessions and repeating these as often as possible.

Increasing the *repetition* gives the information your horse's brain receives during training a greater priority for transfer into long term memory, as described above, in direct proportion to the amount of *repetition* achieved. If you increase the number of *repetitions* sufficiently, you can counterbalance the negative effects of emotions on learning. Increasing the frequency of *repetitions* of action–reward trials and repeating these well beyond the point where your horse has clearly 'got it' and established the desired response to your training is called *over-learning*. While these 'extra' trials will not increase the rate at which your horse will learn, i.e. it will still take as long for the desired behaviour and reward link to be committed to his long term memory, they will markedly increase the chances of the desired behaviour being produced in times of emotion, fear and stress. This is what army drill is for! Training using a very high frequency of repeated simple movements helps soldiers to better remember and carry out the procedures they have learned in times of crisis when they are under great stress, which for a soldier is the kind of situation in which he is most likely to need to carry out these drilled manoeuvres perfectly. When training horses, *over-learning* can be very useful, especially when you are teaching your horse to get used to something he is genuinely frightened of or which may have caused him pain in the past. *Over-learning* may also work by helping to reduce the overall arousal and extra brain activity caused by emotions such as fear and anxiety as total brain arousal is reduced by familiar repeated stimulation, leading to increasing feelings of calm. Any such reduction in arousal and general brain activity also leaves more *neurotransmitters* available for processing, storing and retrieving information, again speeding up the learning process.

So, if you are training towards behaviour you may need in times of stress or trying to get your horse used to something he is frightened of, you should try to include as many 'extra' or repeated trials within a session as possible and as many such sessions as you can reasonably manage to take full advantage of the phenomenon of *over-learning*. He may have 'learned' the task in six trials but will benefit in this way from a further sixty.

Drugs

I am often asked by horse owners to advise them on which 'calmer' or herbal potion is best to augment their training and even by vets whether there are any drugs available which will help horses to get used to certain procedures. The simple answer here is that there are none currently available which actually work in my experience! Most 'calmers' sold over the counter in tack shops and feed stores are mainly chalk and contain less of the herb advertised than the average hedgerow or acre of rough pasture. Do remember that not all natural products are good for your horse – many poisonous plants such as deadly nightshade for example are one hunded per cent 'natural organic herbs'! Most feed supplements you can buy are usually however quite tasty and should not do your horse any harm, providing you make sure that the overall balance of minerals, especially magnesium, calcium and phosphorus, in his diet is correct. Feed additives sometimes help by the 'placebo' effect - in that the user may feel more confident when feeding them and improve their handling or riding accordingly. If the active ingredients were present in sufficient quantities to have any actual physical effect on your horse's metabolism, then they would be classified as pharmacological agents by law, and have to be prescribed and sold only by vets. Interestingly, some 'calmers' have a high concentration of tryptophan in a form which can increase brain levels of the *neurotransmitter* serotonin for a few hours after feeding. This does not count as a 'pharmacological agent' from the legal point of view as tryptophan is an *amino acid*, a constituent of many proteins and can be found in similar concentrations in some ordinary feedstuffs. High doses of tryptophan will reduce some stereotypic behaviour patterns such as pacing and head-twisting, and could be said therefore to have a transient 'calming' effect.

Many owners are upset to discover that despite having had their horse sedated half a dozen times for clipping or travelling that he has still not 'got used to it'. This is because many of the drugs used to sedate a horse work by interfering with *neurotransmitter* activity. Unfortunately this interference also gets in the way of desirable information processing, storage and retrieval and so these drugs also inhibit learning. Phenothiazine-based drugs, such as Acepromazine, which is one of the most commonly used sedatives in horses, is particularly likely to prevent learning in this way. There is no point trying to train a sedated horse. Similarly, some tricyclic antidepressants like Clomipramine and Imipramine, which are sometimes used to prevent stereotypic behaviour such as self mutilation in stallions, inhibit learning.

MEASURING PROGRESS

Once you have planned your training schedule and have begun to train your horse, it can be most reassuring to try to quantify and chart his progress as time goes on. This keeps you going when things go wrong, as they usually do. I have never produced or come across a training schedule which actually did go exactly according to plan. You can improve morale all round by giving your horse's problem or performance a subjective score, say points out of ten. If you write down his score every session and note the dates of these sessions in your diary, you will see what progress you are making. This can also help you predict how long it will take to reach your training goal.

Stick to your planned sessions as far as you can and do not be tempted to 'carry on' until any particular goal is reached. Simply do what you can in the time you have available and score your horse's progress at the end of each session. For example if you are using *shaping* to teach him to load (see Chapter 7 on Practical Re-training Techniques), note how close to the trailer he is at the end of your session and roughly how many trials were needed to get this far – how often did you ask him to move forward and how many of these requests were successful? If you are trying to teach him to move over on command or pick up a front leg, note how often you asked or tried to get him to do what you want and how many times he did it right. An approximate count will do for lots of tiny requests, such as those given as aids when teaching your horse a ridden manoeuvre for example.

Look out – here comes the science bit! Once you have quantified your horse's performance in this way, you can plot the results on a graph. If you put time or the cumulative number of attempts or trials along the bottom (called the x axis in mathematical convention) and the number of 'correct' responses or 'successful' attempts up the side (called the y axis in mathematical convention), you will end up with a series of dots which will eventually take on the approximate shape of those given in Fig 3.1. The line which more or less follows this pattern is always the same elongated 'f' shape and this is called a *learning curve*. Most people have heard of a *learning curve* – now you can draw one!

The distinctive shape of a *learning curve* is due to the fact that initially when starting to learn something, the number of successes is relatively low. These quickly build up and rapidly increase in the middle of the training as the trainee gets the hang of things. Eventually, things settle down when the trainee always gets the maximum number of 'correct' responses and the *learning curve* levels off when attempts are always 'successful'. These curves are always symmetrical, and the top levels off in the same way as the turn up began i.e. at each end of the elongated 'f' shape always matches the other. Many people use the phrase 'on a steep learning curve' incorrectly to describe times when they felt they had a great deal to learn. You can see from the graph that once you are on the 'steep' part of the curve, learning is taking place very rapidly and you are more than half way there with the end in sight!

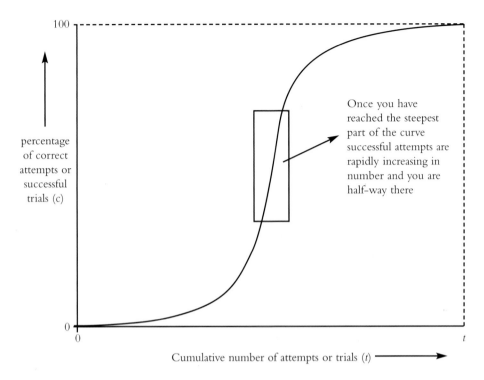

100 ┄┄┄┄┄┄┄┄┄┄┄┄┄┄┄┄┄┄┄┄┄┄┄┄┄┄┄┄┄┄

percentage
of correct
attempts or
successful
trials (c)

Once you have
reached the steepest
part of the curve
successful attempts are
rapidly increasing in
number and you are
half-way there

0

0   t

Cumulative number of attempts or trials (*t*) ⟶

After '*t*' number of attempts in total, sucess rate will be 100% i.e. your
horse has 'got it' and *t* represents the number of trials needed for him to
learn this task.

Fig 3.1. This diagram shows the classic shape of a learning curve.

When you are plotting your horse's progress, you know you have nearly
reached the half way stage when successes suddenly start to escalate and the
line through your more recent dots starts to turn up. This lets you predict
how many more training sessions and therefore how much time you will
need to complete the training task in hand.

The constancy of shape of a *learning curve* in any situation is an illustration
of the fact that rate of learning depends largely on the total number of trials
or attempts made. This means that it will take longer to fix a 'slight'
behaviour problem – one where the problem behaviour occurs infrequently
or less often – than a more 'serious' or frequently occurring problem. While
some people may be disappointed that a relatively 'minor' or infrequent
problem takes a long time to fix, they can also be pleasantly surprised when
they find that the 'worst' horses will learn 'to behave' more quickly than
those which were not so 'bad' in the first place.

SUMMARY

It takes time to train. To be successful you need to *plan ahead* and try to organize your training schedule around your own commitments and daily yard routines as well as your horse's diurnal rhythms. Attention to detail can help you incorporate what is currently known about the effect of varying *reward systems* and *schedules of reinforcement* as well as how your horse's *brain* and *memory work* to maximize the return you get from the time you spend.

The way in which your horse's brain processes information means that the smaller or less attractive your reward, the more *repeats* or 'trials' it will take for learning to take place and that your horse will learn more quickly when he is calm and in a quiet, peaceful environment without distractions.

Variable ratio schedules of reinforcement, where your horse sometimes gets a reward for every correct response and sometimes only for several correct responses makes these rewards more valuable and can speed up training, particularly when rewards are relatively less attractive. *Overlearning* or repeating training many times after your horse has 'got it' will help when you are teaching your horse to get used to frightening situations and to produce the learned response – his 'good behaviour' in times of great excitement, fear or stress, as when away from home or at a competition.

It can take up to three days for your horse to commit some learned behaviour to his *long term memory*, and if your training sessions are difficult or expensive to set up, you can maximize the benefits from these and minimize your efforts by organizing them at least three days apart.

You can predict how long any training task may take by plotting early progress along a *learning curve* and there are more tips on maximising your effectiveness as a trainer given in Chapter 8. It is best to train little and often, so take your time and plan ahead.

Chapter 4

The Learning Process

The basic process by which behaviour is modified and horses learn to respond to commands or to react differently to the world is called *conditioning*. This process has been understood and used to train horses since at least the days of Xenophon, who wrote in some detail about its application to the training of the Greek cavalry around 400BC. The learning process of conditioning is traditionally divided into the two main forms in which it is usually seen in everyday life, known as *operant conditioning* and *classical conditioning*. *Operant conditioning* is also called *instrumental learning* in America, and this chapter explains the way in which these two main forms of learning work.

OPERANT CONDITIONING

This is the simplest form of learning and is how most horses learn things by themselves. It is sometimes called 'aha!' learning and learning 'by accident'. In Chapter 1 on the ABC of Learning I explained how learning can be summarized as the process by which if a horse does something which has a pleasant consequence he is more likely to do it again, and if it has an unpleasant consequence, he will be less likely to do it again. This change in probability of any particular activity being seen is how learning can be measured in scientific terms i.e. when the natural behavioural tendencies of your horse have been modified in this way and the frequencies of certain activities altered, we say learning has occurred.

Say your horse does something that is part of his everyday behaviour such as sniffing and touching something new with his muzzle. This is a common form of exploratory behaviour in horses. If what he is investigating is a new

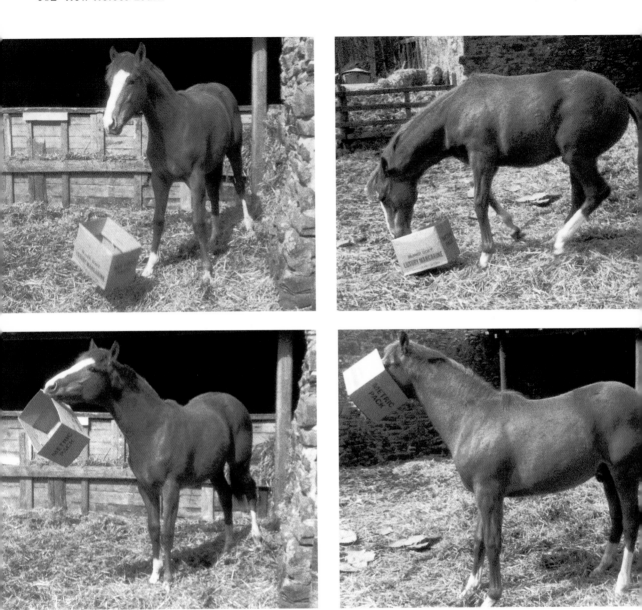

Fig 4.1a, b, c, and d. This series shows instinctive play behaviour being developed by operant conditioning into some very cute attention seeking poses!

electric fence that is switched on, he will get a nasty shock, and be a lot less likely to touch it again. The process whereby his brain 'remembers' the connection between the 'urge' to touch the fence, the action of touching the fence and the unpleasant <u>C</u>onsequence is called *operant conditioning*. The next time he feels this 'urge' and is tempted to reach out and touch this kind of fence, nerve cells in the frontal cortex area of his brain are stimulated into reminding him of the previous unpleasant _Consequence_ and stop him doing this. His _Behaviour_ (e.g. reaching out to touch) in relation to the _Antecedent_ (e.g. sight of new fence) has been altered and we can say he has learned to avoid this sort of thing.

If alternatively your horse investigated a feed bin with a loose lid in the same way as he had done the electric fence, and instead of the shock, got a _reward_ of access to feed as a _Consequence_ of this _Behaviour_, he would be more likely to do this again. The next time he saw such a feed bin, the nerve cells in his frontal cortex would remind him of the pleasant _Consequence_ of reaching out and touching it and make him more likely to do this again. If the lid was tighter this time, and did not come off at once, natural frustration would encourage him to nudge the lid again and push harder. In this way should he manage to get the lid off again, he would be learning to open the feed bin by the process of _operant conditioning_.

This process of _operant conditioning_ works by linking the nerve impulses created in the brain by your horse's perception of the _Antecedent,_ the input from his muscles when carrying out the _Behaviour_ and the pleasant or otherwise sensations of the _Consequences._ For learning to work properly, this information coming into the brain must be processed and 'remembered' in that particular order or sequence, as described in ABC of Learning and in the Brain and Memory Section of Chapter 3 on Training and Time. In _operant conditioning_ it is the link between the _Behaviour_ and _Consequences_ which is particularly important. The idea of learning being a physical process, where the brain builds links between the activity of the different groups of nerve cells that are involved in processing all the information the brain receives during training is why _Consequences_ are sometimes called 'reinforcers' in America and is probably the basis for the term 'positive reinforcement' for pleasant _Consequences_ and 'negative reinforcement' for unpleasant ones. _Positive reinforcement_ (or _reward_) makes the preceding _Behaviour_ more likely to happen again and _negative reinforcement_ (or _punishment_) makes it less likely to happen again.

In the science of applied learning theory, the most important element of the _Behaviour_ or activity involved or learned here is technically referred to as the _response_ and the specific sight or sound which is part of the _Antecedent_ event creating the natural 'urge' or instinctive motivation to respond to it in some way is called the _stimulus_. Learning is the process where any particular _stimulus_ becomes more likely to be followed by a specific behavioural _response_ and so the _operant conditioning_ form of learning is often described in scientific shorthand as '*stimulus – response*' and even abbreviated to 'S-R'.

Operant conditioning is the process where a natural urge or *stimulus* provokes a specific behaviour or *response*, and is how any instinctive action or behaviour becomes more or less likely depending on whether or not it is followed by a pleasant or unpleasant <u>C</u>*onsequence*.

Learning by operant conditioning

Horses can learn all sorts of things by *operant conditioning*, and this is one of the most common processes by which behaviour problems develop.

Example 4.1. Door banging

Do you remember the door banging example given in Chapter 1 on the ABC of Learning? This annoying habit is learned by the process of *operant conditioning*. The horse seeking attention is standing at the door of his stable, looking for someone to notice him. If he gets no attention for just standing there quietly, he will get frustrated, especially when someone who usually gives them pleasant attention is there but looking the other way, or engrossed in conversation, or busy with something else. He may initially toss his head and nudge with his muzzle out and up, a natural attention seeking behaviour in horses. If this doesn't have the desired result, he will become more frustrated, and in horses foreleg pawing is a common frustration related behaviour. This probably developed from the survival benefits of pawing snow off grass or breaking ice on water. When a horse is standing looking out over a stable door, trying to paw with a front leg, his knee and possibly also his hoof will strike the door, and the racket usually elicits immediate attention! This is a very straightforward example of learning by *operant conditioning*. The horse learns that this accidental striking of the door gets him the attention he wanted much more quickly than standing quietly until someone comes over to him. The <u>A</u>*ntecedent* is someone who is ignoring him, the <u>B</u>*ehaviour* is the pawing and the <u>C</u>*onsequence* is the attention, as even an angry yell constitutes attention (as described in Chapter 1 on the ABC of Learning and Chapter 2 on Rewards, Punishment and Motivation). The *stimulus* is what he notices in the person ignoring him and the *response* is banging the door. This horse is learning by *operant conditioning* to respond in this way whenever he sees someone who is not paying him enough attention, as his natural instinct to do so has a pleasant <u>C</u>*onsequence*.

As explained in Chapter 1 on the ABC of Learning, this is how many people unwittingly reward behaviour they don't like and how many horses learn 'bad behaviour'. This sort of thing is best dealt with by making sure horses are rewarded for 'good behaviour' and not inadvertently punished here instead, e.g. as in this example by being ignored when standing quietly!

Example 4.2. Nipping or mugging people for treats

This is perhaps the most commonly seen example of *operant conditioning* in stable yards, and many horses learn to do this so well that their owners and others who know these people do not want to use treats in training. This is a great pity, as by offering the treat in the correct way (as described in Chapter 3 on Rewards, Punishment and Motivation), food rewards can be a particularly valuable tool when training.

I once came across a delightful little black pony called Billy at a local riding school. He was particularly cute to look at, very interested in people and keen to attract their attention, which made him very popular. He did however have a very nasty little nip which presented quite a problem to the yard manager, as it was difficult for her to keep him away from the children who came to ride and she was most concerned that he would really hurt someone one day. She had tried all the usual precautions, keeping him in an out of the way box in a corner and putting a large sign on the door 'I'm on a diet – please don't feed me!' etc. Unfortunately this only heightened his desire for attention and treats. The yard staff were all instructed to be very careful, tying him up and wearing thick gloves when dealing with him. He was well worth keeping in the riding school, however, as otherwise he was a super little pony and went beautifully for all sorts of riders.

When I met Mrs C, she was quite embarrassed that one of her ponies had such a nuisance habit. 'I don't know where he got this from' she exclaimed with disgust in her frustration 'None of our other ponies have ever done this!' It was indeed a very well run yard with a good selection of generally very well behaved ponies. However, as I investigated further, it transpired that his previous owner, a rather eccentric elderly lady, had spent a lot of time teaching him 'party tricks', including 'Hunt the Humbug'. She had thought it was great fun to sellotape the mints he loved to the inside of her cardigan, or hide these in other odd places around her yard and let him find them!

Nudging, especially with the forehead and muzzle jerking out and up is a natural attention seeking behaviour in horses, and is very commonly seen in response to food related frustration. This probably comes from the way in which a foal can get more milk from mum by nudging the udder in exactly this way to stimulate a milk let down reflex.

Horses will also nudge someone leading them, who has lapsed into wandering directly in front of the horse in the same way, out of frustration and to attract their attention rather like a motorist stuck in a traffic queue caused by someone day dreaming, sounding their horn! If the unfortunate leader does not move quickly enough, they may also get a sharp nip in the small of their back, and this is how Billy learned to nip people. He was trained to look for food, and when he didn't get it, he would get frustrated, first nudging then nipping to try to elicit some attention and a treat. In the 'Hunt the Humbug' game, this would help him get the treats, and his previous owner would have been highly likely to 'give in' when he was nudging her and give him a treat during everyday grooming and handling procedures. He was rewarded for a natural tendency to investigate people's hands and pockets for treats, first by nudging and, if frustrated, then by nipping. In his previous home, he probably always got the treat at the nudging stage, as his previous owner was adamant he had never nipped her.

At the riding school, however, he did not get treats from staff and so the nudging quickly progressed into frustration related nipping, which would have been rewarded at least by the ensuing attention and interruption to tacking up etc. With children, he would have been frustrated by the relative slowness and awkwardness of the usual way a child reasonably new to horses tries to give them something, perhaps proffering the treat in a closed fist and nervously snatching their hand back sometimes when he tried to take it. This would have made him try to grab the treat quicker, often unfortunately thereby inadvertently nipping the child's fingers with his teeth. He could then eat the dropped treat easily from the floor and of course, all the screaming and yelling brought more people around, making him the centre of attention again, which is just what he wanted!

So, this is how a natural frustration response to the changing of any treat giving system can actually create a nipping habit by *operant conditioning*. The approach of people, especially children offering treats or with the smell of treats on their hands or in their pockets was the *Antecedent*. The instinctive urge to grab the treat or nip from frustration when it wasn't delivered immediately was followed by that *Behaviour* and the release of the treat, attention or interrupted tacking up etc. was the pleasurable *Consequence*. Essentially, nudging or nipping for treats often gets a horse what he wants, and most learn this very annoying habit quickly if treated in this way!

If you are a little slow in getting any treat out of your pocket, or you 'give in' when your horse 'asks' for another by nudging you, or give him one just after he nudges you while you struggle with a wrapper, you are rewarding this natural attention seeking behaviour. The conditioned *stimulus* may be your appearance with something in your pocket and the learned *response* his nudging. Your horse will learn by *operant conditioning* that this is how to get you to give him a treat. If you try not to, he will get frustrated and may progress to nipping. If he gets a treat in this way only sometimes, he will then learn to do this more quickly (by *variable ratio reinforcement* as described in Chapter 3 on Training and Time).

One of the most interesting cases I have ever been asked to investigate involved a particularly smart little Highland pony called Hamish. His owner had become very concerned about what seemed initially to be a medical problem. He stopped and strained 'to pee' frequently, sometimes eventually producing a trickle. At other times he produced nothing. Her vet had investigated this very thoroughly and could find no signs of any disease or physical disorder which could be causing this kind of problem. According to the vet Hamish seemed perfectly healthy in every other way. He drank as usual and produced the usual amount of wet bedding in his box every night.

Hamish was on loan to a riding school at the time, and I asked if I could sit in on some lessons to see for myself what was happening. I discovered that Hamish was not very popular at this riding school and there were great moans and groans from some of the riders when they were told that they had him for their lesson. I was surprised as Hamish moved very well and had the most magnificent trot I had ever seen in a Highland pony. The manager of the riding school had famously got a '9' for one trot movement when riding him in a local dressage competition. However, after watching Hamish in a few lessons I began to understand why some riders found him difficult. He was in reality a very lazy pony and had discovered (by *operant conditioning*) a 'thousand and one ways' of avoiding work. He tried all of his tricks on every new rider and discovered which one they were most put off by. This became how he would go for them. With some people he jogged, with others he dawdled. Some people were rubbed up against the wall, while with others he would wander off the track, falling in and cutting the corners. The list was endless. With one of my regular riders, who was quite capable, he just stopped after a few paces and tried to lie down! He was however a very useful pony to have in the riding school, as it was very easy for the instructors to see where each rider's weaknesses lay!

When everything was done absolutely correctly, he could go brilliantly, but he took advantage of every window of opportunity he got to have a rest. It was now fairly clear to me that his 'straining to pee' could simply be another one of these devices for getting a rest. I looked very carefully at the times when he did this, and sure enough, it fitted the pattern you would expect if this were the case. He was just 'pretending' he needed to pee as had discovered by *operant conditioning* that if you stop and straddle and strain a little, your rider and the instructor will wait patiently until you produce something. If you do this frequently enough, they will get off, put you in your stable and phone the vet!

His owner had bred Highland ponies for many years and seen just about every naughty trick these often wonderfully clever ponies could come up with, and as she put it – this one really took the biscuit! It also showed us that horses can act or even 'tell lies' and Mrs L was quite embarrassed by 'Hamish's low moral standards'!

Pleased to have solved this unusual case, at first I defended Hamish, saying that on the other hand he showed great initiative and perseverance. I had a course coming up for vets wanting to learn more about behaviour problems, and I was very keen to include Hamish 'pretending he needed to pee' in the practical session to illustrate some of the key differences in pattern of performance between learned behaviour problems and physical disorders. Mrs L kindly agreed, and Hamish was duly transported to the yard where the practicals were to be held. It turned out to be a very cold day and we had a few inches of snow the night before. I was nonetheless in good form, as the snow created a very scenic backdrop and until then, the course had been going very well. I had arranged for one of my trainees to act as Hamish's owner on the day, as Mrs L was unable to come. I followed her out to the school area a few minutes later with the group to let them have a chance to see the problem and practise their history taking. Imagine my horror when I saw a huge steaming yellow patch in the snow on the track leading to the school! He went around that school like a perfect angel and I had to rustle up another less capable rider to let him show off some of his other much less spectacular evasions instead. It might have been the cold, but to this day Mrs L believes that Hamish did it on purpose to get his revenge for my exposure of his useful little trick!

Once Mrs L had explained Hamish's behaviour to the riding school manager, they decided that Hamish would no longer be allowed to stop and rest while 'straining for a pee' in the arena! Instead, he would be given a few moments at the beginning and end of each forty-five minute lesson to relax and 'do the needful' on a patch of long grass beside the school, and kept going if he tried to stop and 'ask for a pee' while working. He quickly learned that this little trick no longer worked, and stopped trying it on in lessons within a couple of weeks.

This is also how clever horses can learn to spook and distract a rider from asking for more demanding work. They learn by *operant conditioning* after a genuine spook that this behaviour puts the rider off and earns them a little break. Even a few steps' respite when schooling will count as a rewarding rest here. If your horse seems always to spook just when everything is starting to go really well, it is likely he is putting this on to put you off!

It usually requires a strict programme of *counter-conditioning* to undo any 'bad behaviour' learned by *operant conditioning* in this way (see Chapter 7 on Practical Re-Training Techniques).

Horses can also learn useful things by themselves by the process of *operant conditioning*. This is frequently how they learn to avoid things which are painful (like electric fencing as described above) or unpleasant.

Example 4.3. Finding shelter

Horses unfamiliar with any field may initially suffer a little more that the rest in wet or windy weather. They do not initially know where all the 'good spots' are, and where to shelter from any prevailing wind, or to go to avoid flies etc. The naturally strong social tendency of horses to follow others and stick close together helps here. When it starts to get windy, or rain, or the flies get really bad, the horses who know the field will go to where they will get the most shelter from the bad weather or relief from flies on a sunny day. The new horse will follow them, and he will 'discover' that that bit of the field feels less cold or uncomfortable in those weather conditions. This is why *operant conditioning* is sometimes referred to as 'aha' learning. You can imagine your horse thinking 'aha – this is the place to be when it rains'! He will then be more likely to go to these areas himself in the future in those weather conditions. We can say he has learned by *operant conditioning* to seek shelter there.

Broadly speaking, the <u>A</u>ntecedent is the bad weather, the <u>B</u>ehaviour is going to a particular spot and the <u>C</u>onsequence is relief from wind or flies etc. In applied learning theory jargon, the *stimulus* is a specific element of that particular weather which he notices and the *response* is his stopping whatever he was doing and starting to move to a particular bit of the field. Your horse has learned by the process of *operant conditioning* to react to that sort of weather by going to the best part of the field to be in for those conditions.

Training by operant conditioning

We can use *operant conditioning* in training, for example:

Example 4.4. Avoiding electric fences

Earlier in this chapter, I explained how if a horse gets a nasty shock when he first touches an electric fence, he learns for himself, by the process of *operant conditioning,* that it is best to avoid these in the future. Many people worry that when their horse is exposed to an electric fence for the first time, his reaction might be so extreme that he panics, dashes off or otherwise hurts himself. They cannot be sure exactly when he might take a special interest and touch the fence for the first time. Many people facilitate their horse's instinctive interest here by calling him over or offering treats from the far side of the fence to encourage him to experience the fence while they are around. They might also try to get him to touch the fence when there are no other horses near it to avoid accidents between horses should his first reaction be a violent one. They can then make sure their horse is all right afterwards. This sort of encouragement can speed up his finding out for himself that touching the fence hurts and so helps him learn by *operant conditioning* here.

Example 4.5. Training to catch by curiosity

Horses are instinctively attracted to novelty, and if the person who has been trying to catch them for half an hour hunkers down in the field, waves the headcollar at him and looks the other way, most horses cannot resist coming closer to see what is going on. Treats scattered nearby can reward this, and begin to train him to approach the person waving the headcollar. The unusual behaviour of the handler encourages him to come over, and this desirable behaviour is initially facilitated using the learning process of *operant conditioning.*

> I had one client who spent a long hot summer reading a series of 'trashy novels' in her 'impossible to catch' horse's field where Silver was kept in a small section of the field on his own during this time. Once Miss M could reliably get Silver to come over to her using *operant conditioning* in this way, she was able to build on this by offering the treats closer and closer until he had to take them from her hand underneath the headcollar, eventually only giving him a treat when he let her put the lead rope around his neck and later only for also putting his nose into the headcollar and so on (using the technique of *shaping* explained in Chapter 7 on Practical Re-training Techniques). She completed the training to catch process here by repeatedly giving him treats and letting him go again immediately she had caught him (using the technique of *counter-conditioning* also explained in Chapter 7 on Practical Re-training Techniques).

The Learning Process 111

This method works very well for horses who are genuinely nervous of people and who may have been abused in a previous situation.

Example 4.6. Training to catch by chasing
Operant conditioning is also the learning process employed when a horse which is difficult to catch is finally caught by chasing him around the field until he is too tired, hungry or thirsty or just plain 'fed up' to keep moving off and decides to come and be caught instead! Some people discover this method when they are increasingly frustrated by a horse grabbing treats and dashing off or playing with them such as by running in circles around them. They are finally pushed to the point of telling him to 'clear off' or some such phrase, accompanied by an expressive gesture with the headcollar or lead rope! The game where he enjoys his owner's undivided attention for ages is over and the horse discovers that he is punished for dashing off by being chased. Chasing is a very domineering thing to do in equine etiquette, and the horse is punished here by having to keep on going and not being able to snatch a bite to eat. This technique is most effective when the horse is very relaxed and confident and really just 'being naughty', although it can be difficult to 'harass' this kind of horse sufficiently to stop him eating etc in a large field, and sometimes a team of helpers is required here. While it can work, it is difficult to do properly and because it works by punishment, this is not a training technique I usually advise.

In the same way as in this last example, *operant conditioning* using punishment is also the process by which the part of the handling system popularized by Monty Roberts and promoted by Richard Maxwell and Kelly Marks known as 'join up' works. The horse is being chased around a circular enclosure, around 60 feet (20m) in diameter. This is the optimum size of circle to use here, as it is small enough to physically stress a horse to the maximum, particularly a young or relatively unschooled horse, but just big enough to allow the handler to stay far enough away from the horse so that the horse thinks he has enough room to run away and he is not tempted to lash out and kick the person chasing him. It is no coincidence that the method popularized by Monty Roberts uses a 60 feet diameter circle and that traditionally horses are lunged and worked in a manege of around 20 metres (i.e. the same diameter), whether this is to help start his training, improve his dressage or perform in the circus where the ring is also about this size!

The enclosure has to be a 'round pen' or circular shape, without corners, to encourage the horse to keep running and to prevent him looking into the corner and using it to stop or turn around and kick out at the handler. The horse has strong natural instincts to run away from any movement just on the edge of his peripheral vision, particularly in the area of his flanks, which is where predators leap to catch and bring down animals like horses, by tearing the large abdominal and hind leg muscles that help him run and of course also help him defend himself by kicking out. In 'join up' the handler initially gets the horse going by throwing a rope at his flanks, where the end flicks in and out of his peripheral vision in exactly the same way as a lungeing whip does when flicked 'correctly' to encourage forwards movement.

The chasing continues while the handler watches for signs of tiredness in the horse, such as slowing up, puffing and particularly, dropping his head and increasing the frequency of looking back into the middle. The handler then reduces the chasing actions which makes the tired horse more likely to stop. When the horse has had enough of this very strenuous physical work, he stops and then the handler stops chasing him. This 'rest' is the reward for stopping i.e. the handler initially sets up a chasing system whereby the horse is punished for not standing still and the horse learns by *operant conditioning* that stopping and standing still is the only way of getting a rest. The handler then changes the 'rules', and moves towards the horse and chases the horse on until he is so tired he stops and this time he only gets a rest if he stops and looks at the handler. If he doesn't, he is chased on again and is effectively punished for not standing still and looking at the handler. Then the 'rules' are changed again, and this time the horse only gets a rest for standing still, looking at the handler and tolerating the handler's approach, closer and closer. This goes on until the only way the horse gets a rest is by following the handler. The horse must stay close beside the handler, even when the handler moves away from him or he is punished by being chased around the ring again. If he doesn't 'get it' quickly, he is chased around the ring again and again.

As you can imagine, this is physically exhausting for any horse and also quite intimidating as the 'rules' keep changing. The horse has relatively little opportunity to process all this information and transfer the essentials into his long term memory, and the physical tiredness and associated anxiety as the 'rules' keep changing further impede this process. Horses can injure themselves easily here, especially when they get very tired and some very sensitive horses find this all too stressful and panic, rearing or falling or becoming aggressive, all of which can cause serious injury all round.

One of the loading systems used by some Natural Horsemanship trainers works in a similar fashion, also using punishment and the learning process of *operant conditioning*. Here, in a kind of 'back to front join up', the horse is punished for stopping, when being loaded into a trailer for example, by being chased backwards or spun around quickly in a series of tiny circles. The handler hisses in a snake like fashion and waves their hands in the horse's eyes to elicit the natural survival response of horses throwing their head up and rapidly reversing in such a situation. This is physically very difficult for any horse, especially when going down a trailer ramp backwards, and horses which are being 'naughty' here quickly learn by *operant conditioning* that the only way of avoiding the nasty shock of the handler 'in his face' and the exertion of the dash back down the slope is not to stop, but to keep going forwards. Many 'naughty' horses quickly work out that trotting into the trailer is the safest option here and this is an impressive result if you have been trying to gently cajole your horse to load for hours! Unfortunately, this system is very dangerous for genuinely frightened horses and will only make them much worse. Their 'worst fears' and instinctive distrust of dark enclosed places will have been realized and they can panic, rear and fall over. People promoting these systems usually select the horses they are going to use at a demonstration beforehand, choosing those which are misbehaving through 'naughtiness' rather than genuine fear, to ensure impressive results on the day. You should be very careful about trying this at home with your own horse unless you really know he is just being 'naughty'. If you are not sure, it is safest to seek properly qualified advice (as described in Chapter 8 on Maximizing your Horse's Learning Potential) before choosing a re-training technique.

CLASSICAL CONDITIONING

Classical conditioning also involves <u>B</u>ehaviour-<u>C</u>onsequences linking exactly as in *operant conditioning*, but here, the role of the <u>A</u>ntecedents becomes more important. In *operant conditioning* it is the horse's conscious desire to do something that sets off the learned 'memory' and changes his behaviour. In *classical conditioning*, the animal learns to react to a signal which is linked with a particular element of the <u>A</u>ntecedent events or situation, and this sort of learning does necessarily involve conscious control.

You may well remember from school the story of the Russian scientist Ivan Pavlov who trained dogs to salivate at the sound of a bell. This is one of the best known examples of *classical conditioning*, and also illustrates the fact that this sort of learning does not always involve conscious 'remembering'. In *classical conditioning*, the brain develops and 'remembers' the link between a particular _Antecedent_ and the subsequent _Behaviour_ in sub-cortical areas of the brain and so it does not always require conscious effort here. This is also the learning process involved in hypnotism.

Pavlov noticed that his dogs sometimes began to salivate when he was preparing their food, and realized that he could get them to reliably salivate very early on in their food preparation process if he always did things in exactly the same way. He thought that this showed a form of learning, but some of his colleagues argued that this could be happening just by natural instinct. So, to prove his point, Pavlov rang a bell before starting to get the dogs' dinner ready, including this very unnatural 'signal' in the preparation process. As he knew they would, his dogs 'learned' that the sound of the bell was always followed by food preparation which resulted in the tasty _reward_ of being fed. They began to salivate just at the sound of the bell, and his colleagues could no longer argue that this was a natural instinct! This sort of learning process is now called _classical conditioning_. You can say that Pavlov's dogs learned to respond to the sound of the bell by the process of _classical conditioning_.

In terms of the ABC of learning here, the _Antecedent_ is the food preparation, the _Behaviour_ is the salivation and the _Consequence_ is the reward of eating tasty food. Pavlov however also introduced the bell, giving his dogs an extra 'pre-Antecedent' signal or command to trigger the _Behaviour_ he was training them to do.

In scientific terms, the salivation is the learned _response_, the food preparation is the original stimulus, sometimes called the neutral or _unconditioned stimulus_, and the bell is the _conditioned stimulus_. An _unconditioned stimulus_ is the usual _Antecedent_ or natural trigger for any response and the _conditioned stimulus_ is the extra or 'new' signal or command which is introduced into the learning sequence. Making links between new signals which precede the _Antecedent_ and elements of the original _Antecedent_ in this way is the most important part of the learning process of _classical conditioning_. This involves the brain linking the new signal or command (i.e. the _conditioned stimulus_) with the original _Antecedent_ (or _unconditioned stimulus_) and reacting to this instead as the new 'trigger' for the behavioural _response_. For this link to be made the new 'trigger' or command (i.e. _conditioned stimulus_) must be noticed just before the original or _unconditioned stimulus_. These two stimuli must usually be repeated a number of times strictly in this sequence, one after the other, for the nerve cells involved to make the necessary connections for the brain to react as if to the latter (i.e. the part of the original _Antecedent_ event which is also known as the _unconditioned stimulus_) when the former (i.e. the new 'trigger' or _conditioned stimulus_) occurs.

Many people do not fully appreciate the importance of this sequence and simply tell you to give any command (i.e. the *conditioned stimulus*) at the same time as your horse is doing what you want (the <u>Behaviour</u>), and that he will thereby learn to associate these two and eventually react by behaving in this way when he hears the command. This does not usually work very well, as the brain processes information in logical sequences, and you have to give the command just before you make him do what you want in order to train him to react in this way to that command. For example, say you know you can make your horse go from trot to canter on the lunge by cracking the whip suddenly behind him, but you would like to teach him to canter on a verbal command – when you say 'canter'. You have to give your command (the *conditioned stimulus*) e.g. say 'canter' just before you crack the whip (i.e. make him do it by using the 'instinctive' *unconditioned stimulus* of the whip crack) for your horse to learn to canter when you say so. There is no point in saying 'canter' while he is cantering or vaguely trying to say 'canter' around the same time as you crack the whip. Sometimes you will get it right and your horse will hear the command just before the whip cracks, and he will start to learn, but other times he will hear 'canter' after this when it has no effect and nothing happens after he hears the command and your horse will get very confused. Your training will be much more effective if you make use of the learning process of *classical conditioning* and make sure you always give the command (the *conditioned stimulus*) first and just before you use any natural instinct (i.e. as an *unconditioned stimulus)* to get him to react or *respond* as you wish. In this way, *classical conditioning* is the process by which horses learn to respond to most of our handling and the ridden aids.

The process of *classical conditioning* is often described in scientific shorthand as *conditioned stimulus – unconditioned stimulus – response*. *Classical conditioning* is the process where any natural urge or stimulus (known as the *unconditioned stimulus*) becomes linked to a preceding signal or command (known as the *conditioned stimulus*). When the horse's *response* to the natural urge or stimulus is followed by a *reward*, the brain 'learns' to react to the new signal or command in the same way. The *conditioned stimulus* then provokes the same behaviour as the original *unconditioned stimulus*.

Learning by classical conditioning
Horses can learn all sorts of things by the process of *classical conditioning*.

Example 4.7. Riding school ponies
You may well have noticed how riding school ponies often do exactly what

the instructor says as soon as she has said so. This is impressive if you are watching your precious daughter in her formative lessons but can be quite exasperating if you are the pupil and keen to feel that you are in charge at least of your own mount!

Ponies in this situation repeatedly hear the instructor's command for example to trot and then immediately feel the leg aid attempts of their trainee riders. Some will get it right and for others the instructor will assist and the ponies are encouraged into trot. They are then rewarded by keeping up with the rest of their mates, which is one of the reasons why the most capable rider is often given the role of lead file in a group lesson. For some there will also be the reward of relief from the cessation of novice leg aids. In this way these ponies are repeatedly exposed to the sequence of the instructor saying for example 'whole ride trot', the riders using their legs or otherwise being encouraged into trot and a reward for trotting.

The instructor's command is the *conditioned stimulus*, the leg aids and any other encouragement to trot is the *unconditioned stimulus* and the *response* is trotting. In a riding school situation these events nearly always occur in exactly this sequence and within half a second or so of each other, and this sequence is often repeated. This is why riding school ponies often learn quickly to trot when the instructor says so. Their brain has linked the command or *conditioned stimulus* to the *unconditioned* or original stimulus and reacts to the command as if it were the original or *unconditioned stimulus* that makes them trot. We can say they have learned to trot when the instructor says so by the process of *classical conditioning*.

It is nice for beginners when the ponies do what is wanted immediately, and good instructors can make use of the way in which the ponies learn to react to their voice by *classical conditioning* to help beginners here and control the ride. The whole process is even more effective if the *conditioned stimulus* remains as constant as possible, and many instructors develop their own particular tone or inflection which they always adopt in this situation. When teaching more capable riders however, a good instructor will avoid using particular words or phrases with the usual inflections, so that the rider cannot rely on the horse responding to the instructor's voice and the instructor can see how effective their pupil is becoming.

I spent some time teaching in a riding school with one very astute horse and we had to use weekly 'code' words for transitions and the various paces, for example explaining to riders that today 'toffee' meant 'trot', 'cheese' meant 'canter' etc as this horse quickly learned that saying 'the 't' word' or spelling out 'T R O T' all meant 'trot'. We also had to be very careful to ask our riders to perform any transition or movements at particular markers while they were at the other end of the school, otherwise this clever little horse just 'did it' by herself! She picked up new conditioned stimuli or commands and learned by *classical conditioning* what they meant very quickly.

Many good trainers use key words or gestures as *classical conditioned stimuli* and, by ingenious incorporation of these into phrases or simple movements can build into a complex 'showbiz' routine and develop an amusing and entertaining show of 'party tricks'.

On one course on horse behaviour I ran for vets wanting to specialize in horses and learn more about safe horse handling and effective training, I organized a practical session on training using *classical conditioning* after they had had the appropriate theory lecture. I split the participants into small groups with a riding school pony each and gave them the challenge of teaching their pony a new trick using *classical conditioning*. One chap got the hang of things very quickly and his group had some fun teaching their pony to pick up and wave a foreleg when they asked 'Are you in the masons Misty?' They had cleverly used the word 'masons' as the *conditioned stimulus* to make his learned *response* more interesting.

So, it is worth thinking very carefully about what you say when speaking to your horse!

Example 4.8. Lifting a foot when you go to pick it up
Most horses work out the sequence in which their feet are lifted for routine picking out, particularly if this is always done by the same person in the same way, and start to lift the next foot before they have to. This is learning by *classical conditioning*. The *conditioned stimulus* (CS) is the sight of the person moving towards and beginning to reach out or bend down for the foot. The *unconditioned stimulus* is the way the person presses the tendons eliciting a natural reflex which makes the horse lift the foot, the *response* (R) is lifting the foot and the reward the cessation of pressure on the sensitive areas of the lower limb. Because most people have their own routine and way of doing this everyday grooming task, usually doing the feet in the same order, the sequence of *conditioned stimulus – unconditioned stimulus – response* is always constant and this is why so many horses learn this so well.

You may have noticed that your horse does not usually pick the foot up 'all the way' here and that the horse only starts to take his weight off it and bring the heel in particular up. This is because the *unconditioned stimulus* only gets him to pick the foot up this far himself. After that most people take hold of the hoof and complete the manoeuvre themselves lifting the leg into the desired position. If the horse does not 'do it himself' he will not learn to do it (as described in Chapter 1 on the ABC of Learning).

I had one client who described on the telephone how her horse 'went mental' when she tried to pick his feet out to the point of pulling away and wrecking a variety of tying up places before galloping across lawns and flowerbeds. Her husband was very annoyed about this and threatening to file for divorce if that bleep bleep horse ruined his handiwork and beloved garden again!

Initially, the suddenness and violence of the horse's reaction sounded like a genuine pain response, and I asked her vet to check him again for any lameness or back problems which might cause such a reaction. He could not find any physical problems and so referred the horse back to me for a full behavioural assessment.

I went along, and as soon as I arrived I could understand why her husband got so annoyed – the place was immaculate and the beautifully landscaped gardens included the stables area with everything finished in gloriously polished hardwoods, granite slabs and state of the art brass fittings. The horse whose future now hung in the balance was standing quietly tied up outside his box, and Mrs T began to groom him and show me what happened when she went to pick up his feet. Harry stood beautifully for everything else, but as soon as Mrs T picked the hoof pick from the box, he threw his head up and shot backwards. We had tied him up to a very frayed piece of bailer twine and closed off the stable yard from the main garden so that if Harry broke free as he usually did, we were able to limit the collateral damage. He was obviously very frightened of this procedure.

For a moment I was perplexed until I spied Mrs T's immaculately manicured hands with bright red nails at least an inch long! She had accidentally been digging these into poor 'Harry' when she went to pick up his feet. Harry understandably objected and he had learned by *classical conditioning* that the *conditioned stimulus* of Mrs T picking up the hoof pick was immediately followed by the *unconditioned stimulus* of her digging these lethal nails into his delicate forelegs and responded accordingly! So, this apparently tricky case was very easy to solve. Reluctant to change her manicure and image Mrs T bought a pair of very thick leather gloves and followed the *systematic desensitization* and *counter-conditioning* programme I gave her to teach Harry that this part of grooming no longer hurt!

So, a little thought and some common sense goes a long way!

Example 4.9. Games ponies taking off
You may be very impressed with the stand to gallop starts of mounted games ponies and wonder how the kids manage to be so effective in their riding, wishing you could persuade your elderly cob to set off with the same enthusiasm at times. If you watch a games practice carefully, you will see that it is not only the children who gaze intently at the starter's flag. The ponies watch too, as they have learned by *classical conditioning* that when the flag drops the kids' feet hammer the ponies' sides and they are variously encouraged to 'go go go'. The flag dropping is the *conditioned stimulus*, the heel drumming the *unconditioned* stimulus and the *response* a flying start. These ponies learn by *classical conditioning* to set off at the given signal before the kids' heel drumming kicks in.

> This can cause problems sometimes. My god-daughter is in a Pony Club which is very successful at mounted games, and I love watching her and her sister practising. It reminds me of my Pony Club days, when, as keen members of the East Antrim Prince Philip Cup games team, my cronies and I detested this particular Scottish team as they invariably beat us. I never thought that one day I would be cheering on the Eglinton Junior Cs! My god-daughter's friend had been very much looking forward to her first practice on a very experienced games pony that she had the chance to borrow that season. Unfortunately for Julie the much anticipated evening became a disaster as she could not keep up with this pony's 'flying starts' and was most embarrassed to beat the record for the most falls during any practice! Happily I can report that Julie did eventually learn how to stay with this super little pony here in the next couple of practice sessions and began to enjoy games again.

So, it is important to remember that horses and ponies are learning all the time and may pick up on signals as *conditioned stimuli* that we would rather they didn't. For the most part however, the process of learning by *classical conditioning* can be put to good use.

Training by classical conditioning

Classical conditioning can be used in training, and this is how most ridden aids and basic handling procedures or 'ground manners' are taught to horses. It is also a very valuable tool in re-training problem horses. For example:

Example 4.10. Halting safely when led

Some horses learn they can pull away from a handler on the ground (by *operant conditioning* as described earlier in this chapter) often after a period of box rest and when the owner is trying to walk the horse out in hand to graze or start gentle exercise. Most horses are very 'fresh' and excited at this time and easily spooked or highly motivated to pull towards 'long lost' companions or tastier grass and any accidental getting away can become a learned response to the feel of any pressure on the headcollar. This is quite dangerous all round. It is just not physically possible to pull back enough to control the horse here and more severe 'pressure type' headcollars only make the horse pull back harder, eventually teaching him to rear.

The best way of dealing with horses who pull away is to ride the horse with a second person leading him by a headcollar over the bridle. The handler should stop and then say 'wait' or some other command that has not been used before in any unsuccessful attempts to stop him. The rider should then use the usual ridden aids to stop the horse. The handler can then give the horse a treat as a *reward* from just in front of the horse's sternum. This makes him stretch his head and neck into the 'desired' ridden outline and helps him use his back and legs properly to halt more easily. The ridden aids are the *unconditioned stimulus* and the command 'wait' the *conditioned stimulus*. It is very important that the rider only gets the horse to halt immediately after the handler gives the command to 'wait'. The desired *response* learned by *classical conditioning* in this way is to halt correctly when asked to 'wait'.

This process can be further refined to help re-train a difficult horse here (see sections on strings of *conditioned stimuli* in Chapter 5 and *counter-conditioning* in Chapter 7).

Example 4.11. Canter on a particular lead

Riders can train their horse to canter on a particular leading leg in response to a particular leg movement using the process of *classical conditioning* by moving their leg in that way just before otherwise making the horse canter on that lead.

For example, in Britain it is common for riders to use the signals of sitting a beat in trot and then a sharp 'nipping' nudge with the inside leg when going into a corner to encourage the horse to canter out of the corner, leading with his inside foreleg. Here, the rider's inside leg aid is the *unconditioned stimulus* (helped by the corner bending the horse's head and neck to the inside naturally encouraging him to canter with the inside leg leading). The *conditioned stimulus* is the 'sit a bump' with the initial movement of the rider's inside leg in preparation for the actual aid. Some horses learn to recognize other changes in the rider's upper body position the relative weight of each seat bone as a *conditioned stimulus* here also. In this way horses learn by *classical conditioning* that when the rider sits for a beat in trot and then moves their left leg, to canter with the left foreleg leading.

In the rest of Europe, most people still use the 'full' three part aid to canter, which involves the rider first brushing their outside leg back, then sitting a beat and nudging with the inside leg. The first element of a true canter step is a higher, quicker step with the outside hind leg and this is encouraged by the tickling of some abdominal muscles as the rider's outside leg brushes the horse here. The next element in a true canter step is actually exactly the same as in trot where the outside foreleg and inside hind leg come forward together in a diagonal pair and it is easier for the horse to balance in a corner or strike off into canter if the rider is sitting at this point. This is why you are encouraged to sit on the 'correct' diagonal i.e. sit when the inside hind leg and the outside foreleg are on the ground together when trotting on a curve. The third and final element of a true canter step is the easy to spot higher and further forward reaching of the inside foreleg, referred to as the 'leading' leg. When the rider asks the horse to canter in this way, the first or earliest signal the horse gets is the brush with the outside leg and so in this case, the *conditioned stimulus* is the rider moving their outside leg and the horse learns by *classical conditioning* to canter with the inside foreleg leading when the rider moves their outside leg in that way. The British system is sometimes adapted to include a hint of the full aid here by having the rider tuck the outside leg slightly behind the girth first of all, which helps a little by organizing their weight so that it is more comfortable for the horse to canter with the inside leg leading.

You can imagine how a horse trained one way and then ridden the other could get confused:

I was once investigating some problems a client of mine was having with canter in an otherwise superb big horse. Miss McF demonstrated how, no matter when, where or from what pace she asked for canter, Foxy would invariably strike off on the wrong leading leg. Miss McF was a very capable rider and quite miffed at this communication problem. I looked carefully at the way Miss McF used her legs and realized that although she used the 'British' system of aids correctly, Foxy was reacting to the leg movement as if it was the 'continental' style aid and so always struck off on the 'wrong' leg. It was quicker to teach Miss McF the continental system than to retrain Foxy here and Miss McF's chagrin was mollified somewhat by being able to boast that her horse 'spoke German'!

The continental method is technically a better system to use as a canter aid. It does not require use of a corner and it stimulates all three of the leg movements required for canter in the correct sequence and encourages the horse to strike off 'cleanly' i.e. making the very first step a 'true' one in the new pace. This is however a little more difficult for the rider to do, as all three movements must be carried out in synchrony with the diagonal pairs of the legs when trotting (i.e. you need to be on the 'correct' diagonal for this to work) and the timing of the three parts of the aid must match the rhythm of the canter. This may be one of the many reasons why the Germans usually beat the Brits in dressage!

Example 4.12 Move over in 'ground manners'
Do you remember the story of Miss N and her very bossy little mare from Chapter 2 on Rewards, Punishment and Motivation? I explained that we used *classical conditioning* to teach her to 'be polite' and move her hindquarters away from Miss N on the command 'over'. This is how we did it. I showed Miss N first of all how to stand on the left of the horse facing Clara's tummy where the saddle would go and to say 'over'. Then I showed her how to tickle or gently pinch Clara with her right hand on the abdominal muscles near the last rib in front of her stifle (which elicits a natural reflex to lift the hind leg and start to step under). Then I showed Miss N how to offer Clara a treat with the left hand to encourage her to turn her head and bend her neck towards Miss N, which also encouraged her hindquarters to move in the opposite direction, away from Miss N.

The command 'over' is the *conditioned stimulus* here, the pinch and offer of a treat are the *unconditioned stimuli* and the *response* to the desirable movement of Clara's hindquarters away from Miss N. This bending of the head and neck also moves the shoulder blade away and would help Miss N get free should Clara try to pin her to the wall again! After several repetitions on both sides, Clara quickly learned by *classical conditioning* that the *response* of moving her hindquarters away from Miss N resulted in a tasty treat. In addition to giving Miss N a technique for moving Clara out of her way, this manoeuvre also helped with the social dominance problems as to move over in this way is a socially submissive or the 'polite' thing to do in equine etiquette.

Classical conditioning is the learning process involved in most of the Natural and intelligent Horsemanship systems of training including that promoted by Pat Parelli and is also how the rest of the handling system popularized by Monty Roberts works. For example, when the handler is chasing the horse

Fig 4.1a, and b. These two pictures show this horse learning to 'move over' using the process of classical conditioning.

around the round pen to establish 'join up' in the first instance, they throw a rope at the horse's hindquarters. In order to do this, the handler turn away from the horse and swing their arm back in a stylized manner. The horse learns by *classical conditioning* that this gesture (the *conditioned stimulus*) is followed immediately by the rope and encouragement to run (the *unconditioned stimulus*). After a few repetitions, the horse will *respond* to the person turning their back and hunching their shoulders in preparation to swinging the rope, and move on before the rope is used. The horse has learned to respond in this way by *classical conditioning* and the handler no longer needs to swing the rope. He just has to turn his body as if he was going to swing the rope. This *classically conditioned* effect is often interpreted by people promoting this system of handling horses as the horse reacting 'instinctively' to the person's body language. Turning away is a submissive gesture in equine etiquette, and it is not possible for bodies our size and shape to mimic that of a horse. It does not matter what the handler actually does in the middle of the pen just before swinging the rope (the *unconditioned stimulus*) as long as they always do the same thing. Mr Roberts could be singing opera or dancing a jig here and it would have the same effect on the horse, although changing the *conditioned stimulus* in this way might be even more entertaining for his audience!

The hand signals and hissing noises promoted as 'Natural Horsemanship' techniques and various stick and rope movements used in the system of working with horses developed and promoted by Pat Parelli as a series of 'games' work using *classical conditioning* in the same way. The handler's movements are the *conditioned stimuli* and the sticks and ropes then encourage the horse to respond or move in a particular way using natural reflexes and the physics of how horses balance as *unconditioned stimuli* just as in traditional ground work and European riding techniques. Some of the equipment used and movements suggested by these kinds of 'alternative' handling systems may cause problems however. Pulling a horse's head and neck around causes a variety of musculo skeletal problems and this could make a particularly 'strong' or frightened horse fall on top of the rider, especially on hilly or uneven ground and on very smooth roads. The very long rope used could also become entangled around the horse's legs in an accident and cause rope burns or even trip him up causing potentially fatal injuries. The knotted rope headcollars used in these systems are versions of the 'Indian war bridle' and the knots hit all the pressure points at once, being very severe and preventing any form of more subtle communication with the horse's head end. It worked well for native Americans as an emergency 'stop', 'go' or 'burl around' device to make their ponies listen to the rider in the chaos and stress of bouts of fighting. But war bridles were made of strips of hide which, like the leather we use today, is kind to a horse being 'skin on skin' and which breaks before the horse's neck will. Many knotted rope headcollars by contrast are nowadays usually made of synthetic materials like nylon and have no 'safety breaks'. The traditional 'Newmarket' style of headcollar is also made of nylon, but it does have safety breaks where the buckles attach. It is not safe to leave a horse tied up with these knotted headcollars and neither should they be used for riding anywhere outside a safe enclosure. The *Highway Code* specifically states that horses must be ridden in a bridle on the public highway. Anyone using these kinds of devices instead of a bridle when riding on the roads will thereby be deemed to have acted with contributory negligence in the event of their being involved in an accident, even if their horse is seriously hurt or killed by any collision.

So, do think very carefully when trying any of these 'new' or 'alternative' systems of working with horses. Any which are effective in the long term do so using the same natural instincts of horses which have been tapped into for thousands of years by traditional European training techniques and work by the learning processes explained here. You should try to pick these out from the rest of the marketing 'package' and adapt any 'new' ideas from 'alternative' systems that you would like to try in order to maximize your own safety and that of your horse.

To finish this section on a jollier note, you can use *classical conditioning* to teach your horse all sorts of 'party tricks'. The training process is quite straight-forward. First of all find out how you can physically get your horse to do what you want. For example, if you hold a foreleg up and offer a treat near the girth area between his front legs he will 'bow' to get it! The actions you make to encourage this movement are your *unconditioned stimulus*. Then choose a novel signal or command to use as your *conditioned stimulus* and give this immediately before you start to encourage your horse to 'bow'. Make sure your horse gets a reward initially for every correct 'bow' or learned *response,* and once he has 'got it' reward him just now and again (i.e. putting him onto a *variable ratio schedule of reinforcement* as described in Chapter 3 on Training and Time). Be careful to first give your command – it can be something you say for example a special key word, a sound such as grinding your teeth or even a sniff or a simple gesture or tiny head movement etc – then encourage him to do the desired actions and reward him. You might have to build up a more complicated movement in baby steps (see *shaping* in Chapter 7 on Practical Retraining Techniques).

The 'smart' bit is in how you dress up the *conditioned stimulus*, hiding the key word in a question or phrase for example, to make the horse's *response* more entertaining.

I remember one well heeled lady whose horses my grandfather shod who was brilliant at this. She would have me on the floor of her yard in absolute stitches when I went round as a small kid 'helping' him in the school holidays. Amongst a variety of all sorts of tricks, she taught a beautiful little pony called Sherry to turn away and put her head down between her front feet in the corner of her stable, as if to hide when she mentioned a very well known local instructress' name. She showed me how to get my pony to do the same, by first saying the name, then throwing a treat into the corner of the box. The best treats here were handfuls of oats that took some time for Sherry to find amongst the straw.

Mrs B would tell a story involving this unfortunate lady or say something along the lines of 'Is that Miss W's car coming up the drive?' and it was just so funny to see Sherry turn away and hide her head in the corner of the box when the dreaded 'Miss W' was mentioned. When Sherry looked like she was going to bring her head up and turn back to us, Mrs B would then say 'Oh it's all right, I must have made a mistake, it's just the fish van' etc. This made the pony's natural behaviour also seem like part of the trick. How we laughed.

As the instructress in question was rather huge and very loud and had yelled at me and my pony many a time during Pony Club rallies at her place, I found this particularly hilarious and of course it was even more fun for me at that age as it was extremely 'naughty' for a grown up to collude with us children like this!

The signals used for such can be very subtle and horses will learn by *classical conditioning* to react to the earliest part of any gesture or movement. Do you remember the story of Clever Hans I mentioned in Chapter 1 on the ABC of Learning? He picked up on such tiny elements of his audience's body language that even his trainer did not know how Hans knew the answers to the questions.

I had one trainee who was particularly bright and after reading about *classical conditioning*, she taught her pony to lift the heel of his left foreleg when she pointed at it and to do the same with the right one when she pointed at it. This was relatively straightforward, using the pointing as the *conditioned stimulus*, then using that hand going on to touch the leg, press the tendons and tickle the pony's heels to get her to start to pick the foot up as if to be picked out as the *unconditioned stimulus*. I was not particularly impressed at this point when she was excitedly showing off her 'homework'. This was fairly standard stuff. Then came the clever bit. Miss H had also taught this pony to pick up the left foot again when she stood in front of her with both arms outstretched as in the 'whatever' gesture often used to 'act' a question, by doing this in sequence after the two leg lifts. She had proceeded from making this gesture to point to and pick up the left leg again. In this way, the pony learned a routine by *classical conditioning*; lift your left leg, then the right as they are pointed at and finally lift the left one again when Miss H stands with arms outstretched, as if waiting for an answer.

I started to be really impressed when Miss H began to ask the pony questions. She would start by pointing at the left leg and saying 'Lift this leg for football team A.' Then she would point to the right leg, saying 'lift this leg for football team B'. Finally she stood with her arms outstretched in front of the pony and asked her 'Which one do you support?' Of course, the pony always 'answered' by picking up the left leg, and in this way she was able to get the pony to 'say' whatever she wanted. By cleverly changing the team or the person's name used in any potential answer from the left leg in one question to the right leg for the next question, she could distract the audience from the left-right-left sequence and had a lot of fun. She also used this trick to be very cheeky! For example, on her first 'demo' she said 'This leg for me' pointing to the left leg and 'this leg for Dr Debbie' pointing to the right and then asked the pony 'who's the best horse trainer?' I couldn't help but smile and at this point I had to agree with the pony here!

Now you will not only be able to impress your chums by teaching your horse a few tricks like this, you will be able to see how equestrian 'showmen' are working using *classical conditioning* and hopefully get some useful ideas as well as entertainment from their performances.

SUMMARY

So, while learning theory can be very complex, it can be summarized quite simply by explaining how learning works by the process of physical changes in the brain known as *conditioning*. This involves the nerve cells that process *incoming information* from the senses, the nerve cells that are stimulated when the body moves and muscles work in *response* to this and the nerve cells used for building *short and long term memory* proteins.

Conditioning is a logical, sequential process depending on these nerve cells building many links with each other, so that in the future, particular elements of *Antecedent* events stimulate particular *Behaviour* or *learned responses* in order to get a pleasant *Consequence* or avoid an unpleasant one.

In *operant conditioning* your horse does something by himself or by accident (the *response*) immediately after noticing something (the *stimulus*). If it has a pleasant *Consequence*, he will be more likely to do it again in that situation. If it has an unpleasant *Consequence* he will be less likely to react in the same way again.

Operant conditioning involves your horse's brain building links between any *stimulus*, a particular behavioural *response* and the memory of the *Consequence*s. This is sometimes referred to in scientific shorthand as *stimulus-response*, i.e. *operant conditioning* is the process where a link is made between a *stimulus* and your horse's instinctive behavioural *response* to that *stimulus*. If that response is rewarded, your horse will be more likely to respond to that *stimulus* in that way again. If the *response* has an unpleasant *Consequence*, he will be less likely to react in that way again. Learning to do something by *operant conditioning* is sometimes described in technical terms as Action – Reward.

In *classical conditioning*, a special signal or command is added just before the 'original' *Antecedents* stimulate any *Behaviour* or natural reaction (the *response*). The new signal is known as the *conditioned stimulus* and the element of the original *Antecedents* which makes the horse react and naturally stimulates the *response* is known as the *unconditioned stimulus*.

Classical conditioning involves your horse's brain building links between the *conditioned stimulus* (the new signal or command), an *unconditioned stimulus* (the original signal or events which naturally make the behaviour happen) a particular behavioural *response* and the memory of the *Consequences*. This is sometimes referred to in scientific shorthand as *conditioned stimulus-unconditioned stimulus-response*, ie *classical conditioning* is the process where a link is made between a new signal or command and any *stimulus*. If your horse's *response* to that *stimulus* is rewarded, he will be more likely to respond to that *stimulus* in that way again. If the *response* has an unpleasant *Consequence*, he will be less likely to react in that way again. Once the link has been made between the new command or signal and the original *stimulus*, your horse will respond to the new signal as soon as it happens, instead of waiting for the original *stimulus* which he has now has learned will follow. Learning to do something by *classical conditioning* is sometimes described in technical terms as Command – Action – Reward.

It can be difficult to remember all the technical details and jargon involved in the scientific description of learning, but I find remembering that all the Cs go together (i.e. Command = Conditioned stimulus used in the Classical form of conditioning) helps. You might also remember 'classic CAR' as classical conditioning = Command Action Reward.

The following diagrams show the sequences of *stimuli* and *responses* and the links between these which are required for the neurological changes to take place in the brain that we call *learning*. They illustrate how learning works by the brain building 'shortcuts' or direct links between *conditioned stimuli* and *rewards*.

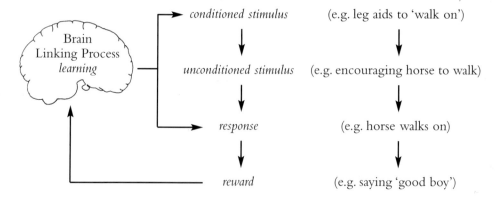

When the desired learned *response* is accidentally punished instead of being rewarded, a different *response* will be added to the chain of events. The horse will usually do something else instead to avoid the accidental *punishment*. Avoiding the punishment acts like a *reward*, and brain links are made between the original signal or *conditioned stimulus* and this different and *undesired response*. Now the horse will react to the signal or *conditioned stimulus* with this undesirable avoidance behaviour instead of the desired *response*. He learns to do the wrong thing and this is how many behaviour problems, especially ridden evasions, develop.

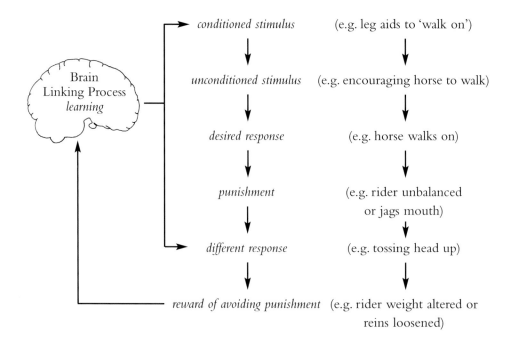

Knowing more about how the basic learning process of *conditioning* works and the importance of the relative order or sequence in which *stimuli*, *responses* and *rewards* must happen, in order for learning to take place, should help you work out how any behaviour problem may have developed. This is often by the process of *operant conditioning*, where a natural instinct (e.g. nudging your pocket) is rewarded (e.g. by getting a treat). Alternatively, you may have accidentally punished the desired *response* to your signals using *classical conditioning* as in the above diagram. I hope this will also enable you to understand how any 'new' form of training or 'alternative' training system works, so you can pick out the useful bits and avoid those based on punishment, which are often erroneously marketed as 'humane'. This knowledge should help you keep yourself and your horse safe, as well as enabling you to teach your horse a few 'party tricks' with which to impress your chums!

Chapter 5

Learning to Respond

All of the ways in which horses learn whether promoted as 'new', 'alternative' or 'traditional' are based on the process of *conditioning* described in Chapter 4 on the Learning Process. There are some variations on this theme however, particularly in the way in which horses perceive and respond to *conditioned stimuli*, which are very useful when tracing the development of behaviour problems and which can also be valuable when training. These are:

- Generalization between stimuli
- Bridging stimuli
- Strings of conditioned stimuli
- Irrelevant stimuli and superstitious learning

This chapter explains the most common variations in the ways in which *stimuli* are perceived and incorporated into the *conditioning* process as horses learn to *respond* to them.

GENERALIZATION BETWEEN STIMULI

Horses sometimes pick out one element of a *conditioned stimulus* and learn to react to just that. Say for example, a horse learned to approach someone wearing a red hat for a treat. We may then start to approach anyone wearing a red hat expecting the treat. This is called *generalization* as the horse has 'generalized' his specific response to the *stimulus* of the sight of a particular individual wearing a red hat, to include anyone wearing this colour of hat.

Not a lot of horsy people wear bright red hats and I used an odd thing here to illustrate the point that it is usually particularly unusual or very noticeable stimuli to which horses develop a *generalized response* in this way. This is because the horse's brain takes particular notice of unusual events, bright colours or loud sounds, as described in Chapter 1 on the ABC of Learning and Chapter 3 on Training and Time. The nerve cells involved in learning are more likely to make connections about these kinds of novel or unusual things and to transfer information about them into long term memory.

This is how horses learn to be generally nervous say of vets or farriers. They will have had an experience which taught them (usually by classical conditioning) that a particular person from one of these groups of people can hurt you. This may have been a vet doing a routine vaccination for example. If the vet looked noticeably different from the people who usually deal with this horse, he may generalize his learned fear response to something unusual associated with the vet's appearance, such as the glint of a stethoscope around the neck or a particular type of overall or 'lab' coat. Many vets' clothes smell of the chemicals they use every day and are stored in their surgery or car. This is often a rather distinctive blend of the particular 'sharp' smells associated with 'antiseptics' etc. and your horse may notice these as the most distinctive feature of the person who 'stabbed' him with a sharp needle, and react in future with fear to this smell. Similarly farriers' clothes carry a distinctive smell associated with the work they do, and this can also become the basis for a generalised fear response.

Generalization can cause problems. To continue with the veterinary example above, the next time your vet approaches, you may need your horse to stay calm for example to allow the vet to examine a nasty wound, or to take his heart rate at an endurance or cross-country competition vet check.

Because *generalization* usually occurs in relation to particularly unusual or very noticeable elements of *conditioned stimuli*, it is usually quite easy to re-train horses with behaviour problems that developed in this way (using the process of *counter-conditioning* explained in Chapter 7 on Practical Re-training Techniques) as it is usually very easy for us to spot the particular element of the *conditioned stimulus* involved. You simply make sure that the horse is frequently exposed to this part of the *conditioned stimulus*, such as the smell of the vet in our ongoing example, just before something nice happens instead. You can ask your vet (or farrier) to keep an old jacket or jumper of yours in his surgery (or forge) or the back of his vehicle for a couple of weeks so that it acquires the blend of smells in question! You then wear this when you are feeding the horse, and he learns by *classical conditioning* again to associate this smell with a pleasant <u>C</u>onsequence instead.

If your horse is frightened of vets or farriers or has had a bad experience with one on their last visit, you can reduce the chances of *generalization* causing problems in the future by being cheeky and asking them to drape one of your jackets that you 'do' the horse in (before you wash it!) around their shoulders when they next approach the horse. Even if your horse then learns to be scared of that jacket, if you continue to wear it for routine stable duties including feeding and so on, you will automatically *counter-condition* the *generalization* effect, and your horse will be less likely to develop any *generalized* fear response to the 'usual' smell or appearance of vets or farriers. This could be handy in an emergency or when out at a competition.

Some horses *generalize* to gender differences in people, and may for example become frightened of men in general if they are usually handled and fed by women and the only men they meet are vets or farriers or 'rough' riders and trainers. You can avoid this happening or help to *counter-condition* your horse into associating men with 'nice' things instead, by bribing all the men you know (husbands, sons, and any male relative, neighbours or friends) to visit your horse with you and give him treats. One or two single female clients of mine have used this very successfully as a 'chat-up line' and unusual way of getting to know someone they are interested in!

Horses can also *generalize* a response to particularly unusual and noticeable elements of the *stimuli* involved in behaviour learned by *operant conditioning*. This is how a horse may learn for example to be scared of black plastic perhaps, after being inadvertently jabbed in the mouth and kicked on the flanks by the unseated rider when genuinely spooking at a piece of a haylage bag stuck on a barbed wire fence.

Individual horses can learn in this way to be frightened of particular elements of areas where they had a bad experience and this can sometimes help with the detective work involved in working out where and why accidents happened. This is also very useful when dealing with the ensuing behaviour problems.

There was one yard where people began to think I had 'gone potty' when re-training a little horse who had become so spooky after a spell away from home that his owner was scared to ride him outside the school. He had been sold to a 'good' competition home, but was returned as 'unrideable' for this reason. Things were so bad that he was actually referred to me by the original owner's vet after a visit where he had been asked to check out Shadow's eyesight. He could find nothing wrong with Shadow's eyes and asked me to investigate the possibility that this extreme spookiness was a learned behaviour problem.

After a little detective work, and riding him out a few times myself, I discovered that this horse only spooked at very particular things which were unfortunately quite common in the fields used for riding in at this yard. These were hoof prints in mud, open gateways, large logs on their side, broken branches crossing others, dandelions and bunches of nettles where one plant was noticeably higher than the rest! I also discovered that Shadow had fallen while spooking in a gateway and hurt himself quite badly in the competition home. I reckoned that I could probably describe the gateway where this happened as containing all the elements listed above and indeed, this turned out to be the case. This supported the original owner's claim that Shadow did not spook like this with her.

I was able to attribute the cause of the problematical spooking to this fall and of course help to absolve the original owner of any blame for selling on a spooky horse! It took quite a lot of time, but we were able to get this partnership hacking out happily again after a complex programme of careful *counter-conditioning* to each of the specific elements to which he had developed the generalized fear response (see Chapter 7 on Practical Re-training Techniques). We also had to combine these elements in various stages as well, and the yard staff and other clients who rode there thought I was absolutely crazy when they saw me out picking dandelions and 'arranging' them in muddy gateways as if still growing and sticking long nettles into bunches of shorter ones to use in our training sessions!

Generalization can also be useful. For example, this is how experienced competition horses learn not to react to new fillers when jumping, or not to be put off by different ways of delineating dressage arenas etc. They *generalize* between some elements in specific fillers or the arena boundaries with which they are familiar and the same elements in new fillers or boundaries, 'recognizing' them as the same sort of thing and therefore do not spook at new ones when they come across them for the first time.

BRIDGING STIMULI

You may recall how, in Chapter 1 on the ABC of Learning, I emphasized the importance of giving your *reward* within half a second of the desired <u>Behaviour</u> in order for the learning process to work properly. This can be very difficult to do in real life, especially when you are some distance from the horse or trying to teach him a complex movement and you just cannot get the reward to the horse in time for it to be an effective training aid. In this situation, you can use a special *stimulus* to 'bridge the gap' between the horse doing what you wanted and giving him his reward. This special *stimulus* is one which can be given just after the correct response as a kind of substitute reward and is called a *bridging stimulus.*

The best signals to use as *bridging stimuli* are those which are very quick and easy to give and which are also very noticeable and arousing and likely to help encourage your horse to continue on, for example through a series of complex steps or other longer movements. It is important that the *bridging stimulus* is quick and easy to give so you can give it within half a second of the initial correct response as you would have done with a 'real' *reward*, had this been possible. You also need to fit the *bridging stimulus* into the interval before the next stage of the desired response. Your *bridging stimulus* acts as a 'substitute' reward for the initial element of your horse's response, and you can then proceed to encourage and *reward* the next element in the same way and so on, until you reach the end of the series of desirable steps or complex movement and can give your horse his treat or 'real' *reward*. A *bridging stimulus* is essentially a *conditioned stimulus* which your horse has learned to associate with a subsequent *reward* and so can be used instead of the *reward* as a temporary substitute for this.

Stimuli which work well as *bridging stimuli* with most animals are clicks, whistles and whip cracks, all of which are quick, easy to give (once you have had a little practice!) and very noticeable and most animals will hear these even if they are in the middle of something very complex, tricky or strenuous. These are commonly used a lot by animal trainers who have to be far away from their animals during training, such as those who work with dolphins or sheep dogs. *Bridging stimuli* are also commonly used where complicated series of manoeuvres are required to complete the desired response – as in circus animals. The whip is traditionally associated with the ringmaster and circus trainers, not because they use it to punish their animals, but because they need to use a lot of *bridging stimuli* in their training and a whip is a very handy device here. It is not a coincidence that most effective *bridging stimuli* are noises. This is because sound travels far, goes round corners or through obstacles and can be noticed even when the trainee is not looking at the trainer. Short sharp blasts on a high pitched whistle or the crack made by a whip also are carried further with less scope for interference than other sounds and are naturally arousing and very noticeable, which is why these are the signals generally chosen by professionals for this kind of training.

One modern training technique that makes extensive use of *bridging stimuli* is 'Clicker Training'. Once the trainer has practised the timing and use of the clicker device, this can be a very effective training tool for horses as well as other animals. It is particularly important here that the trainer first of all teaches the horse that the click is associated with a *reward* so that the click works as a substitute *reward* during training. Initially, you have to teach the horse that a click is followed by a *reward*. This is done by *classical conditioning*, where the click is the *conditioned stimulus* and the trainer getting the 'real' *reward* or treat ready is the *unconditioned stimulus*. So, to teach your horse the clicker *reward system* you first of all make a click, then within half second give your *reward* and repeat this a number of times per session, leaving a few days at least between sessions to let this link be consolidated in your horse's long term memory.

Some horses are initially frightened by the clicking sound and you need to begin by getting them used to this (by the learning process of *habituation* as described in Chapter 6 on Learning Not to Respond and 'Un-learning').

You can then use one click just before giving your horse a small treat to teach him that one click means a little treat. This idea can be developed by using two clicks before giving a bigger or tastier treat, then three or four clicks before even bigger pieces of tit bit etc. to teach your horse that more clicks mean better treats. Finally you can use a series of clicks given in increasing frequency before giving your horse a really super favourite treat to teach him that this pattern of clicks means the very best *reward* of all. In this way you have a variety of clicks at your disposal, each to be used to substitute for various different *rewards*. When encouraging your horse to 'keep going' for example through a grid of jumps or to perform a complex manoeuvre involving a series of steps in sequence, you can use the different click patterns to *reward* him progressively as he goes through the sequence. Use a single click to substitute for a small *reward* for the first step, two clicks as a better reward for the next step and so on until you use the high frequency series of clicks to substitute for the best *reward* for the final step or most difficult part of any sequence. If you listen carefully to people encouraging their horse by tongue clicking you will hear that they often do it in exactly this pattern, naturally giving more or faster clicks as they get more excited (or frustrated!) and the horse gets closer to doing what they want.

I recall with just a little embarrassment my first experience of clicker training. Many years ago, I was very honoured to have been invited to visit and give a guest lecture at Cornell by one of the first lady faculty members in a Veterinary School in America. This particular lady was my heroine, not just because she had done so well in what is still very much 'a man's world', but particularly because she did this while specializing in horse behaviour before it became 'fashionable'! I used her textbook to teach my students and she had developed an equine behaviour clinic which set the standards for this kind of work worldwide.

Professor H had invited a select bunch from the Department to dinner with us at her home, and we had a lovely meal and lots of quite serious academic conversation. Then over coffee one of the girls decided it was time to have some fun. Clicker training was just being developed and she was a keen aficionado. She waited until I had excused myself for a visit to the bathroom, and in my absence involved the whole table in what she hoped would be an 'educational' game. They decided to clicker train me and the chosen task was to pass the milk to a particular person.

After I returned to the table, she began to press the clicker device she had cunningly concealed beforehand in her handbag. When I moved my hands nearer to the designated jug she clicked, and the closer I got the more frequently the clicks came. Unfortunately, I was startled by the click and reacted as if it was a punishment, and she trained me very effectively instead to clasp my hands in my lap and sit very still. The rest of our colleagues thought this was absolutely hilarious and after a few politely stifled giggles began to roar with laughter. What she had forgotten to do, as they were only too quick to point out at this stage, was to initially teach me the reward system that clicks were 'good'. She should have clicked then offered me a cracker, then clicked twice and offered a biscuit, then three times for a chocolate biscuit etc. before starting my training towards lifting the jug. So, in the end, as well as giving me a very red face, it really was a most educational game all round!

Some people use tongue clicks quite effectively in horses, although this does count as 'use of the voice' and is considered cheating and will cost you points in dressage. You will also hear people very experienced with horses, who know nothing of the science of learning theory, using verbal encouragement, such as 'Hup' or 'Go-on' or even 'Good Boy' in this way, making a very effective *bridging stimulus.*

Bridging stimuli are also how a crowd cheering encourages and 'lifts' athletes. For example, an athlete learns by *operant conditioning* that winning (and indeed 'resting' at to the finish) is rewarding. He also learns by *classical conditioning* that cheering is associated with these *rewards*. After getting to the finish line, he hears the cheer and then experiences the joy of winning, satisfaction at making a particularly good shot or relief at finishing as his *reward*. The cheering becomes the *classical conditioned stimulus* for the behaviour or effort that led to this joy or relief. In this way, the *bridging stimulus* of the cheering becomes a substitute *reward* in itself. In a future race, the athlete may have to keep going and put in some very strenuous effort before actually being successful again and if he hears yells of encouragement and cheering from the spectators at the point, these act as a *bridging stimulus* and *reward* the ongoing effort. As the pitch or frequency of cheering increases after greater achievements, he will be further rewarded for these and unconsciously learn to work harder, a *classically conditioned* response to the greater reward of these 'improved' versions of the *bridging stimulus*, as cheering alters in this way when coming to the climax of future competitions. This is how a supportive crowd really can help an athlete do his best. The more excited the crowd become as he starts to do well, the more they will be training him, in a way just like clicker training, to improve his performance! You can use clickers or verbal rewards too in this way when working with your horse and this athletic example can also be applied to equestrian sports. Make use of *bridging stimuli* by asking a few mates to cheer you on next time you are out show-jumping or doing cross-country and station them at the fence you and your horse expect to find the most difficult!

STRINGS OF CONDITIONED STIMULI

When reading previous chapters, you may have wondered if '*Antecedents, Behaviour and Consequences*' or '*stimuli – responses – rewards*' need to follow each other within half a second or so for learning to work, why does my horse start getting excited in anticipation of feeding time half an hour before it happens?' or 'How does my horse know the day before when we are going to a competition or hide at the far end of the field when I start hitching up the trailer?'

These things happen when your horse puts together long *strings of stimuli* or 'chaining' as this is called in America. Horses learn by the usual *conditioning* processes that one signal is followed by another and then another and so on until he reaches the signal at the end of the 'chain' or 'string', which was the original or first learned *conditioned stimulus*. If this 'string of signals' or parts of the 'chain' are repeated often and always in exactly the same sequence, they are more likely to become linked together in your horse's brain. This happens in the same way that the brain links a *conditioned stimulus* with an *unconditioned stimulus*, (as described in Chapter 4 on the Learning Process).

The original *conditioned stimulus* is denoted number one in the chain. The signal learned next which immediately precedes the original one is denoted number two. The signal which happens before that and is added onto the chain next to make the third link and so on. These are usually written CS1, CS2 and CS3 etc. in scientific shorthand, as per the order in which they were added to the chain or string of stimuli.

Most ridden aids are learned by strings of *classically conditioned stimuli* in this way. For example, when a horse is just beginning to be ridden i.e. being 'started' or 'broken', he learns to 'walk on' initially by *operant conditioning* where a handler leading him rewards him for the natural instinct of following. Different handlers have their own versions of tummy tickling etc. to encourage the horse to step forward when they do. This may then progress to training the horse by *classical conditioning* to 'walk on' when the handler says so (as described in Chapter 4 on the Learning Process). The handler's vocal command is the first *classical conditioned stimulus* (CS1). Once this horse had had enough ground work to build the strength in his back sufficiently for him to be able to carry a rider, he will be taught to tolerate someone sitting on his back (by the process of 'habituation' see Chapter 6 on Learning Not to Respond and Un-learning). He is then ready for the next stage of his training and to begin to learn the ridden aids. The handler indicates to the passenger rider when to offer a gentle leg aid. This leg aid is the second *conditioned stimulus* in the chain of commands to which the horse is learning to react (CS2). The handler then gives a vocal command (CS1) if necessary followed by the unconditioned stimulus (US) of tickling the horse's tummy and walking on himself. When the horse walks on (R = correct response) he should be immediately rewarded by cessation of the leg pressure and/or tummy tickling and the giving of a treat (RW). Placing this at the sternum (as described in Chapter 2 on Rewards, Punishment and Motivation) works best here, avoiding teaching the horse to nip and most importantly, encouraging him to stretch his head and neck and use his back to halt properly here. The handler might even offer a *bridging stimulus* such as saying 'good boy' here as soon as the horse takes a step i.e. in between the desired response and giving up the reward. If this *string of stimuli* is repeated in exactly the same order (CS2-CS1-US), the horse will learn by the process of *classical conditioning* to respond by walking on when he notices the earliest signal in the chain, in this case CS2, the rider's leg aid.

It is important that a young horse is not confused by extra unintentional movements of the rider here and that the rider does not accidentally punish the horse by inadvertently changing the rein contact or getting 'left behind' when the horse initially moves off. The handler and rider must also carefully co-ordinate their various *stimuli* to make sure that they are always given in the same order i.e. the leg aid (CS2) must always be given before the vocal command to 'walk on' (CS1), and so on. This is why good handlers prefer to use experienced riders that they know well for this job.

You can use *strings of conditioned stimuli* in this way to improve many aspects of your horse's performance in response to your aids. Transitions become much easier and smoother if taught to your horse using a 'chain' or *string of stimuli* for example. Start with use the usual leg aids (CS1). Then add other signals before this, e.g. one *string of stimuli* which is commonly used here for an upwards transition, say from walk to trot, is lean a little forward just enough to noticeably lighten the pressure you can feel between your seat bones (CS2) and the saddle just before you give the usual leg aids (CS1). Then add breathing in (CS3) just before you lean forward (CS2) and give the usual leg aids (CS1). If you repeat this a few times i.e. (CS3) – (CS2) – (CS1), your horse will learn to get himself ready and trot on in immediate response to the 'earliest' *classically conditioned stimulus* he notices in the *string* and recognizes as part of the 'chain' i.e. your breathing in (CS3). In this way you will get a more obedient and balanced transition.

Many people who are naturally very good riders instinctively give all of their signals to the horse in this very structured and reliable way, building *strings of conditioned stimuli* without knowing it, and horses quickly learn to respond to them. You will also now understand how accidental movements can really confuse things when you are riding and how useful it is to develop awareness of and control over what your own body is doing.

You do have to be careful when selecting your *stimuli* for incorporation into any string.

A friend of mine thought she was being very smart in adding a little sniff to the *string of stimuli* she was using to improve her horse's downwards transitions. He was quite a strong and forward going 17.2 hh Cleveland Bay cross Clydesdale, and was often marked down in dressage, for poor downwards transitions, soliciting comments like 'running into walk' or 'fell into trot' etc. At first all went well, as she went through sniff (CS4), tighten tummy and hold shoulders very tall (CS3), breathe out (CS2), half-halt (CS1) and finally the usual aids for each transition (US). Unfortunately, the day came when she had a cold and could hardly get her now very confused horse to keep going!

Horses will always learn to respond to the earliest signal or *conditioned stimulus* (CS) they recognize in any 'chain', and you can also cause problems by forgetting which signals you have used in the past when training your horse to do something else using the same *conditioned stimulus*.

When teaching a little chestnut Arab gelding recovering from spavins to move straight, I used a fairly standard 'right leg back' aid to control his hindquarters which he tended to allow to drift to the right. He quickly learned to respond well to this (by the process of *classical conditioning* described in Chapter 4 on the Learning Process), and we progressed happily with further ridden exercises and he began to do some nice turns up the centre line keeping straight, with his hindquarters under control care of the 'right leg back' aid and then making some very good square halts. I was very pleased and decided to give him a rest before checking out his response to canter aids, which can be tricky after spavins as the hind leg movement used to start canter is similar to movements which would have been painful when the arthritis causing spavins was active.

First I asked for canter on his best side which happened to be the right rein. No problem and a reasonable few transitions ensued. Then I changed rein and asked for canter at the 'A' end of the school in my usual fashion, involving brushing the outside leg (now my right leg) back. This delightful little horse recognized the right leg back in the corner as the earliest *conditioned stimulus* in the chain which he had just learned led to halt. Obligingly he halted! I regret to have to say that I did not, and instead did a beautiful somersault over his head, luckily landing more or less on my feet beside him. He just stood there, head tucked in, 'doing' his dressage halt for the regulation four seconds or so of immobility, before slowly turning his head to give me a filthy look which I interpreted as 'Well, I did my bit right – What happened to you?'

Apart from these kinds of 'human errors', *strings of classical conditioned stimuli* are a very useful way to improve your horse's response to the standard aids when riding. You may know someone whose horse does beautifully obedient and balanced canter transitions, and been exasperated when, trying to find out how to emulate these with your own horse, you ask them how they do it and they beam happily and say 'I just think canter!' The answer you needed is that they do it by 'chains' or *strings of classical conditioned stimuli*, where their 'thinking canter' is the earliest *conditioned stimulus* or signal in the chain of preparation and aids they use and proceed to give to get canter. Their horse has learned to recognize this 'thinking canter' *conditioned stimulus* and he now reacts to the very subtle changes in posture and breathing that this person unconsciously does when 'thinking' canter, and canters. So in a way they were telling the truth although not in enough detail to be of any use to you! This is how the sports psychology technique of 'visualization' works and can be applied to horse riding, and is the basis of the success of the very useful self help technique of *Riding with your Mind*, developed by Molly Sivewright.

Operant conditioned behaviour can also be modified by a 'chain' or *string of conditioned stimuli* in the same way. Remember the example on how horses learn to find shelter in a new field, Example 4.3 given in Chapter 4 on the Learning Process. Horses are more sensitive than us to changes in atmospheric pressure, wind temperature and direction and perhaps even cloud formations, and they will learn to react to the earliest environmental indications of imminent weather change in this way. The environmental signals a horse can spot leading up to any weather change are effectively a 'chain' or *string of classical conditioned stimuli*, and he will learn to react to the earliest of these by moving to the best place to be in the field for that sort of weather. This sort of learning is probably the basis for many folklore weather forecasting tips – predicting imminent weather change by what the animals in the fields are doing. If you study your own horse's behaviour enough here, you may find he can help you get the washing in off the line a few moments before the rain arrives!

These simple examples illustrate learning using relatively short 'chains' or *strings of conditioned stimuli*. Longer chains can be built to take effect over a day or two and this is how horses learn to anticipate a trip in the trailer or a competition. This is more likely to happen with unusual events or those with particularly 'good' or 'bad' *Consequences*, as described in the Brain and Memory Section of Chapter 3 on Training and Time. Feed arriving is a common example of a very 'good' consequence and some horses get very excited about competitions and regard outings as particularly 'good' also. For other horses, competitions, involving perhaps a day away from mates without grazing and a lot of hard work, may be regarded as a very 'bad' *Consequence* from some horse point of view, and they learn to react to the preparations accordingly. Particular steps in the preparations become the *conditioned stimuli* here, and as most people get ready in the same sort of way each time, whichever elements of the routine your horse can see or hear become the *conditioned stimulus* elements of the string.

If you find your horse's anticipatory behaviour a nuisance here, you can help to diminish this by varying your preparation routine and sometimes doing isolated elements of this without proceeding to the next step on days when you are going nowhere, thus breaking the chain and *extinguishing* his learned responses to the various elements of the chain (see more in Chapter 6 on Learning Not to Respond and Un-learning). This is sometimes essential where the anticipatory behaviour is detrimental to a horse's performance at a competition, as for example in some endurance horses who box-walk. The endurance rider planning to do fifty miles tomorrow does not want their horse to notch up twenty to thirty miles around the box the night before. These horses have learned to anticipate the next day's work using *strings of conditioned stimuli* and this causes changes in hormones and neurotransmitters (such as increasing thyroid stimulating hormone, adrenalin and beta-endorphin levels) which trigger the stereotyped behaviour. It is interesting that these hormone and neurotransmitter changes also help the horse's body cope with physical stress and to perform better, so learned 'anticipatory' behaviour is biologically useful. These helpful physical changes are what an athlete is trying to create when he concentrates on an imminent event to 'psyche himself up', and to this end it might be beneficial to set up a warm-up routine which will teach your horse in this way to anticipate his imminent performance when at a competition whatever the discipline.

In the same way, salivating at the smell or other signals associated with imminent arrival of food aids digestion. Pavlov's dogs (mentioned in Chapter 4 on the Learning Process) actually learned a whole string of *classically conditioned stimuli* until the bell was included as the earliest (CS) signal. It was vital that he prepared the food strictly in the same way each time, to build the 'chain' or *string of stimuli*. This also tells us that not only was Pavlov a great scientist, but that he was a very methodical person too!

The problems experienced by Miss S with 'Jigsaw', described in Chapter 1 on the ABC of Learning developed in this way too. The flash of red from the postman's van that he could see was the earliest or key *conditioned stimulus* in the chain which usually led to Jigsaw's morning feed arriving. On the occasions when this did not happen soon, there was trouble and Jigsaw's frustration-related behaviour caused injuries and a lot of damage. The way in which horses learn using *stings of conditioned stimuli* is one reason why a rigid daily stable routine can create problems. Sometimes your routine is unavoidably altered, and if it is usually very strict, your horse will be more frustrated than if your usual routine is somewhat flexible. A more flexible routine reduces the likelihood of your horse learning a long *string of conditioned stimuli* in relation to his daily life and helps to break up any developing 'chains'. So the way in which horses learn here gives you a good excuse for a little laxity when attending to your stable duties!

Strings can lead to anticipatory behaviour in horses which is useful too. Some racehorses become physically overly stressed by their training routine and this is known in the racing industry as 'overtraining'. There is a blood test available today which will measure these changes and tell the trainer when he is pushing any horse too hard in this way. However, before this test was available, good trainers would know when they had reached this point because the horse would tell them by starting to show reluctance in the stable, trying to avoid being tacked up and some would even become most reluctant to leave their box! In Australia, as I discovered when on a trip to help select horses for an owner keen to be selected for the National team in endurance racing, the grooms are very well aware of this phenomenon and save the owners of the horses they work with a lot of money here. At a subsequent conference in Switzerland I also discovered that these behavioural changes happen a day or two before the currently available blood tests showed 'overtraining', so are particularly useful in also preventing the injuries or muscle damage caused by this, as the behaviour change is an earlier means of detection.

Strings of conditioned stimuli also make it very easy to work backwards along the line to detect the 'key stimulus' leading to any behaviour problem. This is why taking a case history sometimes requires a lot of time and why behaviour consultants may seem inordinately concerned with tiny details about the circumstance surrounding your horse's past misdemeanours which you may have thought were quite irrelevant. They are not just being 'nosey', as, once discovered, it is usually very easy to 'fix' these kinds of problems by teaching the horse to react differently to the 'key stimulus'. This is the earliest *conditioned stimulus* which triggers the 'bad' behaviour.

For example, in Example 4.10 in Chapter 4 on the Learning Process, I explained one way of teaching a horse which pulls away to halt safely when led. Using strings of *classical conditioned stimuli* here to further 'refine' this system is particularly useful for horses who have really established this habit to the point where they cannot be led at all. You need to attach a 'jangling' item to the original leadrope, such as a cat's collar bell or a few old keys. In addition to the *classical conditioned* training explained in Chapter 4 the handler proceeds to build a 'chain' or *string of classical conditioned stimuli*. First she pulls on the leadrope (CS4), then makes the bell or keys jangle (CS3), before stopping (CS2), saying wait (CS1) and having the rider give the aids halt the horse (US). With this 'chain', the horse learns to react by stopping when the leadrope tightens and gives the 'pull' – regardless of who pulled it the handler or the horse. The 'jangle' is the key *conditioned stimulus* here, i.e. this is the one just after which the 'chain' now branches off to the end where the rider halts the horse, to get a reward, instead of continuing along the previous route where the horse had learned that a pull (and no jangle) resulted in this horse getting away to be rewarded by freedom and eating grass.

IRRELEVANT STIMULI AND SUPERSTITIOUS LEARNING

Sometimes, a horse co-incidentally does something else just before the desired behaviour in response to a *conditioned stimulus*. This may happen when he accidentally notices and reacts to something unexpected occurring in the interval between any *conditioned stimulus* and the intended *unconditioned stimulus*, causing the first part of the horse's response to the new *conditioned stimulus* to include this extra unintended behaviour. The unexpected extra event, which is noticed in the interval between the *conditioned stimulus* and the intended *unconditioned stimulus*, effectively becomes another preceding unintended *unconditioned stimulus*. The horse learns in the usual way to include his response to this before he reacts to the intended *unconditioned stimulus* as desired.

This means that the horse learns to *respond* to the *conditioned stimulus* by first of all doing some other thing in addition and entirely irrelevant to what was intended, before going on to respond as desired. This extra response is called '*superstitious behaviour*'. It is irrelevant to the reward for the intended behaviour but is included anyway.

The additional irrelevant <u>Behaviour</u> is said to have been acquired by *superstitious learning*. It is maintained as part of the learned *response* to the *conditioned stimulus* even though it was not wanted and is in itself not being rewarded. It is part of a 'mini chain' being an extra *response* to an unexpected *unconditioned stimulus*, which has become linked by *conditioning* to the intended *unconditional stimulus* and the desired *response*. The horse's brain has built the connections between the two *unconditioned stimuli* and *responses* just like it does when building a *string of conditioned stimuli*. *Superstitious learning* is the name given to what happens in response to an unintentional short *string of unconditioned stimuli*.

Superstitious learning is rarely useful, but it is how some entertaining 'foibles' are acquired. For example, say one day your horse was startled into burling around just before you put a new feed bucket down. You were putting it down anyway, and the 'burl' was of no consequence. If the timing was just right, however, your horse may make a connection between this irrelevant 'extra' response to your approach and the release of the new bucket and 'think' he has to do this every time from now on to get the feed. In terms of the learning process, your initial approach with the new bucket is the *conditioned stimulus*, your putting the bucket down for him, is the *unconditioned stimulus* and the desired *response* is him approaching with head down to eat. Whatever startled him into burling around before putting his head down to eat is an extra *unconditioned stimulus*. In terms of timing, if this occurred in between your approach (the *conditioned stimulus*) and you putting the new bucket down for him to eat (the original *unconditioned stimulus*), his brain could make the necessary connections, 'chaining these *unconditioned stimuli*' and add the 'burl' to his coming to eat response. He has incorporated this irrelevant _Behaviour_ into his previously learned response to your approach with a bucket by *superstitious learning*. I have come across some people who capitalize on this sort of thing and show the foible off like a party trick, for example in this instance saying something along the lines of 'dance for your dinner', although most people find this sort of irrelevant behaviour very annoying.

Superstitious learning is also how many ridden evasions are acquired. These can be quite subtle, such as a tiny head tilt, movement of the tongue or playing with the bit during transitions. For example: if an irritation like a fly or piece of food stuck in the teeth is felt by the horse just after a rein aid and just before he reacts accordingly, he may incorporate the co-incidental reaction to the irritation into the transition. This is most likely to happen if he is learning new conditioned responses to the riding aids at that time. Superstitious evasions can also be quite obvious, such as the 'bowing in halt' habit acquired by one little horse I was training for his owner.

Ginger and I were working on square halts and one day when we were beginning to practise for the first time in a nicely laid out dressage arena, he felt a cleg land on his chest and stretched his head and neck in a bowing action to get it just at the point in between me giving the new conditioned aid to halt (a particular movement of my seat) and him actually bringing his last foot into a square halt. If he was halting any old how or indeed doing 'proper' halts in a school or corner of the field, we had no problem. Unfortunately, each time Ginger was asked to halt using this seat movement in a 'proper' arena at 'G', he bowed – although we also always got our square halt here too! For quite some time this amused many a dressage judge and lost us many a point!

Superstitious learning makes it appear as though the horse 'thinks' he has to do the additional irrelevant behaviour as well as the desired response to get his *reward*. The *stimuli* involved in *superstitious learning* are usually rare or transient things, and the handler or rider may not get a chance to see what exactly any such *stimulus* actually was. Once established, *superstitious behaviour* learned in this way is hard to get rid of, as you have to pinpoint the original unexpected 'extra' *unconditioned stimulus*, and re-create it, in order to use this on its own as part of a *counter-conditioning* programme (see Chapter 7 on Practical Re-training Techniques). It can be very difficult to find and re-enact these unexpected extra stimuli to retrain a horse who acquires an evasion by *superstitious learning* in this way. I find the best way of dealing with these evasions is not to try to get your horse to 'un learn' the superstitious behaviour but to bypass it altogether, by avoiding the original *conditioned stimulus* and using a completely different aid instead. It is usually much easier to re-train the horse to perform the required manoeuvre in response to a new *conditioned stimulus* such as a different aid instead, using *classical conditioning* (as described in Chapter 4 on the Learning Process). There are lots of different ways of getting a horse to do any particular movement. In the American Western style of riding, neck reining is used rather than leg and weight aids to encourage horses to turn. In Iceland, where tall men ride very small horses, their feet hang down well below the horse's sides and traditional European leg aids are of no use to them. Instead, the Icelandic traditional aids focus on upper body movement and use of the seat and thighs. Using a different aid as a new *classical conditioned stimulus* you will not stimulate performance of the *superstitious behaviour* which was learned as a response to the previously used aid or 'original' *classical conditioned stimulus*.

Superstitious learning from *irrelevant stimuli* is another reason why it helps to train in a peaceful and distraction-free environment, so that you can minimize the chances of interference from unexpected *stimuli*. You can also reduce the risk of your horse picking up these 'superstitious responses' by keeping the interval between your *conditioned stimulus* and your *unconditioned stimulus* as short as possible.

It is the increasing risk of this sort of accidental interference between *stimuli* as well as some of the physical constraints on *memory* described in Chapter 3 on Training and Time, which limit the length of the chain or any *string of conditioned stimuli* that most horses can cope with when learning more complex manoeuvres.

This is probably a good thing for competitions aiming to test equestrian skills repeatedly over a routine set of particular movements, such as in dressage, for example. If it were not for these limits, a coach would just have to whisper 'Prelim 7' and off your horse would go – which would be no fun at all!

SUMMARY

This chapter describes the main ways in which variations in the way horses perceive *stimuli* affect the learning process. These can cause problems, but sometimes also help training. Knowledge of these is particularly useful when tracing the development of a behaviour problem, as once the key elements involved have been identified, re-training can be more accurately focussed to deal with the root cause of any learned behaviour problem.

Generalization is the process whereby horses learn to react to one particularly noticeable or unusual element of any *conditioned stimulus* and then subsequently react in the same way to any other *stimulus* containing this particular element. This is how horses learn to be frightened of motorbikes or men in general after a bad experience with one in particular. On the positive side, it is also how they learn to respect all electric fences, not just the one they were taught to be wary of and to jump over all brightly coloured fillers, not just the particular ones they have seen before. The process of generalization can be summarised in diagrammatic form:

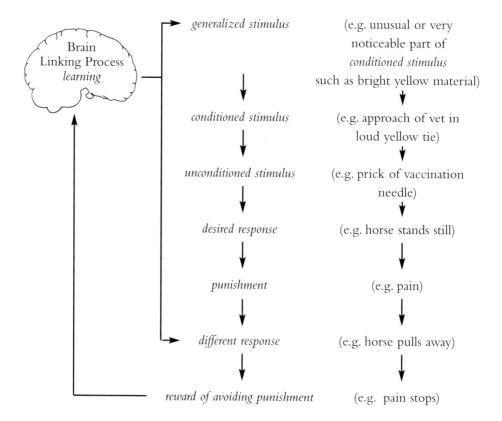

The brain may notice a particularly outstanding or unusual aspect of the *conditioned stimulus* first, and the conditioned link is made with this generalized stimulus instead of the specific *conditioned stimulus*. The horse will learn to *respond* in the same way in future to any other different *stimulus* which includes this unusual aspect, i.e. the horse in this example has learned by the process of *generalization* to pull away whenever he sees anything bright yellow coming closer.

Bridging stimuli are substitute *rewards* which are useful when it is not practical to give real *reward* immediately after the correct *response*. These tend to be short sharp sounds, like whistle blasts, whip cracks and are most useful when your horse is learning complex or a linked series of movements. This is how clicker training works; the 'click' is a *bridging stimulus*.

When *bridging stimuli* are repeated or occur more frequently, they represent a greater *reward* and help to encourage continued, sustained or more strenuous responses.

The use of *bridging stimuli* when training can be summarised in diagrammatic form. This example shows the learning process involved when a horse is learning to jump a complex grid or series of jumps, each element requiring a bounce step only between fences. If there was only one pair of fences, the horse could be immediately rewarded for getting safely over the second element as illustrated below:

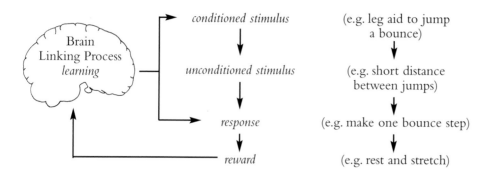

However, to encourage the horse who is just learning to keep going through a small grid, with perhaps two bounce steps required to get safely over three fences in a row, it is necessary to offer a *bridging stimulus* after the first correct *response* which has to go unrewarded and the final rest and stretch reward. The bridging *stimulus* acts like a substitute *reward*, as illustrated below:

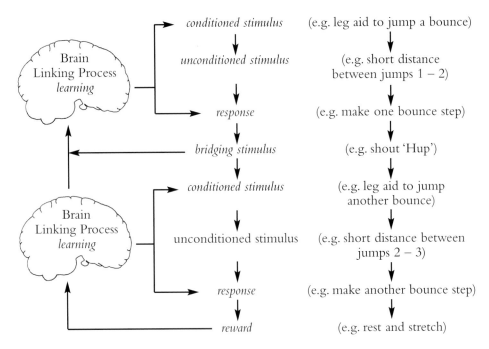

In this way the *bridging stimulus* fills in the gap between any unrewarded but desirable initial *response* and the eventual *reward* for any sequence of movement for example. This allows the brain to recognise the initial part of the sequence as being linked to the *reward*, and build the necessary links for learning to take place.

A *string of conditioned stimuli* is a 'chain' of signals which always happen strictly in the same order and so your horse will learn to react with the correct *response* to the earliest signal in the chain. These are numbered in the order in which they are learned i.e. the original CS or one nearest to the US is denoted CS1, the one learned next is the signal which occurs just before that and is called CS2, with the one learned next being CS3 and so on. It may help you to remember that this system of numbering means that in real time, there is a countdown to the final signal just before the correct response i.e. in real time these signals happen in reverse order i.e. 3, 2, 1.

The series of diagrams below summarise the way in which a chain of conditioned stimuli can teach a horse to react to earlier and earlier elements in any sequence of events which regularly occur in the same order.

Initially when being fed for example, a horse may learn to react with excitement whenever the owner appears carrying a feed bucket, by classical conditioning in the usual way:

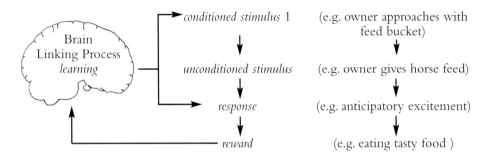

Later, the horse may learn to link the preceding step in the sequence of events leading to delivery of feed, in the same way

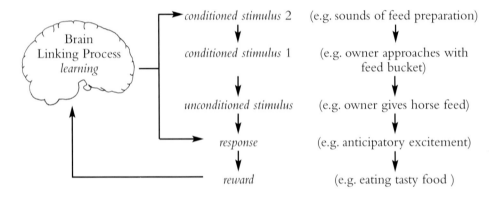

As above, the horse may then learn to react to an even earlier step in the sequence:

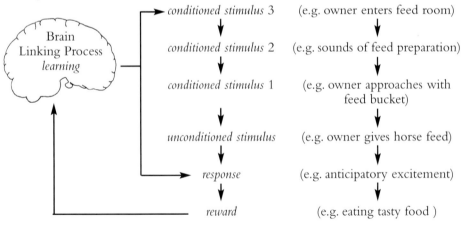

If any sequence of events follow each other strictly enough, a horse will

learn in this way to react to the earliest event in any chain.

Strings of stimuli for most *rewards* are usually quite short, involving four or five stimuli in the 'chain', and are how many useful things such as most ridden aids are learned by horses. *Strings of stimuli* for more important *rewards* can be very long, explaining how horses can learn to anticipate exciting or unusual events in their daily life from your preparations. Some forms of anticipatory behaviour can be useful, but where this causes problems you have a good excuse for building a little flexibility into your daily stable routine.

Irrelevant stimuli lead to *superstitious learning* when they accidentally occur between the desired *conditioned stimulus* and the *unconditioned stimulus*, and the additional unexpected reaction to them is included as part of the horse's correct or desired *response*. *Irrelevant stimuli* interfere with learning and produce additional, odd, 'superstitious' behaviour.

The diagram below summarises the way in which irrelevant stimuli can interfere with training:

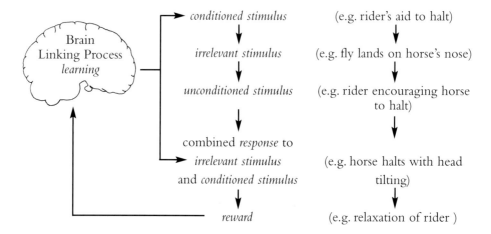

If this *irrelevant stimulus* happened the first time that this horse was being taught these aids to halt, he would learn to halt with his head tilting. The best way to deal with this is to teach this horse a different aid to halt.

Irrelevant stimuli can be very hard to pin point and re-create and many bizarre habits and tricky ridden evasions are learned in this way.

These variations on *conditioning* can all be incorporated into practical re-training programmes and some of the most useful of these are described in Chapter 7 on Practical Re-training Techniques.

Chapter 6

Learning Not to Respond and 'Un-learning'

The process of *conditioning* described in Chapter 4 on the Learning Process and expanded on in Chapter 5 on Learning to Respond is also the basis for the way in which horses learn not to respond, for example to things which may be naturally frightening but actually do no harm and do not hurt your horse. This is often colloquially referred to as 'getting used to things' and the technical term for this is *habituation*. Horses 'habituate' to something when it is of no consequence whatsoever, i.e. it has neither a pleasant nor unpleasant <u>C</u>onsequence from the horse's point of view. Horses learn to ignore such things and do not respond to them in the future.

When the link between a learned response to any signal or stimulus and the associated <u>C</u>onsequence is broken, the learning process is reversed and the horse will no longer respond to the signal or stimulus in that way. This process is called *extinction*, and the learned response is said to have been 'extinguished'.

Essentially, the process of learning 'not to respond' to something is called *habituation* and 'unlearning' a previously learned response is called *extinction*.

HABITUATION

Horses learn a great many useful things by the process of *habituation*. For example, horses which live in a field beside a motorway or an airport very quickly 'get used to' the traffic and low flying aircraft in this way. Initially, the flash and rattle of the heavy vehicles or the sound of the planes acts as an *unconditioned stimulus*. The horses are naturally motivated by instinct to be frightened of these and react accordingly. Initially these *stimuli* are unusual and regarded as 'important', but the more frequently they are repeated without being followed up with any reward or any punishment, the less important they become. In survival terms there is no advantage to the horse in prioritizing the processing of this information and very familiar sights and sound are less likely to be consciously perceived, as described in Chapter 3 on Training and Time. If these sights and sounds are of no <u>Consequence</u> to the horse there is no point in his reacting to them. If he is neither rewarded nor punished for his reactions, he ceases to react and we say he has become accustomed to these stimuli. Technically he has learned by the process of *habituation* to ignore these stimuli. What is happening in his brain is that

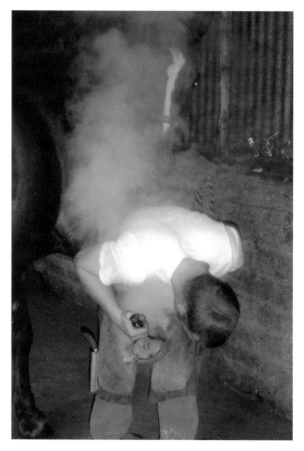

Fig 6.1. Horses can quickly learn to tolerate even the most naturally frightening things such as the smoke from their own hooves burning when these are presented as an inconsequential part of everyday life.

essentially 'no learning' is taking place. There is no *reward* for reacting to such *stimuli* and so no link is built between the *stimulus* and his instinctive *response*. There is no reinforcing process going on and the link is not built. Learning not to respond is really 'not' learning!

This is why it is very worthwhile taking a horse out and about to experience all of the things which are naturally frightening that he needs to learn to get used to, such as travelling and all the sights and sounds and excitement of a show or competition environment, before you need him to stay calm and perform at his best in such situations. Many horse breeders try to get their foals out and about for this reason, as for example mentioned in Chapter 1 on the ABC of Learning in the story of Fiona and the black foal whose training was interrupted by the well meaning Glaswegians! Some people feel that it is best to do this during a foal's first six months, primarily because at this stage they are still very easy to handle, being relatively small and still quite attached to the mare.

An American veterinary surgeon Bob Miller noticed that foals he had had to handle a lot, due to illness or injury when they were very young, were generally easier for him to handle when he was attending to them in a similar fashion when they were much older. These foals had learned by *habituation* that their natural avoidance behaviour when poked and prodded by a vet in this way was of no <u>C</u>onsequence and so, later did not react to this sort of thing in the usual way. Mr Miller developed this idea into a series of handling manoeuvres he recommended people carry out with foals in order to achieve this effect themselves, and used the term 'imprinting' to describe and promote it. However, the word 'imprinting' actually already had a different technical meaning in the science of learning. It describes the process where birds instinctively follow the first moving thing they see at a very precise and critical stage in their early development, usually during the first day after hatching. Many early behaviour scientists created bizarre behaviour in this way, such as imprinting chicks on boxes moved by string, or themselves. True 'imprinting' is a physical developmental process and once done, cannot be undone so you cannot reverse the process. It cannot be altered by subsequent experiences or training. Chickens imprinted on boxes and geese imprinted on a particular person would die if left to their own devices here, as they could not 're-learn' to respond instead to the much more suitable and rewarding *stimulus* of their own mother. Mammals like horses do not have this kind of 'sensitive period' in early life and their brains are much more developed at birth than those of birds. They cannot be 'imprinted' irreversibly in the way that birds are.

Fig 6.2. During his first few months, this foal is being gently introduced to some of the things he will have to tolerate in later life.

The effect Mr Miller had noticed was simply learning by *habituation*. This can be reversed by later life experiences. A foal which learns by *habituation* not to react to balloons for example, can learn to be scared of these again if he has a bad experience in the future. If the foal were hurt say banging his head after being startled by a balloon bursting, he would learn by *classical conditioning* (as described in Chapter 4 on the Learning Process) to be afraid of the sight of the balloon before it burst. Unlike true 'imprinting' which only works during a very short critical period of brain development, Mr Miller's system also works on horses of any age, although it is of course more difficult to shove a bigger horse around in this way and restrain him during his natural avoidance reactions to the various forms of poking and prodding involved!

While in some ways exposing very young foals to all the things they may have to learn to tolerate in later life can be very useful, the process advocated by Mr Miller is very intrusive and could damage foals in unskilled hands. It is also very intense and so each element learned here is less likely to remain in the foal's long term memory due to the physical constraints on this described in Chapter 3 on Training and Time. Interfering with a foal in the first few days of life may also damage the mare/foal bond. Some mares at the bottom end of the 'good mum' scale may subsequently reject the foal, while others towards the top end of this may become overly protective and aggressive to the handler who treats the foal in this kind of way. There is also the danger that, in unskilled hands, the foal may be hurt by these manoeuvres and only learn instead to become frightened of people; quite the reverse of what is intended.

Habituation is often most useful in conjunction with other training techniques. For example, do you remember the story in Chapter 5 about the 'educational dinner party' in New York State, illustrating the importance of making sure that the horse (or behaviour expert!) about to be clicker trained is not put off or frightened by the clicks? The story showed how this form of training can then have the opposite effect of that intended. For those horses which are initially startled by the clicks, this form of training has to be started by *habituating* the horse to the sound of the clicker. The clicker should be repeatedly pressed without there being any <u>C</u>onsequence to the horse, i.e. no reward and no punishment. Once the horse has learned to ignore the clicker by the process of *habituation*, training can proceed to teach him that it is instead associated with a reward as described in Chapter 5 on Learning to Respond.

The story of Blue and the 'P' family in Chapter 1 illustrates the importance of selecting exactly the right element of any naturally frightening stimulus when training by *habituation*. This can be tricky at times. For example:

Early in my career, I had a client whose daughter's pony jumped beautifully over rustic poles and cross-country fences, and did very well in Working Hunter classes. However, Rory would not jump coloured poles under any circumstances and Mrs F was really disappointed that Sarah could not take advantage of Rory's obvious talent in the show-jumping arena. 'Easy peasy' I thought and advised Mrs F to buy some coloured poles and scatter them all over their place anywhere these would not get in the way, including Rory's field, in front of his stable and on the lane on the way to and from his field and so on.

Initially, as expected Rory learned by *habituation* that these poles were of no consequence, and happily walked past and then over them in his everyday life. We progressed to including a coloured pole in a line of rustic poles for Sarah to school over, first leading him and then riding him. So far, so good. We began to include coloured poles with their rustic fences at home, with great success. Eventually we built fences with coloured poles at home and Rory jumped them beautifully.

Sarah was delighted and with great anticipation off they went to a Pony Club rally, keen to show everyone that Rory was 'cured'. Much to our disappointment however, at the rally, Rory still refused to jump over the show-jumps they were using. I was really very surprised, as one red, blue or green and white striped pole looks very much like any other, and although it was theoretically possible that Rory had only got used to his own poles at home, I had expected that *generalization* (as described in Chapter 5 on Learning to Respond) would have helped here. I asked to see the Pony Club fences, and we took Rory along to the place where they held the rally so that I could see for myself what was going on. The jumps had all been cleared away and were neatly stacked in the arena, so we began to set them out. I suggested to Sarah that she warm up in the usual way and try to walk him over some of the poles I was laying out. Much to our surprise, Rory walked over these beautifully and then dodged sideways around a pair of jump stands which had not been put in place beside the poles! Then it dawned on me – he was scared of going between the jump stands, not over the poles!

The stands used for show-jumps were white and those for rustic fences were plain wood, so he did not mind jumping over coloured poles on rustic stands as had been the set up at home, but at Pony Club, the coloured poles were set up on the standard white stands! So, relieved to have solved the mystery, we had to start 'Rory's *habituation* training all over again, this time using jump stands. We started with plain ones set either side of his stable door and field gate and along the lane etc. and Sarah gradually painted these white, doing a little bit after school on dry evenings. This time we had got it right, and Mrs F was very proud when these two eventually made it into the Pony Club show-jumping team.

In particular, *habituation* is how horses learn to tolerate a lot of early handling and all of the things they have to get used to when they are starting their training. Many of these things, including tack and even the rider sitting 'like a lion' on his back are naturally frightening for a horse and a lot of early handling which is gentle and rewarding makes later training much easier. It is best to leave Mum and foal alone to bond for two or three days and then work carefully with the foal little and often when Mum is close by, and perhaps also occupied with eating her own bucket of feed, keeping the foal between yourself and the mare so she does not worry you are taking the foal away or separating them.

Habituation is usually more useful than not and relatively few 'bad habits' are learned this way. The most common problems learned by *habituation* are seen in riding school ponies which learn to ignore the riders' aids if these are repeatedly given ineffectively or in the incorrect way or with inappropriate timing. These ponies are sometimes, rather unfairly I think, described as 'dead to the leg' or 'hard in the mouth'. Should riders lapse back into this kind of 'nagging' leg habit after learning the correct way to use their legs, they may be chided by instructors and humorously accused of polishing their boots! This reminds them that using their legs in this way is of no _Consequence_ to their horse. It can be very difficult to teach someone _not_ to do something. When a rider constantly moves their legs without effect, this movement becomes of no _Consequence_ to both horse and rider. The horse will get used to this movement and learn to ignore it (by the process of _habituation_). The rider will also get used to doing this leg movement and by the same learning process their own brain begins to ignore the signals received from the legs about this movement. The rider is now genuinely unaware of what their legs are doing, and actually believes they are still! There is no point in an instuctor saying 'stop moving your legs' and this approach can be very frustrating all around! I find video-tape very useful 'evidence' here and it is much more effective for an instructor to give the rider a different positive signal (such as the feel of their seat bones rolling back for example) to concentrate on which helps to tell them when their legs are moving.

I recall one client who was terribly upset that her new neighbour at a large livery yard constantly yelled at her own horse. The horse didn't seem to mind, and just stood there quietly munching hay while this rather large and untidy lady fussed and clattered and worked around him. Eventually however, Mrs D couldn't stand this any more and felt she had to say something.

Much to her surprise, when Mrs D complained to the new neighbour about the noise, the neighbour was unabashed 'Oh don't worry' she said 'Minton [the neighbour's horse] is thick as two short planks – it's the only way to get through to him!' Of course Minton was really very smart and had long since learned by _habituation_ that all the yelling was of no _Consequence_ and so ignored it! The unfortunate Mrs D also had to try to do the same. Relations were somewhat strained for a while! However, I had tried to cheer Mrs D up a little when we first talked about this by the thought that, in any emergency if she had to get Minton's attention, she should just speak very quietly to him. I explained that this would be so unusual for this horse that he would be much more likely to take notice of anyone speaking to him in this way.

One day, Minton was startled by a small bird flying into the stable corridor where he was tied up for grooming. He leapt back, broke the string and accidentally landed with his front foot right on top of our noisy neighbour's foot. Minton was standing transfixed with his head up, breathing heavily and staring at the place to which the bird had flown. The poor neighbour was screaming all sorts of things at him. Of course, Minton ignored her. He was used to this and her yelling was generally of no <u>C</u>onsequence to him. His owner had inadvertently trained him by *habituation* to ignore this sort of thing. Being a kind soul, rather than standing back and enjoying her revenge, Mrs D went carefully up to Minton and whispered 'move over darling!' Of course, this was so unusual to him that it got his attention immediately, and as he turned his head to look at Mrs D, he naturally took some weight off the foreleg and Mrs D was able to push his shoulder enough to encourage him to lift the leg, releasing her noisy neighbour! The neighbour was most impressed. Once she had recovered and caught her breath, she asked Mrs D how she had done it. Mrs D explained the principles of learning theory and how horses learn by *habituation* as I had explained them to her. I am delighted to report that his was the start of these two becoming friends and a much more peaceful stable yard ensued.

Sometimes horse are so frightened of something that it is difficult to expose them to it safely and learning by *habituation* is limited by the increasing levels of fear related hormones and associated changes in neurotransmitters in the brain of a frightened horse as described in Chapter 3 on Training and Time. Take the American method of getting a horse used to tack etc. known as 'sacking out'. Here the horse is exposed to a constant and extreme form of all the movements around him which people want him to tolerate. This form of training is referred to as *flooding* or *saturation therapy*. It is quite extreme and carries a high risk of injury all round. Imagine the reaction of a horse scared of clippers should these be switched on and left running beside him in his box all the time! He would eventually become exhausted and less able to react. At this point some *habituation* could take place and this horse will stop reacting to the clippers or the sacking out. This is a rather drastic approach, and while it is the quickest way to begin to see some results, the risk of injury is high and any learning achieved in this way less likely to be retained in long term memory.

When trying to 'habituate' a horse to particularly frightening *stimuli*, it is better to break the *stimulus* down into short little bursts or reduce its extremity where possible, e.g. using a tape of the clippers, initially played very quietly for just a second or so over and over again. This can be increased in 'baby steps' by playing the tape for a little longer after a few sessions, then increasing the volume and so on, allowing the horse to 'habituate' to each part of whatever frightens him in stages, gradually building up to the full original stimulus. Training using the learning process of *habituation* in this way is called *systematic desensitization* and is described in more detail in Chapter 7 on Practical Re-training Techniques.

This is why the traditional European way of starting a horse's training with early handling, lungeing and ground work to strengthen his back muscles and gradually gently building up to teaching him to tolerate a rider on his back works so well. A horse worked in this way is less likely to be injured and will remember his 'lessons' for much longer than one 'broken' by the traditional American 'cowboy' method of a single exhausting 'bucking bronco' session or being chased around a pen for half an hour first until he is too tired to buck.

Where I come from in Northern Ireland, it is common to see children working quietly with ponies and young horses starting their training with great skill, instinctively using *habituation* as this makes everything easy all round. These children are usually much smaller than their horses and do not have enclosures or ropes and this cultural knowledge is built on thousands of years of tradition and experience. The first American cowboys did not have this background knowledge and experience to rely on and were relatively much bigger than the little horses frequenting the 'wild west'. They used their weight and ropes to subdue their horses and bully them into submission, at great risk all round. The macho kudos of being able to 'sit a buck' led to the exciting sport of rodeo riding. The modern rodeo horse is actually trained to buck by *operant conditioning* using a bucking strap to irritate the horse into bucking. If this was not done, these horses would quickly learn by *habituation* to tolerate a rider and be of no more use to the event. The riders also have to kick the horse on the shoulder to encourage bucking or lose points and risk disqualification. I spent some time in Canada working on behalf of the RSPCA investigating the welfare of horses on farms there and discovered, when chatting to the youths who worked with these horses, that these lads enjoyed the thrill of breaking a horse in a 'bucking bronco' session and that they were not at all interested in easier and less risky ways of doing this! As one particularly charming fellow put it, with his big blue eyes twinkling away as he leant back proudly against his truck, after showing off his numerous scars and lumps and bumps from various breakages – 'I like a good buck!'

Learning by *habituation,* however, is generally a widespread and useful tool for horse trainers whose horses and personal health are precious to them!

EXTINCTION

Extinction is the scientific name for the process of 'un-learning', where a previously learned response is 'extinguished'.

Extinction occurs when the reward or punishment is removed from the end of the ABC learning 'chain' of *stimulus – response – reward*. To use an analogy here, you might take a job because it has a good salary, and continue working away happily for the monthly pay cheque. If for some reason you stopped getting paid, you would eventually stop going in to work.

The *rewards* or *punishments* that are involved in any learning process are called 'reinforcers' because they are necessary to maintain the link that the brain builds between any *stimulus* and a *response*. They need to happen now and again to keep this link working and without them it 'falls into disrepair' and is eventually broken.

This is how many handling problems can develop. For example, most people initially give their horse a treat as soon as they get the headcollar on when training him to be caught in the field. Then, once he has learned this, they stop giving him the treat. However, they are often disappointed to find that one day he does not come up to them to be caught. If they cease giving the *reward*, the horse will eventually cease giving them the correct response. They have 'extinguished' the previously learned response to come to be caught.

Extinction is the major reason for any 'relapse' in 'bad behaviour' of horses once they come back home after being sent away for retraining for example. This is also why many horses gradually revert to their old habits after an intensive 'alternative' training course. Any useful learning that has happened while a horse is 'on a course' or away for re-training and the associated improvements in behaviour will eventually be extinguished if this learning is not regularly maintained at home afterwards by continued training.

This is why it really is worthwhile 'revising' exercises used in re-training for example on a weekly or at least monthly basis after the problem has been resolved. You need to keep rewarding learned behaviour every so often in order to maintain the physical links within the brain and the learning that has taken place. Luckily because of the beneficial effects of a *variable ratio reward* system (as described in Chapter 3 on Rewards, Punishment and Motivation), rewarding your horse now and again is also the most efficient way of teaching your horse to do what you want and making sure this gets into in his long term memory.

Extinction is how a less skilful rider can spoil the way in which a horse has learned to perform. For example, a horse might have been brought on to move really well, have had some competitive success and be sold to someone who hopes to achieve the same. If they are unable to ride sufficiently well as to still *reward* the horse in the same way when he moves as required, this horse will gradually move less well. He will become less obedient to the aids if all the tiny alterations in balance and softness in the rein he had previously learned were his *reward* for doing this no longer happen. The desired responses are said to be 'extinguished'. In the same way, riding school horses often cause problems for their new owners should they be sold to a private home. In a riding school, the riders are constantly helped by the instructors to ride as well as they can, and for the most part this brings out the best in the horse. In good riding schools, horses will also be schooled regularly by an instructor to maintain a certain level of obedience and performance. Once this horse is only ridden by a novice rider without supervision, he may lapse and the process of *extinction* results in a decline in his obedience and performance. There are also some other reasons why horses moving from a riding school situation may develop problems, including the fact that they usually get a lot less work in their new home. Changes in their equine companions can trigger or exacerbate social dominance related problems. Some horses thrive on individual attention and small social groups but many become bossier in this kind of situation and this can lead to handling problems and so on. This highlights again the usefulness of regular lessons, and if your horse's behaviour declines markedly after you buy him, it is often well worth having some lessons, for example, taking him back to the riding school he came from now and again for a private lesson, employing a freelance instructor who can come and teach you on him at your place or finding a more experienced rider to help you exercise and school him, just so that any previously learned 'good behaviour' is not lost by *extinction*.

While in some ways like this the process of *extinction* can be a nuisance, it can also be used to help with re-training. The undesirable response in any learned behaviour problem can be 'extinguished' in the same way. Firstly, the *reward* must be identified and remember what matters here is the horse's point of view. Then, the *reward* should be removed from the 'chain' of *stimulus – response – reward* and the *stimulus – response* section only repeated until the horse stops responding to the *stimulus* in that way.

For example, the common problem of pulling back and breaking free can be resolved by extinction. This problem develops usually by the process of operant conditioning, where something acting as an *unconditioned stimulus* genuinely spooks the horse; he pulls back, this is the *response* and he breaks free which is the *reward*. The *reward* element here can be removed by simply passing a long rope or lunge line through the tie-up ring. Attached to a piece of bailer twine between the clip and the headcollar as a safety break and hold at the other end. When the horse tries to pull back, the handler releases the line gradually so that there is no tension on it. The horse cannot have a tug of war with nothing to pull against and so cannot beak free, so no more *reward*! The handler should wear their riding hat, footwear with a good grip and ideally with steel toecaps, and stout gloves. The horse should also be protected with boots or stable bandages and knee and hock boots or his usual travelling gear.

Initially the horse may try harder to pull back, i.e. when things do not go according to plan, his natural instincts will encourage him to try harder, and he may even run backwards, throw his head up and in some extreme cases rear. A helper should be on stand by, also wearing protective gear, just in case, to be ready to encourage the horse forward at this point. This procedure should only be carried out in a large hazard-free enclosed area with sound footing and preferably also a soft surface to minimize the risks of injury all round. Most horses stand looking very surprised when this little party piece no longer results in their getting free. It does require a certain amount of skill to handle the long line in this way, and you should practise first of all on a helper before trying to re-train your horse this way. It is also now possible to buy a 'bungee' leadrope which expands when the horse pulls back, and providing this is attached to a safety break and is designed to expand quickly and far enough, this can be helpful if you need to tie your horse up in between training sessions before training is complete. Otherwise you will need to have someone hold the horse for you here until training is complete. This requires a secondary programme of *counter-conditioning* (see Chapter 7 on Practical Re-training Techniques).

Extinction is the basis for the TEAM TOUCH system of horse handling as promoted by Linda Tellington-Jones. As with all 'new' and 'alternative' systems this is not a panacea or remedy for all behavioural problems, but it can help with those where the horse is scared of being touched or has learned that a certain piece of tack or procedure involving touching certain areas hurts. The 'rubbing' all over habituates the horse to touch and he learns by *extinction* that this is no longer associated with pain. It has no <u>C</u>onsequence, and he stops flinching or trying to avoid being touched. Similarly the repeated movements used to manoeuvre the horse here get him used to doing this kind of step or turn without any subsequent good or bad <u>C</u>onsequences and so he stops trying to avoid these naturally difficult movements. This can be helpful for horses which have experienced discomfort from a poorly fitting saddle as a <u>C</u>onsequence of such movements. These manoeuvres also work as mini 'warm up' stretches, although the touching pressure used is too light to have any massage effect on the muscles. Linda Tellington-Jones also promotes some pressure-point massage techniques which may help ease some muscle spasms. I have a very busy American colleague who does not have the time to write up detailed *habituation* re-training programmes and simply tells clients whose horse will benefit from this to buy a Linda Tellington-Jones video!

As another example of the use of *extinction* to deal undesirable behaviour:

I was once investigating the problem of 'hay-dipping' in a couple of retired racehorses who repeatedly dipped mouthfuls of hay in their water before eating it. This dunking very much annoyed the groom who looked after these horses, as it caused a lot of mess and the hay clogged up their automatic drinkers leading to spills. Mr M had tried to stop them doing this by hanging their hay-nets as far away as possible from the water supply, but this only made things worse as the horses moved back and forward between the two creating even more mess. He had wondered if they were making 'hay soup' (or even 'hay beer!') and liked the sweet (or slightly fermenting) taste of the water after it had had hay soaking in it. Mr M even went to the trouble of putting their left-over hay in a bucket of water through the day and then 'straining it' to provide a bucketful of 'hay soup' which he gave them in the evening with their hay-nets. Much to his chagrin Valour and Sally continued to dip mouthfuls of hay in their automatic drinkers and did not drink the 'soup'. He was concerned that this behaviour might therefore have been a stable vice or stereotypy, indicative of stress in genetically sensitive horses, and as I was studying this sort of behaviour problem at the time, asked me to look into this possibility.

I observed them very carefully over the next few weeks, counted the number of dips per hour and examined the pattern of the dipping in great detail using twenty-four hour infra-red video recording. Mr M was very impressed with this 'high-tech' approach, but most disappointed when I had to report that the 'hay dipping' behaviour did not fit the pattern of a stereotypy. I did notice however that large mouthfuls were 'dipped' for longer than small mouthfuls, and there was one other possibility that Mr M had overlooked when trying to find out why these horses dipped their hay in this way. I wondered whether or not they just wanted to dampen the hay before eating it, rather in the same way I ate my cornflakes (wasting good milk as my mother used to scold!). We tested this by soaking their hay nets for half an hour before tying them up in their boxes. Much to Mr M's delight, they began to gradually stop dipping and after two weeks, neither dipped at all. He was surprised that Valour, who originally dipped his hay more frequently than Sally, stopped dipping sooner. I explained that the process of *extinction* is really *conditioning* in reverse, and that Valour would have had more chances to work out that dipping the hay himself no longer had any benefit, as he dipped his hay more frequently, so he would have discovered this more quickly than Sally. We had 'extinguished' their hay dipping response by removing the reward, as there was no extra benefit in dipping the already pre-soaked hay.

This hay dipping example shows that 'un-learning' by *extinction* follows the same rules and time scales outlined for the basic learning process described in Chapter 3 on Training and Time. Valour's hay dipping behaviour was extinguished sooner than Sally's as Valour's higher frequency of dipping gave him more 'trials' in any period of time.

People are often surprised by this and while they are usually pleased that the 'worst' horse 'gets better' quicker, they can lose patience with the horse whose problem did not occur very often at first, but still drags on taking a lot longer to 'fix'. Keeping a training diary here helps (see Chapter 8 on Maximizing your Horse's Learning Potential). Remembering that just as learning rate depends on the number of 'trials' so does the rate of 'un-learning', should help you persevere when re-training horses whose learned misbehaviour occurs less often. This is why sporadic misdemeanours take a lot longer to deal with than those that happen frequently and horses with particularly 'challenging' behaviour improve much more quickly than those which are just 'a little bit naughty'.

A particularly skilful rider can use *extinction* to re-train a horse that has learned to spook to avoid work (e.g. by *operant conditioning* as described in Chapter 4 on the Learning Process). Here the rider has to sit still and try not to become unbalanced or alter the contact during a 'pretend' spook. He can devise a pattern of ridden exercises so that the horse is encouraged to spook just at the point where the workload increases. This helps the rider as he is better able to predict when a spook may happen. It is important that the rider does not lose his patience also and be tempted to *punish* the horse here by kicking or pulling etc., and he must also continue to ask for the movement he wanted when the spook occurred. The aim here is to make the spooking behaviour a *response* of no <u>C</u>onsequence, neither rewarding the horse by being put off riding as usual nor punishing him, even by inadvertent changes in contact or becoming unseated. Removing any *reward* (or *punishment*) in this way 'extinguishes' the spooking response to imminent effort. If the rider is not quite up to this and finds the spooking frightening or too irritating to ignore, there are also other re-training techniques which work well here and which any rider can use (see *counter-conditioning* as described in Chapter 7 on Practical Re-training Techniques).

SUMMARY

While initially 'learning not to respond' and 'un-learning' may seem similar, *habituation* and *extinction* are different forms of interruption in the *stimulus-response-reward/punishment* 'chain' of learning.

  Habituation is the technical term for 'getting used to' things, such as no longer reacting with fear or avoidance responses to *stimuli* which are naturally frightening, or 'learning to ignore' ineffective ridden aids. It describes the process where horses discover that any natural or instinctive response has no <u>C</u>onsequence, it is neither rewarded nor punished and so does not become linked by learning to the preceding *stimulus*.

  The process of habituation is illustrated in the diagram below;

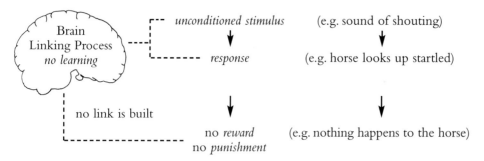

Extinction describes the process of 'un-learning' where the *reward* (or punishment) ceases and is no longer given after the desired response. Over a period of time, the response ceases also i.e. it no longer occurs after the *stimulus* is given, as there is no longer any reward (or punishment) to reinforce the link between the *stimulus* and the *response* which the brain previously developed or 'learned'. It is as though repeated unrewarded effort chips away at the link or learned reaction which was built by the rewarded effort until the link is broken.

The process of *extinction* is illustrated in the diagram below, using the example of a horse which had learned to become excited when his owner approached with a bucket of feed. If the owner repeatedly approached this horse with an empty feed bucket, he would soon 'unlearn' the excited response and begin to ignore this.

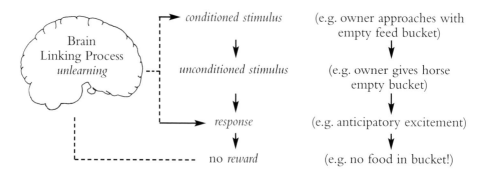

Both *habituation* and *extinction* can be used, along with all of the other variations on the *conditioning* process by which horses learn already described in Chapters 4 and 5, to help unravel the cause of any learned behaviour problems and when training as in Chapter 7 on Practical Re-training Techniques.

Chapter 7

Practical Re-training Techniques

All of the forms of learning and variations of the basic *conditioning* process described in previous chapters may be used when re-training horses and can be helpful when dealing with behaviour problems. There are probably as many variations on these themes used when training horses as there are trainers and problems. However, there are three classic adaptations of the learning process which are particularly useful when re-training 'difficult' horses or horses with 'challenging' behaviour. These are:

- Shaping
- Counter-conditioning
- Systematic desensitisation

SHAPING

Sometimes it is difficult to get a horse to do the whole sequence of movements required when training or to tolerate something difficult or frightening for long periods of time all at once. Simple *conditioning* becomes tricky in practice because you may need a lot of repeated or different *unconditioned stimuli* to create the complete desired response or end goal. This is where the training technique of *shaping* can be very useful.

Shaping is a variation of *operant conditioning* (as described in Chapter 4 on the Learning Process). When *shaping,* the horse is initially rewarded for responses which may not be the desired end result but which are a 'step in the right direction'. In this way *shaping* is very useful when trying to teach a horse something complicated, such as lateral work or '*haute ecole*' or 'airs above the ground'. *Shaping* is also invaluable when you need to work towards the desired result 'one step at a time', as for example when teaching a genuinely nervous horse to load.

Essentially, when *shaping* a response you *reward* the horse for his first step in the right direction. You then only *reward* him for the next step in the right direction and it is very important that he is subsequently only rewarded for a response which is closer to your goal than the previous response. In this way the rewarded response gets gradually closer and closer to the desired end result.

A common situation where *shaping* can be used to great effect is when loading a nervous horse (as mentioned in Chapter 3). Here you do literally give a treat for each step in the right direction! For example, the horse may start 20 feet away from the trailer and be trying to birl round and nip off in the opposite direction. Initially you need to calm him and encourage him to stand and look at the trailer. This is the first 'improvement' or part or the desired response and a *reward* can be given. The horse should then be asked and encouraged to move on a step closer to the trailer. This is an *unconditioned stimulus*. When he takes another step (R2), another *reward* should be given. This process can be repeated, until he is placing a foot on the ramp for his *reward*, then both front feet and so on until he is finally only rewarded for staying in the trailer while the ramp is done up. If at any point progress is interrupted and the horse goes backwards, ending up farther away from the trailer than where he was previously rewarded, he should not be given another *reward* until he gets, not only back to where he was before, but just a little closer than that again. It is often very tempting for people to start again should they overdo the encouragement and accidentally send the horse shooting backwards instead. They want to *reward* the horse for standing still again, even though he is actually now farther away from the goal. Should they do this, the horse will gradually end up farther and farther away from the trailer and in effect he will be training the people by *shaping* to give him treats farther and farther away from it!

Note when working with horses around trailers you should always wear

Fig 7.1. *Opposite*: This horse is being trained to approach the tractor trailer she is very wary of by the process of *shaping,* being rewarded (with apples!) for each stage in the process of coming closer to it.

your riding hat, gloves and footwear with a good grip and ideally also with safety toe caps. It is vital that no-one is allowed to go behind the horse at any time – take the long way round the front of the vehicle to get from side to side if necessary. This is especially important when working with the ramp – stand to the side when putting this up and down, or when fastening and unfastening catches. A horse panicking, kicking or backing out for any reason will easily bring the ramp down on top of anyone close to it and the associated injuries are usually very serious and can be fatal.

The reward system used in *shaping* is an incremental *fixed ratio* system (as described in Chapter 2 on Rewards, Punishment and Motivation). First of all, one step gets the horse one *reward*, a *fixed ratio* of 1. This is usually denoted FR1 in scientific shorthand. Then, as measured from the original starting point, two steps are required for a *reward*. Two steps for one *reward* is usually denoted FR2 in scientific shorthand. Three steps for one *reward* would be denoted FR3 and so on.

For the sorts of problems where *shaping* is useful, it is usually not possible to achieve the desired goal in one session. Some pernickety people do manage to count steps and note the FR score they achieve each time. This is often a bit tricky to do in real life for ordinary mortals, although you do need to remember how far you got at the end of each session. I have seen clients using a piece of chalk to mark where the ramp was and where their horse got to for his last *reward* in a *shaping* to load session, and it does help here if you make a rough note to yourself of where you got up to in a training diary (see more about this in Chapter 8 on Maximizing your Horse's Learning Potential).

In Chapter 4 I used as an example of the use of *operant conditioning* to train a horse to be caught 'by curiosity'. Here, Miss M sat down in the field to attract her horse's attention. This was the first part of an *unconditioned stimulus*. She scattered treats initially as far away from herself as she could throw them, completing the *unconditional stimulus*. Ben was initially rewarded for coming close enough to eat these. Natural instincts helped us here as he ate those he came to first and then came closer for the rest. She then threw the treats less vigorously, and Ben had to come closer to get these. She sat on a strategically placed log in the same spot each session and marked the closest point reached at the end of each session with little twigs stuck into the ground. Once Ben came close enough to Miss M, she was able to use a different *unconditioned stimulus* to encourage him to put his nose into the headcollar for the treat and so on until he tolerated her putting the headcollar on completely to get his treat. Ben was kept in a separate piece of the main grazing paddock at his yard during this time to help with this training. Obviously, this approach is only suitable for a horse left on its own in a paddock, as other horses will be interested too and the source of the treats mugged for more or accidentally injured in the inevitable scrum!

Shaping can also be used to extend the length of time for which a horse will behave as desired, such as standing still, holding a leg up for shoeing, or staying quietly in a trailer and so on. Here you initially reward him for doing what you want for one second, then for two seconds, then four, five, ten, twenty seconds etc. gradually building up to the required length of time that you would like him to be able to manage this for. As time goes on you can make the intervals between increments longer, speeding up the process. Simply remember or make a note of the time you got up to at the end of each training session and start at this point next time.

Shaping is also how many top competition horses are traditionally taught complex dressage movements. Their riders and trainers may not know the technical term for the way in which they work with the horse here, but usually manage this very skilfully. For example, a horse will be taught each element of the movement sequentially, first bending their head and neck in a certain way for a rest, then being required to do this and step under with a hind leg in a certain way before given a rest or slight reduction in leg or rein pressure, then doing both of these movements and stretching the shoulder as required and so on, doing first only part and then only one step of the complete movement, before being asked to do more and more steps in the sequence before the rewarding rest, change in seat or reduction in rein or leg pressure is given.

The effective use of *shaping* requires patience and some degree of attention to detail, in particular to make sure that *rewards* are only given for responses which are closer to the goal than the previous response. However, with a little forward planning it is a most useful technique and can be applied to almost any behaviour where the desired end point can be reached in sequential parts.

COUNTER-CONDITIONING

Counter-conditioning is one of the most widely used re-training techniques. It uses the process of *classical conditioning* to teach horses a positive response to something they would naturally be frightened of and trains them to react with a different response to any given signal or *conditioned stimulus* they have previously been conditioned to avoid.

> A friend of mine once kept her very traffic shy horse beside a sawmill yard, and was most relieved but a little embarrassed one day when, instead of the expected fidget or 'explosion' as a huge timber truck appeared from the opposite direction on the road she was riding along, her horse tried to spin around and follow it! The driver had kindly slowed down to pass her, and, as she discovered upon further enquiry, her horse had become used to getting a sandwich from the drivers coming into the sawmill yard past his field. His previously acquired fear response to the approach of the truck had been changed by the process of *counter-conditioning* to 'here comes my treat'!

In this example, the truck appearing is the original *conditioned stimulus*, this horse's past bad experiences of traffic the *unconditioned stimulus* and his originally learned *response* is to shy, with his *reward* being the avoidance of expected pain. After living at the sawmill for a while however, logging trucks appearing are followed by the different *unconditioned stimulus* of a nice chap in overalls proffering a sandwich, and the new *counter-conditioned response* of approaching the truck has the different *reward* of a tasty sandwich instead.

Counter-conditioning is a particularly useful technique for re-training horses where an *undesirable response* has been learned as a reaction to a particular *stimulus* (the original *conditioned stimulus*). When *counter-conditioning*, this *stimulus* is used in association with a different *unconditioned stimulus* to elicit a different desirable *response* resulting in a different *reward*. The original *conditioned stimulus* becomes the signal for this different *desirable response* instead.

For example, if a horse had learned to try to avoid the clippers, perhaps because he had been burned by them in the past, the noise of the motor could be the *conditioned stimulus* for this undesirable avoidance behaviour. The learning process by which this problem developed can be described as: sound of clipper motor (*conditioned stimulus*) – burning sensation (*unconditioned stimulus*) – fear and avoidance reaction (*response*) – burning stops (*reward*). The horse's brain has linked the signal or *conditioned stimulus* to the *response* which resulted in a *reward* and he will react to the sound of the clippers by trying to avoid contact with these in future. This is simple *classical conditioning* as described in Chapter 4 on the Learning Process.

If the noise of the clippers is then used as a signal for something nice happening to this horse instead, such as feed arriving, for example he will learn by the same process of *classical conditioning* to react differently when he hears the clipper noise. The learning process here can be described as: sound of clipper motor (*conditioned stimulus*) – sight of food arriving (*unconditioned stimulus*) – pleasure and approach (*response*) – eating tasty food (*reward*). The horse's brain has now linked the original signal or *conditioned stimulus* to a different *response*, which resulted in a different *reward*. In future, this horse will now react to the sound of the clippers by approaching the stable door looking for food instead. This way of training horses to react differently to stimuli which used to elicit undesirable responses is the basis of *counter-conditioning*.

It is vital in order for *counter-conditioning* to work to be able to correctly identify the specific nature of the *conditioned stimulus* involved. This is sometimes called the *key stimulus*. For horses scared of clipping as in the above example, the *key stimulus* may not be the noise of the clippers, but could instead be the vibration they make, the tickling sensation he feels when they first touch him, or maybe a tug on the hair or a subtle change in the sound of the motor as it labours or the blades heat up.

Once the *key stimulus* has been identified, *counter-conditioning* is really very easy to carry out and this makes it a particularly useful tool when dealing with behaviour problems, as illustrated by the frequency with which this technique is mentioned (fouteen times!) in previous chapters.

> For example, in the story of Blue, the little Highland pony who was scared of the news-stand, in Chapter 1, we eventually discovered that the 'key' *conditioned stimulus* he had learned to react to was the new and different headlines which appeared every day. So, Miss P had to re-create these when re-training him, which she did very well cutting out words from all sorts of headlines in old papers and photocopying her own 'new' ones each day. She amused herself by making good copy out of inventive and interesting slants on P family life. She would tie Blue up around the corner and while he was out of sight attach her new headline. Then she would bring him back to his box past the stand and give him a treat after he went past it. Blue learned by *classical conditioning* in the usual way (as described in Chapter 4) that a new headline on the borrowed stand outside his stable signalled the imminent treat. Miss P left the headline up and took him past many other times without giving him any treats. In this way, he learned by *habituation* to ignore the stand with a previously seen headline on it. He also learned by the process of *counter-conditioning* that a new and different headline now meant

he was due a treat. So, instead of shying at these in the future when passing the shop, he would peer at them rather hopefully. Miss P told any interested onlookers as she rode proudly by that he was keen to keep up with current affairs!

In the case of Shadow's story in Chapter 4, I had to go through a similar procedure using all of the various elements he shied at in different combinations to get the correct *key stimulus* for the violent shying he developed after a bad fall in a particular gateway containing these, and persevere despite the giggles of the stables staff at the 'great doctor' arranging dandelions in the mud!

In another story used in Chapter 4 on the Learning Process, for example, Harry, who was kept in the most beautiful surroundings, had learned by simple *classical conditioning* to break free and run away when his well groomed owner Mrs T picked up the hoof pick. Her picking this up was the original *conditioned stimulus*, the subsequent inadvertent digging of nails into his heels the *unconditioned stimulus*, his *response* avoidance behaviour and his *reward* avoiding the pain. This undesirable reaction would have eventually been extinguished had Mrs T just worn gloves and picked the feet up as I had shown her to do. However, Harry would have initially continued to escape and this was an unacceptable risk in her situation, as her husband was very keen on his immaculate lawns. Instead a *counter-conditioning* re-training programme was required where Mrs T picked up the hoof-pick before feeding Harry treats in his stable, then she repeated this outside with a helper holding him, then again when he was tied up, with the stable yard temporarily barricaded off from the rest of the garden just in case! She also practised the new way of picking up his feet with her helper holding him to teach Harry that this no longer hurt (using the technique of *habituation* described in Chapter 6 on Learning Not to Respond and Un-learning). For the *counter-conditioning* part of his re-training, Mrs T picked up the hoof pick (original *conditioned stimulus*), then rustled the treat packet in her pocket while approaching him (new *unconditioned stimulus*), and as he waited here (new *counter-conditioned response*) he got his treat (*reward*). So, Harry learned to look forward to Mrs T approaching him with a hoof pick (in a gloved hand!) instead of running away.

In this way, *counter-conditioning* is a very valuable re-training technique. It is useful in all sorts of situations as mentioned in earlier chapters, including teaching horses that the smells of the vet or farrier which were previously associated with discomfort are instead associated with food (as described in the examples used in Chapter 2 on Rewards, Punishment and Motivation) and so on.

Counter-conditioning can also be used to turn genuinely 'naughty' evasions into work for example, removing any *reward* and instead setting things up so that the evasion results in more, not less work for the horse. For example, if a horse 'pretending' to spook is turned in a small circle immediately whenever he does this, he will learn by *counter-conditioning* that this is not really worth his while any more! Instead of a rest immediately after a spook he has to work harder, to turn the small circle. He is rewarded however for continuing with the on-going work instead whenever he gets the urge to spook, as this is less strenuous than the little circle. Here, the urge to spook becomes followed by continued work on the ongoing exercise instead. When in an arena or schooling, the turn should always be made to the inside, keeping the bend that was required at the point the horse decided to spook. The advantage of this is that it also helps to rebalance the horse and the rider is less likely to become unseated or fall as she knows which way the horse will be birling! The turn should be made using a strong inside leg aid, and 'body turn' i.e. the rider turning their hips and shoulders in the direction they want to go, keeping their back straight, while taking care to keep a firm contact in the outside rein and not tilting their hands or upper body.

The same effect can be achieved using *counter-conditioning* in this way on the ground with confident and naughty horses that evade by running backwards for example when not wanting to load. These horses should be encouraged to turn their hindquarters away from the handler as quietly and gently as possible (as for example described in Chapter 2 in the case of Miss N and her bossy mare). It is important to use the correct turning procedure here in order to avoid accidents and excessive stress or strain. As soon as the horse tires or wants to stop, only one more turn should be made before asking again for the originally requested manoeuvre. This is the basis for the success of the 'birling' method of loading 'tricky' horses which some people use. This does not work, as they often try to explain, by 'disorientation' – the horse knows fine well where the trailer is even if he is a little dizzy! It works by *counter-conditioning* and is only appropriate for genuinely naughty horses. To do this with a frightened horse is dangerous and will only exacerbate fear-related handling problems in a genuinely nervous horse.

Counter conditioning is however most frequently used in conjunction with other forms of learning to complete a re-training programme. In Chapter 6 on Learning Not to Respond and Un-learning, I described the initial use of *extinction* when re-training a horse which has learned to pull back when tied up for reasons other than the obvious one Harry had in the example above. To complete the re-training process by *counter-conditioning* in this situation, the handler needs a helper to stand near the tie-up ring ready to offer treats. The tug on the line is the original *conditioned stimulus* for the pulling back (original *conditioned response*) to get free (original *reward)*. Once the horse stops running backwards as the hander plays out the long line, the handler should slightly tighten the line she is holding. This recreates the original *conditioned stimulus*. The helper should then provide the *unconditioned stimulus* of proffering treats and they can both encourage the horse to walk on back up to the ring (new *counter-conditioned response*) for a treat (new *reward*). This stage of the re-training may require the additional use of *shaping,* as described earlier in this chapter, should the horse initially be reluctant to walk all the way back to the tie-up ring. The handler can walk towards him at first, to proffer the treat, giving it after the horse takes his first one step in the right direction. The horse should only get another treat each time for more steps in the right direction, until he goes all the way back to the tie-up ring to get his treat. If the horse is very difficult to move forward, *classical conditioning* can also be employed in addition to teach him to walk on when asked e.g. when riding, by saying 'walk on' or some such phrase just before giving the usual leg aids, as described in Chapter 4 on the Learning Process. This can then be used to help to encourage him forward for his treat when *shaping* his *counter-conditioned* response.

This shows how *counter-conditioning* works together with all of the variations on the theme of *conditioning,* or the basic learning process explained in earlier chapters, to build an effective re-training programme.

SYSTEMATIC DESENSITIZATION

As described above, food is one of the handiest alternative rewards to offer when training by *counter-conditioning*. However, sometimes a horse is so frightened, for example of the clippers or loading, that he is too anxious to eat, rendering the usual sorts of *counter-conditioning* impractical in the first instance. He may also be so scared or have such an extreme reaction to something that it is dangerous to expose him deliberately to it, and of course, as described in Chapter 3 on Training and Time, fear inhibits the learning process and long term memory storage in particular. For very nervous horses you need to first of all use an adaptation of learning by *habituation,* known as *systematic desensitization* to reduce fear and extreme responses to the point where you can safely begin to use *counter-conditioning* or some other training technique to complete the training process.

In *systematic desensitization* the horse is exposed to only part of the frightening original *conditioned stimulus* at first, building up gradually in 'baby steps' to expose him to the complete stimulus. For example, with horses showing extreme avoidance responses to the sound of clippers, instead of using real clippers whirring away in the usual fashion, you can use a tape recording of these in your training. This can be played to the horse in short bursts at very low volume and used as the initial *conditioned stimulus* in a *counter-conditioning* or *habituation* re-training programme. Once the horse has learned to tolerate this, the tape volume and duration of play can be gradually increased in stages until it approaches the real thing. It is best to use a tape of your own clippers for this as other machines may sound a bit different to your horse.

It is important when training by *systematic desensitization* to consolidate each stage by using the same level of *stimulus* for two or three training sessions and ideally to leave a few days between the last session at any stage and the first session at a new stage. This facilitates long term memory storage and employs the process of over-learning (as described in Chapter 3 on Training and Time). Consolidating your training in this way makes your horse more likely to produce the desired response at stressful times in the future, and this is particularly useful when training by *systematic desensitization*, as this form of training is usually carried out to teach horses to tolerate something frightening or previously associated with pain.

The most common mistake people make when trying this technique for the first time is to push too hard too soon. By 'baby steps' I really do mean absolutely tiny increments. With the clipper example, this would involve increasing the time the tape was played by a couple of seconds of play at volume level one every few sessions until a few minutes were tolerated and then repeating the whole process step by step at volume level two and so on. You can make the increments bigger as you progress though the training process here. This is because initially, moving from one second to two seconds (i.e. an increment of one second) represents a one hundred per cent increase in the level of the stimulus used. Later on, e.g. moving from one hundred seconds to one hundred and ten seconds (i.e. an increment of ten seconds) only represents around a ten per cent increase in the level of the stimulus used. When getting a horse which scrambles in the trailer used to the trailer moving, for example, you must only drive for a metre or so in straight lines at first before stopping and rewarding the horse for not 'panicking' or 'scrambling'. You can then build this up metre by metre until your horse can travel quietly for around fifteen to twenty metres. You can then usually get away with increments of five metres until fifty metres, then increments of ten metres until one hundred metres, then increments of fifty metres until five hundred metres and so on! Once he is OK travelling half a mile or so in a straight line you need to repeat the whole process on curves, initially using very large circles with gentle curves and working up to the size of curve needed to turn right or left at road junctions. This kind of training is best done off road, and this example shows how effective *systematic desensitization* can be a very laborious process.

If you make any increment too big, you will see the extreme fear response again. In this instance, simply return to the last successful level used, consolidate this again over at least three sessions and then make the next increment half the amount tried before. If this also fails, return to the last successful level, consolidate this again and try a smaller increase and so on until you reach the size of increment which works.

For *systematic desensitization* to work properly, you need to expose the horse to the frightening *stimulus* just to the point where he begins to get nervous. If you do not reach this point, you are not progressing as he is not actually frightened of the level of *stimulus* being used. It is vital to stop exposure before real 'fear' and the extreme response or dangerous avoidance behaviour begins. You can choose the best level of attenuated *stimulus* to use at the start of your *systematic desensitization* programme by first of all gradually building this in a pre-training 'discovery' session until the point where you begin to see the avoidance behaviour. If you look very carefully at your horse here, you will see some of the first signs of tension before you see the main elements of early avoidance behaviour. In the order in which they appear, the most obvious signs of tension are: straightening of the lip line (the commissure of the mouth where the lips join together and which curls down in a relaxed horse), tightening of the 'chin' so that the lower lip appears tucked in and tightening and tucking, kinking or flinching of the tail. When these signs are seen, tension is rising and the increasing levels of the hormones and neurotransmitters which initially cause these tiny muscle changes in the face and in the back, affecting the way the tail is held, will soon be enough to cause the much more dramatic ones of fear-related avoidance behaviour.

Sometimes the level of *stimulus* required to reach this point is already known. For horses which are traffic shy, most riders know by bitter experience how far away the vehicle needs to be to begin to cause distress. If a horse panics and 'scrambles' in the trailer, it is usually pretty obvious at what point in the journey this occurs. Some horses will panic when the engine starts, others may not panic at all until the extended turn of a large roundabout for example. For many horses the trigger for their panic, which becomes the original *conditioned stimulus* here, is the manoeuvre which occurred just before they slipped or lost their balance and began to scramble to try to right themselves. This is often a sharp right or left hand turn at a junction. This explains the seemingly bizarre willingness of these horses to load. It is not going into the trailer that they are scared of, but the trigger for their panic is a particular movement of the trailer. It is this movement which triggers the panic response in future, so these horses load easily and then 'freak out' along the way whenever this particular movement of the trailer occurs in future.

Any *stimulus*, frightening event or previously painful procedure can be broken down into 'baby steps' for a *systematic desensitization* programme.

For example, in the case of Mrs B and Ally mentioned in Chapter 5 on Learning to Respond, Ally was terrified of having his rug removed after this had caused him a lot of pain from an untreated wound sticking to the rug lining. Here the 'baby steps' involved Mrs B initially just touching the rug, in various different places, then fiddling a little more as she touched it, then touching the straps, then moving these, then just unclipping and re-clipping these, progressing in each few sessions until Ally would stand quietly while she opened the front, then in later sessions to fold the rug back a little and so on, very gradually building up to moving the whole rug loosely over him and eventually in the final sessions removing it. In each session Mrs B would repeatedly do just each tiny element over and over again, changing to the next level in later sessions. It took weeks before Ally could tolerate the whole process sufficiently well for Mrs B to be able to safely proceed with a *counter-conditioning* programme. Ally's routine grooming during this time was effectively a bed bath here, and the training was done in the wintertime using a lightweight, breathable, 'combo' style rug to help to keep Ally comfortable. The *counter-conditioning* stage of his re-training involved Mrs B feeding him his bucket feed one handful at a time immediately after removing the rug, before replacing it to repeat the process for the next handful of feed. Mrs B learned the hard way to check her other horses under their rugs properly every day and was very careful to do this most thoroughly before whisking them off in the future!

Thankfully most *systematic desensitization* re-training programmes are not quite so tricky or laborious. For example, the shoeing process can be broken down into tiny pieces of the whole procedure and an owner can do much of the early re-training here using borrowed 'broken' or old tools as in the example given in Chapter 3 on Training and Time. Initially the horse may need to get used to just having his feet picked up by someone who smells like a farrier, then to tolerate this while the handler is holding a farriery tool in the other hand, then to stand with their leg held up to have their hoof tapped gently with these and so on. This saves some time as the farrier is only required to become involved at the stage where the tools have to be used in a more realistic fashion.

People can be quite inventive when breaking down *stimuli* linked with undesirable reactions. For example:

> I had one client who was really fed up with her horse shying at the flapping loose pieces of wrapper on the big bales of haylage stacked around the farm where she kept him. She had tried to tidy these up and altered her hacking routes on windy days and so on but inevitably more bits came loose and flew onto fences to catch them out. After I had explained the principles of *systematic desensitization* to Miss R, she got busy cutting tiny strips of this and tying these to her horse's stable door bolt handle. Every few days she cut bigger pieces and combined these with various raggedy bits rescued from around the farm. After a few weeks her horse was sufficiently used to these to tolerate them on her feed bucket handles, and she was then able to begin a *counter-conditioning* programme. Miss R began by feeding Zak out of buckets festooned each day with more and more bits of black plastic and built up to laying a plastic version of a 'paper chase' trail for him to find treats all over the place beside the biggest most raggedy pieces! In the end, Zak amused everyone at the farm by developing a great attraction to the big bales he used to be so frightened of.

Re-training using the technique of *systematic desensitization* can be a long and laborious process, but it is often essential to tone down extreme reactions in the first instance before it is safe and practicable to carry out further training. It is particularly useful to help a genuinely nervous horse to relax sufficiently to allow further training to be carried out to complete a re-training programme.

SUMMARY

There are three re-training techniques which are particularly useful when re-training horse with behaviour problems, *shaping*, *counter-conditioning* and *systematic desensitization*.

Where it is difficult in practice to get the horse to do all of the movements required to make up the complete desired response at once, the technique of *shaping* allows you to teach him to do this bit by bit. You *reward* the horse for each 'step in the right direction' making sure each successive reward is only given for steps which are progressively closer to the final goal.

The technique of *shaping* is summarised in the following series of diagrams, using training to load as an example:

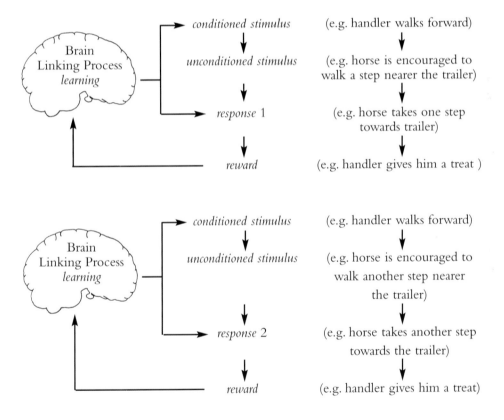

This procedure is repeated and the horse is rewarded each time he gets closer to the trailer.

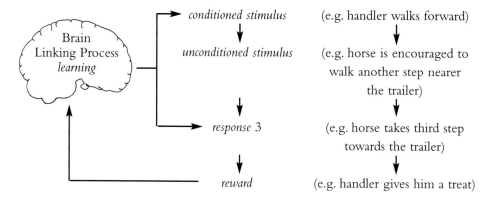

It is very important to *reward* the horse only for each further step in the right direction.

Counter-conditioning is one of the most widely used re-training techniques. Here the horse is trained to react differently to any particular *stimulus* to which he may previously have developed an undesirable *response* using the learning process of *classical conditioning*. The original *stimulus* or trigger for the undesirable behaviour must be correctly identified and then followed by a different *unconditioned stimulus* creating a different desirable response which gives the horse a different *reward*. The most common use of this is to train horses to associate something which previously frightened them with a positive *reward* such as a food treat instead.

The technique of *counter-conditioning* is summarised in the following diagram:

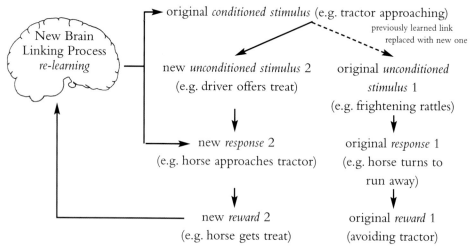

Sometimes a horse is just too scared for *counter-conditioning* to be carried out safely. He may show extreme reactions or become to anxious to eat when exposed to the original frightening *stimulus*. In this case you need to use the technique of *systematic desensitization* to expose the horse to the fear inducing *stimulus* bit by bit, gradually building up to the 'full Monty'. It is particularly important here not to push for too much too soon, to consolidate each stage and to keep the increments between stages very small. This can sometimes be a laborious and time consuming process but is often essential to get a horse to the stage where *counter-conditioning* or another technique can be used to complete his re-training.

The technique of systematic desensitisation is summarised in the following diagrams. Initially, for example, a horse may have learned to be frightened of the sound of clippers in the usual way:

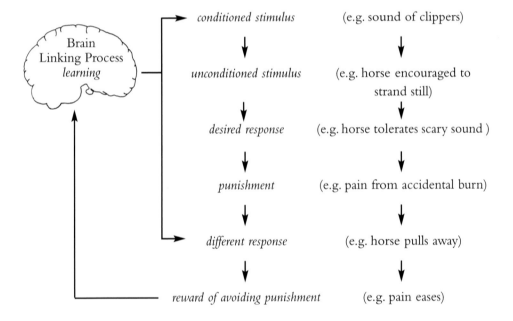

By using a much reduced version of the original *conditioned stimulus*, the undesirable response can be progressively extinguished:

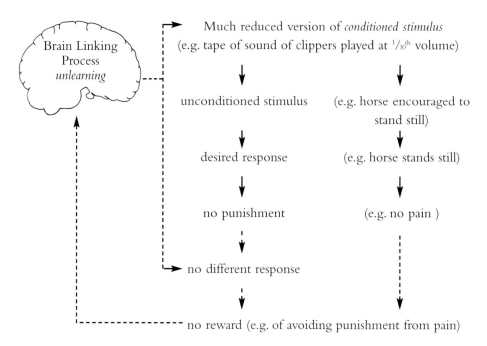

Brain Linking Process *unlearning*

Much reduced version of *conditioned stimulus*
(e.g. tape of sound of clippers played at ¹/₁₀ᵗʰ volume)

↓

unconditioned stimulus   (e.g. horse encouraged to stand still)

↓

desired response   (e.g. horse stands still)

↓

no punishment   (e.g. no pain)

↓

no different response

↓

no reward (e.g. of avoiding punishment from pain)

Once a horse has learned by *systematic desensitization* to tolerate the reduced form of the *conditioned stimulus*, you can begin to train him by the process of *counter-conditioning* to associate this with something *rewarding* instead.

Most successful retraining programmes make use of all of these techniques, and with a little thought they can all be adapted to suit whatever facilities are available and the individual needs of most horses and riders.

Chapter 8

Maximizing Your Horse's Learning Potential

Obviously there are limits on how much and how quickly any horse can learn. This is primarily determined by his genetic make up, his health and the physical constraints on memory as described in Chapter 3 on Training and Time.

There is not a great deal you can do to influence these factors. Many studies have looked at the effects of breed or type of horse, gender and age on rate of learning and retention of learned behaviour and generally found that these factors had no significant effects on learning ability, concluding, as for similar studies in people that learning ability for the most part was an individual characteristic. Young foals are probably learning a great deal more than older horses in the same way as babies acquire information at a phenomenal rate compared with children and adults, but as yet, there are no measured age effects on rate of learning in horses, and it is quite easy to train very old horses – thirty plus. You probably know one horse who is a little 'slow on the uptake' and another who is just too smart for his own good, and can rate all the other horses you know somewhere in between.

A smart horse that learns quickly is not always the easiest to handle as they can learn 'bad' behaviour just as quickly as 'good', and this can lead to problems.

I usually meet my clients at the point when they are at their 'wit's end' with their horse, and when the 'story so far' is a particularly bleak one, I try to brighten things up by pointing out something positive about their horse and his

Fig 8.1. Foals acquire many social and feeding behaviour patterns by operant conditioning from their instinctive responses to Mum's behaviour.

behaviour. It is usually quite easy to find something good about most horses, but there are times when it can be a struggle. There was one horse in particular I shall never forget. She was a 17.2hh Irish mare called Polly, who had completely terrorized her loving owner during the first six months she had owned her.

Polly had repeatedly jumped out of her field over (and through!) all sorts of increasingly reinforced fencing. When electric fencing was used, she discovered how to operate the 'gate' by lifting the insulated handle, which shorted out the fence allowing her to walk through it. She had jumped out of a variety of boxes and kicked holes in any stable where the top door was shut. She could no longer be led as she just pulled away and was manoeuvred from stable to field and back again by bribery with a bucket of feed. She galloped around her field screaming when left in it by herself, even if there were horses in the field next door, but chased and kicked any horse left in her field as a companion. She bit when being groomed and would not let anyone pick up her front feet. On the rare occasions Mrs L had managed to actually tack up and get on this mare, much to Mr L's dismay, she had napped and reared. Polly had been asked to leave a number of local livery yards and a few weeks before I met her, the farrier had 'left in a huff' after an 'altercation' informing Mrs L that neither he nor any of his local colleagues were prepared to try to shoe this mare again.

Most concerned about her increasing inability to take care of Polly, Mrs L had asked her vet to visit to see what he thought could be done to 'settle her'. Being a sensible chap, he took this sorry history from a few feet away from the stable door and suggested she see me first before he proceeded any further with a physical examination!

When I first saw Polly, she was standing loose in small yard calmly eating hay from the ground 'as if butter wouldn't melt'. Mrs L and I leaned over the gate (from the safety of the outside!) and we watched Polly while Mrs L gave me the edited highlights of her recent misdemeanours. She was an ungainly looking horse, with a slightly roman nose and was an odd speckled 'pinkish' roan colour with a very thin and straggly mane and tail. I realised that my options for finding something nice to say about this horse were limited and declining fast as the story unfolded. As Mrs L went through her litany of disasters, Polly stood like an angel, just glancing over at us now and again. I heard how she had kicked the trailer ramp clean off the hinges at one side and then refused to come out until the haynet inside was finished! She had once escaped from her box in an American barn style of yard and opened several other stables, finishing off their horse's haynets and was found lying on a pile of rugs outside the only box with any hay left while their rudely evicted occupants huddled at the far end of the corridor. The tales of further crises went on. When we reached the part where Mrs L was telling me about the farrier and how no-one could pick up this horse's front feet, Polly looked up at us, very casually, and then picked up her front leg herself and stood holding it up! Mrs L was mortified. I had a stitch in my side from trying to keep a straight face. When I finally had to burst into laughter, I found the 'good' in Polly – 'Well,' I said, consolingly 'She's clearly extremely clever.' 'Hmmn' said Mrs L woefully, 'a lot smarter than me that's for sure!' It was just coincidence of course, the leg being lifted peremptory to frustration related pawing as the hay was running out and Polly was keen to get Mrs L's attention by threatening to paw the concrete with her slightly crumbling unshod foot. Luckily, Mrs L could see the funny side too, and we continued with the assessment.

Most of the difficulties with Polly were due to social behaviour and social dominance-related problems. She was very keen to boss other horses around but was not very good at it. She treated people exactly as she treated other horses, and may well have had very limited equine social contact in the past. By finding an appropriate bunch of companions for this mare, to teach her equine social skills in a controlled manner, teaching Mrs L how to behave like a dominant horse with Polly, and teaching Polly some basic 'ground manners', Mrs L was finally able to manage this horse safely, and have all the fun and success show jumping that she had hoped for when she bought her.

So, maximizing your horse's learning ability may not always be desirable! However, should you wish to make the best of your horse's inherent potential here, some of the more practical ways in which you can help are as follows:

- Increase motivation
- Feed memory
- Improve physical fitness
- Minimize distractions
- Minimize stress
- Avoid confusion
- Build on success
- Improve the trainer!

INCREASE MOTIVATION

You may well have tried to encourage your children to do well in exams by promising them a huge present or holiday when they get the desired results. It is much more difficult to explain this sort of deal to your horse!

You can however help to increase your horse's motivation to learn (see Chapter 2 on Rewards, Punishment and Motivation) by increasing the value of *rewards*, like food for example, using variable schedules of reinforcement and training when he is hungry and not trying to sleep as described in Chapter 3 on Training and Time. One study found that very thin horses learned more quickly than fat ones and concluded that this was due to the fact that the thin horses were more highly motivated to work for the food *rewards* being used. Obviously, your horse should be kept well nourished and not too thin or 'starving', but you can manipulate your training schedule to take advantage of the fact that his natural appetite is best after two hours of not eating and this is the point where your horse will be most likely to be motivated by food.

You can also increase motivation for food by using particularly 'tasty' treats. It is much easier to encourage children (and other people) to do things for chocolate than for broccoli. Usually sweet treats work well for horses too at any time of the year. Succulents and juicy things like carrots and apples may be more highly prized in the winter time when there is relatively little juicy grass around and there are many 'healthy' packet crunchy treats available which your horse might be particularly keen on in the summer when his diet, if grazing most of the time, will be relatively soft and low on fibrous material. It also helps to experiment with all sorts of treats to find out which your horse likes best, as there are many individual differences here, as described in Chapter 2 on Rewards, Punishment and Motivation. Rate of consumption is an excellent guide to palatability, and while greed is not usually considered a virtue, it does make a horse much easier to train!

If you are using companions as *rewards* e.g. for a napping horse, these become more attractive if they are absent for a couple of hours, as in such a social animal as the horse, it is not so much 'out of sight, out of mind' as a case of 'absence makes the heart grow fonder'.

Similarly, a 'rest' from ridden work is really only a valuable *reward* if the horse is physically a little tired, so you need to set up this kind of motivation in your pre-training warm up.

FEED MEMORY

Although it has been shown in one study that thin horses learn more quickly than fat ones, this is most likely to be due to increased motivation for food in thin animals, as described above. It would be very interesting to see if this is still the case if something other than food, such as freedom, access to companions or physical comfort were used as the *reward* in this kind of study. However, it is generally assumed that any individual's learning ability is maximized when they are well nourished and not 'starving'. People lose their concentration when they get very hungry, and some surveys of schoolchildren found that a sensible breakfast and lunch which maintain blood sugar levels over a longer period help them concentrate better on their studies. The same is likely to be true for horses as well, as your horse's brain also needs energy from sugar to work. This is also partly why you 'get the munchies' when studying or thinking a lot, as changes in neurotransmitters and other chemicals in your brain create a craving for sugar and high energy tasty things.

Chapter 3 described the way in which your horse's brain prioritizes incoming information, transferring only a tiny part of this to long term memory using neurotransmitters and amino acids to build 'memory' proteins. Neurotransmitters are themselves built from amino acids, and for his brain to work efficiently, a horse must have enough amino acids in his diet. Amino acids are the building blocks of protein, and so it is very important that your horse has enough protein in his diet to maximize his learning ability and literally with which to create his memory.

Many people are concerned that too much protein will make their horse 'hot', 'fizzy' or more reactive and thereby more difficult to manage, and a variety of 'cool mixes' are now available with a low protein content to cater for this market. Generally these 'non heating' feeds have a protein content of around ten per cent. Horses need at least this amount of protein in their overall diet, and as a lot of hay can have a protein content as low as five per cent, many horses do not get enough protein in the winter time.

It is a myth that a high protein diet will make your horse excitable, as any excess protein is simply 'de-aminated' in the liver after digestion and turned into energy stores. In Britain, people think that oats are 'heating' in this way and we replace oats with maize in 'cool mixes'. In America it is maize or 'corn' which gets the blame for excited horses and they use oats instead in their 'steady mix'!

It is actually the balance of particular amino acids which matters here and not really the overall protein content. Grains like oats, maize, soya, split peas and beans are all relatively high in the amino acid tyrosine which is used to make the neurotransmitter dopamine. It is the dopamine which makes a horse alert and reactive. Beans were fed to horses in days of old – and it is likely that the dopamine increasing effect of this is the basis for the saying 'full of beans' to describe liveliness! Grass and rice bran is also very high in protein (usually fifteen to twenty per cent), but grass proteins contain a lot more of the amino acid tryptophan which is used to make the neurotransmitter serotonin. Serotonin makes your horse sleepy and less alert. So, if you want to keep the protein content of your horse's diet high to help with learning and memory, but worried about excitability, it is best to give your horse his protein from feeds like haylage ('pickled' grass with twice the protein content of hay) and cubes made with a high proportion of dried grass (such as traditional pony cubes, including grass nuts) and make sure you feed as much fresh grass and grass based forage as you can as part of an overall balanced diet, reducing the amount of his diet based on cereals and grains. So, not all 'concentrates' help increase concentration!

Ten per cent is the protein concentration of a feedstuff at which tryptohan is most efficiently transferred from the general circulation into the brain across the 'blood brain barrier'. However, if the bucket feed is made from cereals it will be relatively low in tryptophan anyway and represents only a small part of the total daily diet as most horses will eat hay or grass just before and immediately after their bucket feed, so feeding a ten per cent 'cool mix' in this way doesn't really affect neurotransmitter levels and excitability at all in the long term.

It is likely to improve learning ability and be more cost effective in the long term to maximize the grass element and quality of forage in your horse's diet and to make sure his overall diet contains enough protein. If you are feeding only average quality hay, this is best done by feeding a high protein content (e.g. fifteen to twenty per cent) bucket feed.

INCREASE PHYSICAL FITNESS

Obviously, it does not matter how skilful your training, your horse cannot learn to do something he is not physically capable of. Most people are aware of this with regard to height of fences when jumping for example, but forget about complexity in combinations or the athleticism required to work continuously on a circle or to do some relatively simple pieces of lateral work. So, the fitter your horse is physically, the better able he will be to actually do what is being required of him in training.

Most horses show 'handedness' and left to their own devices turn more frequently one way than the other. This makes them move better on one rein than the other and in many horses one hind leg is stronger than the other. Usually, the shoulder opposite the weaker hind leg is stiffer. When moving on a curve with a little inside bend of the head and neck, the inside hind leg has to work a little harder and the outside shoulder has to stretch more. The way horses' legs move in each of the gaits usually means that a horse will walk and trot better on one rein and canter more easily on the other. You can get an approximate indication of the relative strength of the hind legs by comparing their 'curviness' when viewed from a safe distance behind the horse. When he is standing square, the better developed muscle tone of the strongest leg makes this appear 'curvier'. If you offer your horse a treat beside first one shoulder, then the other, you will find out which side he can bend his head and neck most easily towards. This is the stiffest shoulder as the one on the 'outside' of the neck bend is the shoulder being stretched more or the most supple of his shoulders. It helps when teaching your horse a new movement to try it on the rein which is physically the easiest for him i.e. using the strongest hind leg on the inside and the most supple shoulder on the outside, before doing this on the other rein. Obviously it helps his future performance if you work to strengthen the weaker hind leg and increase the suppleness of the stiffest shoulder. Training is facilitated if you teach him a new movement with a few trials on his 'best' side, then work on the other side for around four times the number of trials or length of time used initially and then finish any session with another few trials on the 'best' side again. This makes it physically easier for your horse to carry out new movements correctly and ensures you finish each session on a 'good note', giving you both an easier task on the 'better' side, while improving his physical development by working twice as much all together on his 'weakest' or 'stiffest' side.

One study found that younger horses learned to go through a maze more quickly than older ones. The young horses were mainly three year olds and were also generally a lot more active than the older horses involved in this study. Their greater activity may be why they learned more quickly as a more active horse gives himself more 'trials' (see Chapter 3 on Training and Time) or chances to learn in a maze than one who is naturally less active in this kind of situation, as other studies controlling for activity levels do not find age differences. If your horse is fitter, he will naturally be more active and this may help him to learn tasks depending on voluntary physical activity such as loading into a trailer or lorry.

Training is best done when it is within current levels of physical fitness, as it is important that your horse does not become over tired physically when you are trying to teach him something. If he is physically stressed, his body's natural reaction to this means that his brain will be physically less able to process and store information. Riding an exercise beyond his current level of fitness is necessary to increase his fitness for that movement, but at this point it is harder to *reward* him for doing the movement correctly, as the work involved will be an inadvertent punishment. So, it is best to teach your horse a skill e.g. a step or two of lateral work or a grid exercise when he is physically warmed up but not tired and to be careful to separate the learning skills part of your training from the physical fittening part of any ridden work. Once your horse is fitter, you can then speed training up by packing more 'trials' into any ridden exercise without tiring him or spoiling training by inadvertently punishing him with physical discomfort for doing any demanding movement correctly.

Increasing fitness also improves learning ability in another way. When animals are physically fitter, they have lower base levels of chemicals called endorphins in their circulation. Endorphins are involved in creating the sensations of 'pleasure' or feeling good, in the brain. These feelings are stimulated by a rise in levels of endorphins. For example, when your horse eats something tasty, his levels of beta-endorphin rise for a short time and he 'feels good'. The brain notices the rising effect more readily when base levels are low and where a relatively small increase in beta-endorphin levels has a bigger effect on the overall amount present in the circulation. This means that the same piece of soggy carrot will give a better 'feel good' effect and seem tastier to a fit horse with low base levels of beta-endorphin than it will to a less fit horse with higher base levels in the first place. If your horse is very inactive and 'unfit' then even the tastiest treat may just be a 'drop in the ocean', in terms of changing endorphin levels, making food *rewards* less valuable and training will take longer (as described in Chapter 3 on Training and Timing).

Rising endorphins also stimulate the brain cells that use the neurotransmitter dopamine, where activity results in a generally more reactive and excitable horse. These create the 'buzz' many people experience from exercising beyond their current levels of fitness, as beta-endorphin levels increase for a short time immediately after the exercise in response to the 'stress' of the physical exertion. This is why you feel better or refreshed, more lively and alert immediately after exercise. This is also why your horse seems 'fresh' and may be spookier if he has had a rest from work for a day or two or some time off! Both of you will find learning a little more difficult at this point, and it is better to wait till the 'buzz' is over and your horse gets rid of the 'tickles in his toes' before you try to learn something new that you would like to stick in long term memory. Take a fresh horse for a short hack to settle him before doing any training involving learning skills. In the same way, increasing fitness long term will reduce basal levels of beta-endorphin and result in a generally more relaxed horse, which will be easier to train and also be physically better able to process and store information about your training in his memory!

MINIMIZE DISTRACTIONS

Most teachers will tell you that it is very important to get children's attention in order to teach them effectively. Focussing attention in a distraction-free environment helps free up amino acids and neurotransmitters for the processing and memory storage of information about the task in hand, as described in the Brain and Memory Section of Chapter 3. Keeping your horse's attention also makes him less likely to spook or shy and helps you concentrate on what you are teaching him without wasting time while you are training having to deal with spinning, bucking or napping etc.

This is best done when schooling by frequent changes of bend e.g. every half dozen steps or so with a few steps of 'straight' in between and changing rein in as many different ways as you can think of, never using more than half the school on one rein, as well as including as many transitions as you can manage, even just from walk – halt – walk will do. Walk – trot - walk – halt is an especially good way to settle a livelier horse, and you will keep his attention better if you vary the routine here. Similarly, varying the routine and manner of changing rein really encourages your horse to listen to you. Try riding uneven zig-zag shapes or 'squiggles' or tracing the letters of your name in the school! When hacking out you can use leg yielding or shoulder-in along a lane or track and frequent transitions or little detours to hold his attention.

The most common distraction I come across which can lead to serious problems is discomfort and pain. I cannot emphasize enough the importance of making sure that your horse's 'bad' behaviour or poor performance is not a reaction to discomfort or pain, and the best way of ensuring this is to take advantage of the appropriate professional help which is currently easily available to all horse owners as described below.

MINIMIZE STRESS

The effects of physical stress, pain and the emotions of fear or anxiety all result in changes in brain neurotransmitter levels and the availability of certain amines which reduce your horse's ability to store information about on-going training in his long term memory as already described in Chapter 3. This is why 'cramming' for an exam the night before is only effective short term learning, as information processed against a background of 'stress' and 'tiredness' only lasts a short time, and you forget most of it within a few days. Information processed in this state usually only makes it into short term memory as it is much more difficult for your brain to transfer anything into long term memory under these conditions. This is also why your horse appears to 'back slide' when you take him home after a short intensive course promoting the latest 'alternative' system of working with your horse. The way in which learning is 'crammed' in to these courses means it is unlikely to remain in your horse's long term memory, so do not worry that it is your fault or that you are doing it wrong back home – impressive immediate effects rarely last. It is very important if you want your training to be effective in the long term to keep your horse relaxed, comfortable and pain free.

The only way to ensure that your horse is physically comfortable and pain free is to get appropriate help from properly qualified professionals. The rise in popularity of riding over the past decade or so has led to a corresponding rise in people offering their services in the horse industry. There is a huge increase in people who have 'qualifications' which are gained on a short course, or a series of weekend 'courses' from a non regulated source such as a private individual or company. Unfortunately the law has very little control over quality of service provided by such people and these 'qualifications' might look good on a business card, but in reality mean very little. While some of these individuals join forces and even form associations for marketing purposes and may choose to protect themselves with third party and public liability insurance, they often do not protect their customers by holding full or professional indemnity insurance for the work that they do. These people are not fully accountable for any advice they may offer and the customer is left to pick up the pieces when things go wrong. It is much safer (and more effective and cheaper in the long run!) to use someone whose qualifications are at least degree level from a nationally recognized institution, which has to meet certain standards and be assessed frequently by external examiners who are completely independent and not part of the institution.

The specific qualifications you should look for and how to access proper professional help with most aspects of horse care given below:

Health

Veterinary surgeons

Your vet is the best place to start here. British law requires anyone working or advertising themselves as a 'veterinary surgeon' in England, Scotland, Wales and Northern Ireland to be registered with the Royal College of Veterinary Surgeons (RCVS). Properly qualified vets (i.e. people with certain degrees and experience) are allowed to put the letters MRCVS after their name, signifying that they are 'members' of the Royal College of Veterinary Surgeons. The phrase 'veterinary surgeon' is a protected title, which means that it is a criminal offence to call yourself a 'veterinary surgeon', if you are not MRCVS. As well as maintaining a register of vets, the RCVS is a disciplinary body and will deal with any complaint or concerns you may have about any MRCVS. They can give you the contact details of vets in your area. The British Equine Veterinary Association (BEVA) also keeps a list of its members, who are vets with a particular interest in horses and so may also be able to help you find as local 'horse vet' (see Appendix for list of useful addresses).

There are a great many other people offering services here, including back men, teeth men, dentists, osteopaths, chiropractors, cranio-sacral therapists, horse whisperers and all sorts of massage and alternative therapists. I believe that if your horse could choose, he would phone the vet every time! The most humane and the only safe way in my opinion to ensure your horse's health is properly taken care of is to use your vet. It is a false economy to try various other 'therapies' first. Your vet can diagnose and treat immediately any injury and disease as a cause of pain and undesirable behaviour. Some vets use homoeopathic remedies for some conditions in horses and traditional Chinese veterinary medicine uses acupuncture among other treatments quite successfully for some equine disorders. Your vet may find no obvious physical cause for any problem and he can then refer you to the professional most likely to be able to help, including behaviour consultants, saddle fitters or physiotherapists. He may refer you back to your farrier for corrective shoeing, which is an important part of treatment of many injuries and other diseases or disorders causing lameness. Many vets prefer to refer clients to a properly qualified behaviour consultant after a negative or an inconclusive initial examination to rule out 'naughtiness' or 'learned misbehaviour' before proceeding further with expensive diagnostic tests looking for a physical cause for the presenting problem. In this case, most equine insurance companies will pay or reimburse you for the behaviour consultant's fee as this saves everyone time and money in the long run.

Dentists

Many people advertise themselves today as equine dentists. I believe that this gives the misleading impression that they have a medical degree like a human dentist and are as competent in dealing with equine tooth matters as a human dentist is in dealing with people's teeth. There are short courses available today which anyone, without any previous medical training or any academic or science related qualifications, can attend and thereafter be allowed to call themselves an 'equine dentist'. There is no protected title for equine dentists i.e. it is legal for anyone to print a business card and advertise themselves as an 'equine dentist'. These people may be quite capable of 'floating' or rasping the sharp edges off horses' teeth, but they are not nearly as well qualified as your vet to deal with the many other mouth and teeth related disorders, including abscesses, which cause pain and can lead to behaviour problems. Your vet can treat all these other problems and 'do' your horse's teeth using sedatives which help him make a really thorough examination of your horse's mouth and make the work much easier, safer and quicker for both him and your horse. He can check your horse's overall health at this time too, as many diseases show early signs in the mouth. Most horses need their teeth checking every six months and if you organize a 'teeth checking' visit half way between your annual vaccination check ups, your vet will have a good chance of picking up some health problems before you see major signs yourself.

Most equine vets prefer to do the dental work in their client's horses themselves, but some vets are not particularly good with horses and do not like rasping teeth. It is physically demanding and a particular skill and some veterinary schools now run courses for 'tooth men' and people advertising themselves as equine dentists to teach them how to do this safely and properly. These people can then work under veterinary supervision as an equine dental technician, and this is an excellent way for a busy horse practice to get the routine tooth work done. The vet examines your horse, and treats any problems as required, advising the technician on rasping and any other routine work which the technician can then carry out. You and your horse are safeguarded by the professional veterinary involvement and your vet can manage a lot more equine dentistry with properly trained help.

Physiotherapists
There are many people who refer to themselves loosely as a 'physio' or 'back man' and ply a trade in massage and manipulation, claiming to help your horse. Physiotherapy, as practised by a properly qualified Chartered Physiotherapist is the only sort of manipulation of any kind that I would allow anyone other than a vet to do to my horse. Most horse muscles are too deep below the skin and too large and toned for anyone to physically affect them with their hands from the outside of the horse! It is not physically possible to 'put back' a pelvis or vertebra which is 'out'. Those who claim they are doing this are actually reducing superficial muscle spasms. This only has a temporary effect and may not deal with the problem causing these spasms in the first place.

People with the academic and professional qualifications that allow them to register as a Chartered Physiotherapist have the appropriate degrees with scientific and anatomical training to be able to do this safely on people and operate under strict ethical codes of practice. They are identified by the letters MCSP (Member of the Chartered Society of Physiotheraphy) after their name. Those working with horses or other animals have taken further post graduate training and qualified to specialize here at a nationally recognized academic institution, identified by the letters ACPAT

(Association of Chartered Physiotherapists in Animal Therapy). They will treat your horse at home if possible and only take him in for treatment if they need to use specialized equipment or work so frequently with him that this is the most cost effective way of doing it. They will often show you specific exercises which you can continue at home to complete his rehabilitation and reduce the risk of any relapse.

MCSP Chartered Physiotherapists work by veterinary referral, carry full insurance for this kind of work and are accountable for their professional activities to their registration body. Again, this safeguards you and your horse, as you have some comeback in law should anything go wrong. If your horse is injured whilst being massaged or manipulated by anyone else, you may have no comeback in law at all and your insurance company is unlikely to pay for any veterinary or other treatment required to deal with this. Your vet should have access to the list of registered MCSPs further qualified to work with horses in his area and this can also be obtained from ACPAT (see the Appendix).

Farriers

In Britain, only a registered farrier is by law allowed to shoe a horse or trim feet in preparation for shoeing, and it is also against the law for an unqualified person to call themselves a farrier. Trainee apprentices are only allowed to work under the supervision of the registered farrier training them. The institution which is responsible in law for registering farriers is the Farriers Registration Council (FRC), which registers farriers who have gained the necessary qualifications and experience. Training and professional standards are overseen by the Worshipful Company of Farriers (WCF) and a qualified farrier is entitled to advertise as DWCF, indicating that he has gained his Diploma from the WCF and agreed to work to the professional codes of conduct laid down. He can undertake further training and further qualify as an Associate or a Fellow and advertise AWCF or FWCF accordingly.

If your vet feels that a change to the way your horse is shod or 'special shoes' would help with any lameness or other disorder, he can refer your horse for 'corrective' shoeing. Some farriers do a lot of this kind of work and your vet may be very familiar with someone in your area whom he recommends for this type of work. However, most registered farriers are quite capable of carrying out 'corrective' shoeing to your vet's specifications, and there is often no need for you to suffer the inconvenience of changing farriers. Your vet can check with your current farrier as to his capabilities. The FRC provide a referral form for vets to use and there are ongoing developments aiming to facilitate effective communication between the veterinary and the farriery professions.

If your vet seems critical of the way in which your horse is shod, do let him know how long ago your farrier attended to this, as the foot continues growing and noticeably differs from the 'ideal' shape within a few weeks. If your vet feels that your horse may benefit from a change in the way he is shod, you should give him your farrier's name and details and ask them to deal directly with each other. This allows your farrier to explain to your vet the reasons why he shoes your horse as he does, perhaps already compensating for gait and conformational peculiarities, or to minimize wear or the stresses and strains on the foot to help your horse in his particular discipline or with the kinds of surfaces he is kept and usually ridden on. This way, your horse benefits from the collaborative expertize of both these professions rather than suffering from any breakdowns in communication between them.

It really is also well worth your while being there when your horse is shod whenever you can manage this. You can learn a great deal about your horse from what your farrier sees in the way he wears out his shoes, and you can help your farrier do the best he can for your horse by telling him what work you are doing and what kinds of surfaces you plan to ride on. You should keep strictly to the shoeing interval your farrier recommends for your horse, and most large livery yards have a weekly visit from their regular farrier, so your horse can be slotted in whenever required. It also helps your farrier do the best job he can for you if your horse (and his feet in particular of course!) is reasonably clean and dry, and standing ready for him in a well lit, dry and sheltered area with reasonably level smooth hard standing. It is very difficult for any farrier to shoe a horse well if it is leaping around in a sea of mud on the side of a hill at dusk with the rain lashing in his face!

It is particularly important to use only registered farriers, not only to safeguard your horse's welfare, but you may also find that your insurance company may not pay out for any feet and lameness problems if your horse has been shod by an unregistered person. You can contact the Farriers Registration Council to check whether anyone shoeing horses in your area is registered with them (see the Appendix).

Behaviour

Choose someone with a science degree and ideally a post graduate specialist degree (e.g. MSc or PhD) in animal behaviour from a recognized University, who works by veterinary referral and has not just public liability or freelance instructor's insurance but also holds full professional indemnity insurance for advice on equine behaviour.

There are a great many 'qualified equine behaviourists' or 'horse whisperers' plying a trade today whose qualifications are based on a few weekend courses and who do not safeguard their clients with professional indemnity insurance. They represent a very high risk to insurance companies and the premiums for these people would be prohibitive. They often use only one particular system of handling, based on the guru whose celebrity and methods they are trying to promote and whose videos or gadgets they need to sell to keep the franchise. There is no particular handling or training 'system' which works for all horses and all problems, and you should beware of anyone suggesting that putting your horse through their system will solve your horse's particular behaviour problem. To use a medical analogy, the medicine which cured your neighbour will only help you if you are the same kind of person suffering from exactly the same disease. As some problems are fairly common, like some diseases, promoters of any particular system have a certain amount of success, as occasionally their system is suitable in some cases. Treating all horses or even all 'misbehaving' horses in the same way however is inappropriate.

I was once asked to see a gorgeous Highland pony called Katy whose very knowledgeable owner had 'tried everything' to fix a problem without success. Katy would not let any of her feet be picked up, and had developed all sorts of ingenious ways of throwing her weight around to avoid this. Katy was a little tricky to mount at times, but tolerated most other routine grooming procedures very well. She had a wonderfully full flowing mane, and stood beautifully to have this prepared for showing, but remained intractable when it came to feet. When routine foot care and shoeing were becoming impossible, a variety of people offered all sorts of suggestions. They tried 'being firm' and 'getting really tough', without success. They tried being gentle, working gradually up to offering treats for picking up feet , without success.

When I was finally asked to assess Katy's behaviour, it transpired that the difficulty with her front feet was due to a social dominance-related problem, but the difficulty with her hind feet was due to genuine discomfort and fear which we ultimately traced with veterinary assistance to a very stiff back. This was dealt with (ultimately by having the saddle fit corrected) and two different techniques were required to 'fix' this pony. Using the same technique on all four feet would only have made the problems with two of them much worse, which was why 'all the usual things' had not helped this pony. The girl who rode Katy was given specific exercises to deal with the social dominance issues and 'firmness' advised when picking up the front feet only.

A gentle approach (using *counter-conditioning* as described in Chapter 7 on Practical Re-training Techniques) was advised for picking up the hind feet only, and within a few weeks, this pony was behaving much better – all round, much to the owner's relief!

It is very unusual for two different problems which seemed superficially similar, both causing difficulty in picking up feet, to occur in the same horse at the same time, but this case is a classic example illustrating the importance of a diagnostic approach to re-training horses with 'challenging behaviour'.

A properly qualified professional advisor will ask a lot of questions to first diagnose the root cause of any behaviour problem and then, should this not be pain or discomfort requiring veterinary attention, offer the most appropriate exercises from every known humane and effective training method to help and teach you how to safely manage your own horse at home with everyday equestrian equipment.

Properly qualified behaviour consultants working on ridden problems should also hold some riding instructing qualifications, such as the BHS PTT for example, and have freelance instructors' insurance in addition to that they hold for 'behaviour' work.

If you are not sure what the qualifications any 'behaviourist' advertises actually are, do ask! Unlike the protected titles for veterinary surgeons and farriers, there is as yet no protected title or law to protect you from unqualified people offering behavioural services and it is perfectly legal for anyone to print up a business card as a 'qualified equine behaviourist' and offer their services. They may have some impressive letters after their name which actually only means that they have paid to join some association or other. This does not give you any comeback when things go wrong, as there is not yet any independent professional body overseeing 'behaviourists' in Britain. There is an academic group in America called the Animal Behavior Society (ABS) which has set appropriate standards of academic qualifications and professional experience and registers people who meet their stringent requirements. Unfortunately these are too high to be popular yet in the UK as relatively few people offering help with behaviour problems would qualify for ABS accreditation. There is a however a growing number of suitable post-graduate specialization courses now available in Britain and some academics are working towards the development of a professional register with similarly high standards in Britain via an Association of Chartered Behaviour Consultants which should help here. Any 'behaviourist' with recognized academic and instructing qualifications safeguarding their customers with full professional indemnity insurance will be happy to tell you about it.

Tack

Saddle Fitters

Many tack shops offer a saddle fitting service and some saddle manufacturers run short courses for sales staff on fitting their particular brand of saddle. I believe it is misleading for these people to advertise themselves as 'qualified saddle fitters'. People qualified in the making of saddlery and working in repair and selling of saddlery are entitled to call themselves Master Saddlers under the auspices of the Society of Master Saddlers. A Master Saddler however may not necessarily be qualified in saddle fitting. The Society of Master Saddlers further trains members of their Society in saddle fitting and has developed their own qualification of Qualified Saddle Fitter. Those who pass their rigorous examination are entitled to advertise as a Society of Master Saddlers Qualified Saddle Fitter or SMSQSF.

As described in Chapter 2 on Rewards, Punishment and Motivation, a poorly fitting saddle is one of the most common causes of pain I come across, leading to poor performance and often being a major contributory factor to the development of behaviour problems and riding accidents. Your horse can change shape enough within three months to render a previously well fitting saddle sufficiently uncomfortable as to cause a behaviour problem or accident.

Once when I arrived to teach at a new yard, the owner asked to have a discrete word with me about one particular horse before I began the series of private lessons planned for that day. The horse in question was a very pretty little Connemara cross called Maud and Mrs McC was very concerned that her owner might 'play down' the extent of the problems they had been having. 'I wouldn't get on it if I was you' she advised. 'It's absolutely bonkers. It seems fine one minute and then for no reason at all just freaks out – big time and you really have no control whatsoever. I think she should get rid of it!'

Some instructors do always ride a new client's horse first to get a feel for what is going on, but I find I can usually see more from the ground, so was not planning to ride Maud in any case, unless her rider Miss D asked me to. I was however grateful for Mrs McC's kindness in warning me here, as many people do not spare a thought for the hapless instructor and I have come across plenty who imagine that if a new rider doesn't know the horse's 'bad' points these might miraculously disappear. Believe me the new rider usually discovers them very quickly!

When Miss D came in to the arena for her lesson, I made all the usual enquiries about Maud and how they were getting on. I suspect Mrs McC had had a word with her as well because she did divulge some of the difficulties she and Maud had been having during their first couple of months together and in particular described how Maud would suddenly bolt and only stop when she collided with something or fell over. This is typical of true bolting and is nearly always caused by genuine fear or pain. As I enquired further, it transpired that Maud had generally bolted when turning sharply, especially to the right and could not trot round the short end of the area on the right rein. I did not have too far to look for the most likely cause of her discomfort here. The saddle used was very new and very big and I thought it seemed far too long for this horse. I asked where it had come from. 'Oh the local tack shop were very good and gave me a super deal as they had a special offer on these saddles and I had bought so much other stuff' she replied happily. 'Did they fit it for you?' I asked. 'Oh they said there was no need as it was exactly the right size for a 15hh Connemara cross. I love it! It's a lot nicer than the others I got from the show and a much nicer colour than the one I won in a magazine competition! Anyway, it can't be her saddles that are the problem as they are all brand new and well known makes. She's just the same in all of them and this one cost a fortune!'

She told me how much and I had to agree that it had. Nonetheless I was keen to experiment. We tried all the other saddles in Maud's 'wardrobe' and they all seemed to be a very poor fit in one way or another. I had noticed a rather tatty old saddle in the far corner of the tack room which seemed the right sort of size and shape for this kind of horse. Miss D saw me eyeing it up. 'Oh we can't use that old thing' Miss D exclaimed in horror. 'It's ghastly – poor wee Maud only had that when she came to me. I don't know why I didn't just throw it out. I expect that's why they gave it away with her just to get rid of it!'

Cheering up rapidly now I asked how Maud had been when Miss D had tried her and had she ridden her in the old saddle. It turned out she and Maud had been fine, and managed a lot of loops and trotted around the arena on the right rein no problem. Pursing her lips in disgust Miss D was persuaded to let me try the 'tatty old thing' on Maud and indeed it seemed by far the best fit of the lot. I also horrified the kindly Mrs McC by hopping up for a mini 'test drive' in it myself, and Maud, bless her, went really well - considering the discomfort she must have endured for ages when being ridden in all the very smart and expensive new gear that had been bought for her with the best of intentions by her new owner.

I advised Miss D not to ride Maud again until a properly qualified saddle fitter had been out and checked the old saddle for safety and fit and to take their advice when buying the next saddle for Maud.

This story did have a happy ending as the SMSQSF who attended found the old saddle to be safe and an adequate fit with a few minor adjustments, and was able to take one of the other saddles as a trade-in for a nice new one to Miss D's taste which also fitted Maud properly, and sell the rest giving Miss D much of the money spent so ill-advisedly back. She had enough to buy a half share in a good second hand trailer with the proceeds and I am pleased to recall spent what was left on lessons!

Ideally, as Maud's story shows, you should employ a SMSQSF to help you choose a saddle for your horse, and it is very important that you use a SMSQSF as soon as you acquire your horse and/or saddle to check and refit as required, and follow their advice on frequency of follow up checks required to keep your horse comfortable. The cost of these is usually included in the initial fee. The frequency of re-checking required will depend on the amount your horse changes shape and any noticeable change of weight or muscle tone and fitness may mean you need your saddle adjusted to match. The SMSQSF can advise you on checking fit yourself and the signs to look for which indicate when you should ask them back, and can also advise you on the type of saddle which might best suit you and your horse, as well as advising you on the correct fitting and maintenance of most items of tack. A pamphlet of contact details of SMS Qualified Saddle Fitters listed by geographical area is available from the Society of Master Saddlers.

Loriners
Loriners are professional craftsmen who make metalwork for equestrian use, including bits, stirrups and the metal parts of saddle trees. Their services are not well known outwith the saddlery industry, but you can contact the Worshipful Company of Loriners directly for contact details of loriners or

where to get advice and further information about bits and bitting. They may also be able to give you contact details for reliable 'bit banks' in your area, from which, once you have paid to join, you can borrow or hire a variety of bits to 'try before you buy'. The Worshipful Company of Loriners also run courses on the practical selection and use of lorinery especially for the riding public open to all who wish to learn more about the design, fitting and use of bits (see Appendix).

Instructors

There are many good instructors without formal teaching qualifications and many with these who are not so good! Many successful riders move into instructing or coaching, and while some are excellent, others are not. Someone who has had considerable competitive success may not necessarily be a safe and effective instructor. So, it can be a bit of a lottery trying to find yourself a good instructor.

The British Horse Society (BHS) system at least ensures that any BHS qualified instructor has undertaken some formal training and passed a teaching exam by demonstrating safe and reasonably competent teaching. The first level of qualification here is the Preliminary Teaching Test, denoted BHS PTT, which is only open to those who have first passed two stages of exams in riding and stable management (denoted stages I and II), and a separate exam in riding and road safety (R&RS). Anyone with their PTT who then passes a further stage of exams in horsemanship and stable management (denoted stage III), the Health and Safety Executive First Aid at Work certificate and logs five hundred hours of proven teaching experience qualifies for an assistant instructor's certificate (denoted BHSAI). There are two further levels of instructing qualifications requiring passing of further horsemanship, stable management and teaching exams, denoted BHSII (intermediate instructor) and BHSI (instructor). Individuals, who maintain their BHS membership, keep their First Aid at Work qualification current (by repeat examination at three year intervals) and attend BHS approved training courses each year (including a child protection course if working with children) may be included on the BHS Register of Instructors. This entitles them to cheaper freelance instructor's insurance, and separates these from the many completely unqualified people offering their services as riding instructors, coaches or trainers. Particularly well known and successful instructors may be invited eventually to apply for their Fellowship (FBHS) which is the highest level of qualification within this Society.

Anyone can join the BHS, and the Society maintains Safety, Welfare and Training Departments, offering advice and information to members on these topics, as well as an Approvals Department which inspects riding schools and livery yards on an annual basis. A BHS Approved establishment is likely to be of a higher standard than the average riding school and BHS Approved Riding Schools can train clients towards and award BHS Horse Owner's Certificates, which can be a useful way of learning more about taking care of your horse and improving your riding. The BHS Safety Department also trains Riding and Road Safety Trainers and runs exams here which are open to anyone trained by one of their Approved Trainers. If you have to ride on the road (and it is much safer not to!), then taking part in this kind of training will markedly improve your awareness of how to keep yourself and your horse as safe as possible here. If you or your horse are unlucky enough to be involved in a road accident, having done some training and better still passing your Riding and Road Safety Test may stand you in good stead when insurance companies start wrangling to apportion blame. So, the BHS has a lot to offer horse owners.

It is however best to ask around and look for personal recommendations from people you trust when trying to find a suitable instructor. Go along and watch them give a few lessons before you book yourself in and do not be afraid to try a variety of local instructors to find one you get along with and whose personal style suits you and your horse.

British Equestrian Directory

Published by the British Equestrian Trade Association (BETA), this is the equine equivalent of the *Yellow Pages* and a very useful book to have in your yard. It lists most equestrian professionals by area and contains all sorts of useful contact details for just about anyone and everything in the equestrian industry.

Scottish and Northern Equestrian magazine publish the equivalent Scottish listings every year the Scottish Equestrian Directory, incorporating the BHS Scotland Yearbook.

General advice

The plethora of advice offered to horse owners today is often very confusing, and very few horsy people have the confidence to say 'I don't know' when asked about something equestrian. They usually cannot resist offering an opinion, and if you ask around enough you can get any opinion you like!

I really did have one Scottish lady client who came to me via her vet, after requesting her horse be put down when the advice of a neighbour failed to solve her problem. It turned out that this neighbour was eventually asked his opinion because he came from Ireland! Not wishing to offend he made a few imaginative suggestions which unfortunately only made the problem worse.

Articles in equestrian magazines are often very interesting and many offer excellent advice. You should be aware however that most magazines need advertising income to run and many articles (and websites) are written 'for free' by people wishing to promote a particular product or service or sometimes just themselves! So, do take what is being suggested with the proverbial pinch of salt. Look out for the 'ad' placed strategically within or next to these kinds of features and columns. The most useful articles are those which compare products or ideas and are based on information from a variety of sources, offering a more critical or balanced review of any topic.

When seeking help and advice, it really is best to use people qualified as described above. These people are not just those best qualified in these various areas, but are accountable for their actions and advice given. Most belong to professional organizations which set codes of conduct making sure their members treat their customers properly, i.e. do their best to satisfy you or reimburse you any fees paid, and hold sufficient insurance; including full professional indemnity insurance so that you can be paid adequate compensation should things go wrong. If you are not sure how well qualified anyone is, do not be afraid to ask whether or not they hold professional indemnity insurance as the fee for this usually prohibits anyone without proper academic and professional qualifications.

AVOID CONFUSION

When it comes to training, as anyone who has ever been 'on a course' at work can tell you, it is very important to KISS i.e. Keep It Short and Simple!

I had a charming and relatively wealthy young client who shared her horse with a friend who could not afford regular lessons. Miss F enjoyed her lessons very much and was keen to pass on her new knowledge to her friend Miss

S. I was pleased to help her to do this as it would benefit their horse if they were both working with him in the same way. Miss F asked is she could spend one of her lessons with me teaching her about instructing, so that she could help Miss S improve her riding. I thought this was a very good idea, and looked forward to the session. I thought it would be quite easy and rather fun. Unfortunately, as soon as we started, Miss F began issuing a constant stream of criticism and bamboozled poor Miss S with a series of commands which were just impossible to keep up with. My kind and gentle client had turned into the 'instructor from hell' and Miss S was rapidly reduced to tears! It took a lot of tea and sympathy to restore everyone's confidence and I had to work really hard to explain tactfully that Miss F had just tried to do too much too soon and that no-one could be expected to cope with this amount of information 'overload'. The horse had a nice time however and seemed very pleased with the brevity of our 'training to teach' session!

When training your horse, as well as when teaching someone to ride, it is very important to break the overall task down into simple easy steps and be very clear about what you are teaching him at any one time. For example, to successfully complete a turn on the forehand your horse must accept the contact, flex and bend his head and neck slightly to the side, accept a blocking rein at one shoulder and move his hind leg forward and underneath him when you apply the appropriate leg aid. Most horses find this manoeuvre physically difficult and quickly find effective evasions if you try it all at once, rushing, curling their neck around too much and over-bending, going backwards or pulling and walking off, etc. Most riders also find it difficult to remember all of the different aids they must use together to ask for this correctly. So, when teaching this manoeuvre, I break it up into 'baby steps' and work on each little bit at a time until both horse and rider know each bit very well before asking then to put these together to actually do a quarter turn and so on until they can do the required movement easily. This is the best way to teach horse and rider any manoeuvre.

When training your horse you will get the best results if you minimize scope for confusion by working on only one thing at a time. This may mean that you have to tolerate other aspects of his ridden work being less than perfect for a while until you have 'fixed' each of the building blocks that make up any movement. For example, let him trot too fast or too slow while working on your bend. Then forget about bend and work on adjusting the speed of his trot and so on until you can do each element easily on its own. You can then start putting these elements together one by one, until you can ride the perfect trot circle.

It is also very important to avoid confusion by being consistent in your training, and make sure that you react in the same way to any element of your horse's behaviour all the time. It helps here if everyone involved with your horse, especially livery yard staff, know what you are doing and agree to treat your horse in the same way. This is most important for routine handling procedures such as turn out for example, where it is easy for people to forget the 'new' way of doing things and slip into old habits. This can really ruin any training you may have done to date. Making sure all riders and friends and family who are involved with your horse, however infrequently, are working with him in the same way is vital for effective training.

BUILD ON SUCCESS

The best training is progressive. As described above, you can really help your horse learn by keeping it short and simple, and breaking training up into short, easily achievable targets. You can then start to put these together and build on previous achievements. This is the basis for one of the most useful re-training techniques commonly used known as *systematic desensitization* (as described in Chapter 7). For example, say you are trying to get your horse used to being washed down with a hose. You start with a short piece of dry hosepipe, and add a small damp sponge, then put a little more water on the sponge and so on until your horse will tolerate water trickling from a hose which is wiped off immediately with a sponge and keep building up to the 'full Monty'.

One of the most common mistakes people make is trying to do too much too soon. Choose your target for each session, and repeat your training exercises until your target is reached immediately in a few consecutive sessions. You are then ready to move on and try a target just a tiny bit closer to your eventual goal. If you get problems here, you have just made too big a leap at once and you should return to the previous step, re-consolidate this by repeating this stage a few times and then move on by only half the previously attempted amount and so on, as already described.

When you have achieved your goal in any session, do take a break. You do not have to ride for a whole hour just because you have booked the school for this length of time! Make your training sessions short and sweet. This helps to prevent your horse from getting bored or stale and makes training much more enjoyable all round. Don't aim too high too soon and don't push your luck when all goes well. If your horse achieves your target early in the session, call it a day and finish with a fun hack or a thorough grooming. Too often I see successful show-jumpers teaching jumping and, getting carried away by their initial success, spoil a super training session by pushing people and their horses beyond their current levels of fitness and ability, encouraging them to jump higher and higher or pushing pupils through more and more complicated grids until they have an accident and fall. It is much better to leave things on a good note and pick up later from where you left off, gradually building up to your goal over a series of sessions. As well as helping to prevent accidents, this gives your horse's brain time to consolidate any learning and his body time to get physically fitter alongside any progress in his skills training, facilitating his complete development.

Finally here, horses can *learn to learn*. Many circus horses and successful competition horses actually learn about the training process and begin to look for the *rewards* in new experiences. They realize (by *operant conditioning* as described in Chapter 4 on The Learning Process) that any novel challenge may be a 'new trick' and that a reward is imminent when they 'get it'. They are less likely to be scared of or overexcited by novelty, having learned that this usually means tasty treats (by the process of *counter-conditioning* as described in Chapter 7 on Practical Re-training Techniques) and this makes it physically easier for them to learn new things and transfer information about these into long term memory (as described in Chapter 3 on Training and Time and above). Horses that have 'learned to learn' are likely to be more active and try harder when presented with a new challenge and they are a joy to ride and work with. You can see this happening often in ponies which do a lot of Pony Club games and horses being introduced to cross-country or Le Trec, for example, which after a while may begin to work out what is required and how to deal with novel obstacles for themselves. Any horse that is consistently trained properly can develop his learning skills by 'learning to learn' and this is one of the most useful ways in which you can improve your horse's learning potential.

Fig 8.2. While her rider is busy concentrating on the bottle she has to pick up, this clever little games pony has learned by the process of *classical conditioning* to focus on the next stage and get herself ready for the turn and the gallop back to the rest of the team.

IMPROVE THE TRAINER!

It obviously helps your horse if you strive to maximize your own effectiveness as a trainer. This is not so hard to do and by reading this book you are well on your way!

Knowledge

Learn as much as you can about training techniques and the way in which your horse's brain and memory work so that you can take advantage of this when planning your training and structuring training sessions. People will always be coming up with new ideas and ways of applying this knowledge when training, but a horse will always be a horse! His brain works in the same way today as it did thousands of years ago and will do in thousands of years' time. All effective training techniques have to work using the horse's natural instincts. You can now critically assess any 'new' or 'alternative' handling or training 'system' and see the learning processes by which it works to help you decide whether it will be of any use to you and your horse. You can apply what you know about *rewards*, *punishment* and *motivation* to try to work out how any behaviour problems your horse may have developed began and are being maintained. This gives you a head start in dealing with them.

Riding and handling techniques

Obviously your own physical ability and level of skill here is very important, both in keeping you safe and in helping you communicate effectively with your horse. Tips on improving this were given in Chapter 2 and regular lessons are valuable to anyone, no matter what their current level of skill. I try to have a lesson every month or so and I always find it very useful to have another 'expert's' eyes looking at what my body is really doing and what my own little horse is getting away with!

Planning and focus

The advantages of planning your training so that you can do this in comfort and at your own convenience were detailed in Chapter 3. If you are stressed, tired, hungry, rushing or anxious you will not be working to the best of your ability as a trainer and you cannot expect your horse to do his best for you in these circumstances. This is when people are most likely to make mistakes, at best spoiling previous training and at worst causing an accident. Making sure you have a clear training target for each session, and organizing these to minimize distractions and interruptions will help you as much as your horse in the ways described above. Break your goal into 'baby steps' and concentrate on one step at a time. Consolidate achievements by repeating these over the next few sessions. This helps in particular with long term memory retention. You can quantify and record your horse's progress in a training diary or even plot developments along a learning curve to show yourself how well you are doing and encourage yourself to persevere with your training programme. Do not however be tempted to persevere at all costs. There will be times when the weather, various crises and all the things life throws at us intervene and when the only sensible thing to do is to cancel any planned training session and continue from where you left off another time.

Fig 8.3. Lessons can begin at an early age.

Fig 8.4. This rider is learning how to encourage this young horse to engage her abdominal muscles and stretch her neck and back in the early stages of their training.

Fig 8.5. Lessons can be conducted in any area where it is safe to ride and disturbances unlikely.

Patience

When it comes to working with horses, patience truly is a virtue. Some people who are instinctively very 'good with horses' often don't know what it is that they do which works, but you will find that they tend to be naturally laid back, calm and patient types of people. So, when training, try your best to remain calm and relaxed.

I spent one wonderful summer at the University of Pennsylvania, working at their New Bolton Center for Veterinary Medicine which has some of the best teaching and horse behaviour research facilities I have ever come across. It is set in glorious countryside with reliably fabulous weather and I drove everyone mad by commenting on this in typically British fashion every day! I was lucky enough to be invited to stay with the Departmental secretary, herself a very successful horse trainer and breeder. One day we were talking about equestrian equipment and what was necessary and what was not. Mrs

A listed amongst her essentials for teaching horses to load, two jugs. I was intrigued. Imagine my surprise when this very respectable lady divulged that these were for wine for the trainers so they stayed 'mellow' and did not lose their patience, should the waiting game become tedious!

Do take your time and do not be tempted to rush or try to stick to an impossible schedule. Know when to stop and take a break. Remember that five minutes of 'correct' training is much better than an hour of muddling along and it takes time and lots of repetition for most ordinary training to get into your horse's long term memory.

Practise

Experienced trainers can make it look very easy, but successful training is a lot harder than it looks, and it is necessary to practise and the more training you do properly, the better you will become. The choreography of a training session can be as complex as any ballet sequence. Training horses is physically demanding and can be mentally quite exhausting as you really need to concentrate on the task in hand and make sure that you are not doing anything to inadvertently spoil your training as you move around or work with your horse. You can help your horse a lot more here if you practise training on simple everyday procedures or 'party tricks', before you need to do any serious retraining to fix a problem. Very few surgeons would relish the thought of their first solo operation being a life or death matter for a member of their own family! If you need to use a technique, such as lungeing to help to deal with a problem, it is better to first have some lessons and then practise on a well behaved horse who is used to being lunged before trying it yourself on your own 'naughty' or 'fresh' horse.

If you practise and apply the training techniques described in Chapters 4, 5, 6 and 7 to your everyday handling and riding, you may be pleasantly surprised at how much your horse's general performance improves. You will then find it much easier to teach him new skills and movements or to fix anything that goes wrong.

Confidence

Chapter 2 described the dangers of over-and under- confidence. Improving your knowledge and practising will help both here, and you should only attempt anything yourself when you are confident that both you and your horse are capable of it. Training in a safe environment doesn't just help you avoid accidents; it helps you ride and train with confidence. Clear away any old gates, litter, poles and jump stands not in use and all other hazards from your riding area. If the surface is flooded or slippery or too uneven, do not try to do fast work, jump or do complicated grids etc. Have the confidence to cancel a planned session should 'life' intervene and reschedule it. Make sure you, any helpers and your horse are wearing the appropriate safety gear, such as protective boots for your horse, steel toe cap boots for people, riding hats and gloves (especially for loading and all handling training on the ground as well as when riding) to help with confidence all round.

If you are not sure of anything, do ask for appropriate help. This is not a sign of weakness but a sign of strength of character. Knowing when to quit and when you need help is one of the most important aspects of your training knowledge. Knowing 'what you don't know' is a most useful piece of knowledge and being aware of your own limits will help you keep within these when training and enable you to do this training with confidence.

SUMMARY

Your horse's ability to learn is to some extent limited by his genetic make up and other factors. You can however help him to do his best if you keep him relaxed and focussed, make sure he is comfortable and physically capable of what you are trying to get him to do. Be consistent, and break down complex movements into simple elements, teaching him one step at a time. Ignore 'bad' behaviour and reward 'good'. Do not be shy of asking for help if required and make sure you use properly qualified people for advice and assistance where needed.

So relax and be patient. Keep training simple and take one step at a time. Plan ahead, take care for your own safety and that of your horse and most of all enjoy working with him. Finally, if you are stressed the chances are your horse will be too – so take it easy, keep yourself safe and have fun training your horse!

Appendix

Useful Addresses

ACPAT
Association of Chartered Physiotherapists and Animal Therapists,
21 Woodland Close, Penenden Heath, Maidstone, Kent ME14 2EX
secretary@acpat.org.uk or call via CSP on 020 7306 6666

Association of Chartered Behaviour Consultants
PO Box 12981, Dalkeith, Midlothian EH23 4YF

BETA British Equestrian Trade Association
Wetherby, Stockfield Park, West Yorkshire LS22 4AW
www.beta-uk.org or call 01937 587062

British Equestrian Directory
Published by BETA Equine Management Consultants division
www.beta-int.com or call 01937 582111

British Horse Society
Stoneleigh Park, Kenilworth, Warwickshire CV8 2XZ
Call 01926 707700

Chartered Society of Physiotherapy
14 Bedford Row, London WC1R 4ED
enquiries@csp.org.uk or call 020 7306 6666

Farriers Registration Council
Sefton House, Adam Court, Newark Road, Peterborough PE1 SPP
Call 01733 319911

Royal College of Veterinary Surgeons
Belgravia House, 62-64 Horseferry Road, London, SW1P 2AF
Call 020 7222 2001

Scottish Equestrian Directory
Hillaine Publishing, 26 Blairs Road, Letham, Forfar, Angus DD8 2PE
www.scotequest.com or call 0845 130 7669

Society of Master Saddlers
Kettles Farm, Mickfield, Stowmarket, Suffolk IP14 6BY
Call 01449 711642

Worshipful Company of Loriners
Projects Manager and Lorinery Course Co-ordinator, The Sling, Mill
Lane, Eckington, Worcestershire WR10 3BG
patricianassauwilliams@hotmail.com or call 01386 751695

Index

ABC of learning 9, 30
  antecedents 10–20
  behaviour 20–4
  and classical conditioning 114–15
  consequences 24–9
  and operant conditioning 101–4
accidents, traumatic 28, 71–2, 88, 93–4
adrenalin 143
'advance-retreat' training methods 29
advice, sources 208–9
age of horse 188, 194
aids of rider 69, 119–27
  canter transitions 120–2
  developing 'feel' 74
  extinction of responses 162–3
  habituation of horse 158–9
  timing of 19–20
  training of young horse 139–40
  see also riding techniques
Ally 55, 181
alternative therapists 122, 124–5,
    196–7, 198
alternative training courses 162
amino acids 92
Animal Behaviour Society (ABS) 203
antecedents 10–20, 128
  see also stimuli
anticipatory behaviour 142–3
antidepressants, tricyclic 97
anxiety 64–5, 95
Arab horse 53
associations 19, 30
athlete, response to cheering 137–8
attention, focussing horse's 195–6
attention seeking behaviour 31–2,
    69–70, 89, 104–5
  door banging 31–2, 89, 104–5
  nipping/mugging people 105–7

azoturea 64–5

back pain 204–6
'bad' behaviour
  extinction of 162–7
  rewarding 68–70, 89, 104–5
'bad' habits, learning/teaching 22, 71
bandages 51
behaviour 20–4
behavioural consultants 37, 201–4
  qualifications 201–2, 203–4
Ben 83–4, 172–3
beta-endorphins 194–5
Billy 105–6
Bindra 11–12
birds, imprinting 155
bitless bridles 48
bits
  advice on 206–7
  materials 48–9
  types 46–8
Blue 12–13, 175–6
body language 124
bolting 205
boots, horse's 51
brain, function of 89–97
'breaking' of horse 139, 161
breeds of horse 90
bridging stimuli 78, 134–8, 149–50
bridles 44–6, 48
British Equestrian Directory 208
British Horse Society 203, 207–8
brushes, grooming 40–1
Buckley 71–2

calming 73
calming agents 96–7
canter

on lunge 115
  ridden transitions 120–2, 141–2
case history, importance of 144
catching of horse
  by chasing 111–12
  'by curiosity' 110–11, 172–3
cavesson, lungeing 50–1
Chang Tzu 62–3
cheering, response to 137–8
circadian rhythms 84–5
circus trainers 86, 135–6
Clara 75–6, 122
classical conditioning 29, 113–15,
    125–7, 213
  brain linking process 128–30
  learning by 115–19
  training by 119–27
Clever Hans 17, 126
clicker training 13–14, 136, 137, 157
clicking, tongue 136–7
clipping
  fear of 10, 174–5, 179
  habituation to 160–1
  need for 51–2
coat, horses' 52–4
communication, trainer-horse 17
companions 74, 77
conceptual learning 90
conditioned stimuli 114, 116–19
  strings of 32, 138–45, 150–2
conditioned stimulus-unconditioned
    stimulus response 128
conditioning 29
  see also classical conditioning;
    operant conditioning
confidence 66–8, 217–18
confusion, avoiding 209–11
consequences 24–9, 101–3

classical conditioning 128–9
consistency 29
first experiences 25–6
repetition 27–9
timing 26–7
consistency 29, 30
copying, learning by 21–3
counter-conditioning 32, 173–8
brain linking processes 184–5
crib-biting 22
cross-country jumping 22–3
cultural knowledge 161

Dales pony 54
déjà vu 92–3
demonstrations, alternative
horsemanship 80
dentist, equine 47, 198–9
desensitization, systematic 82, 160–1,
178–82, 185–6
diet, and memory 191–3
discrimination learning 90
distractions, minimizing 195–6
dogs, Pavlov's 113–14, 143
'doing it himself' 23–4
door banging 31–2, 89, 104–5
dopamine 192
dressage training 173
drinkers, automatic 16
drugs 96–7

electric fencing 101–3, 110
Ellis, Dr R N W 63
endorphins 194–5
extinction 152, 162–8

farrier 40, 200–1
horse's fear of 132–3
preparing horse for 36, 82–3
qualifications and registration 200
systematic desensitization of horse
182
see also shoeing
fear
habituation to stimuli 160–1
and learning 95, 178–9
systematic desensitization 178–83
feed supplements 96–7
feeding 191–3
feet, picking up 35, 36, 69, 117–18,
176
fencing, electric 101–3, 110
first experiences 25–6
fitness

horse 58–9, 193–5
rider 57
fixed ratio schedule of reinforcement
87, 172
'flashback' 93–4
flooding 160
flying starts 119
foals 23–4, 187, 188
handling 155–7, 158
food rewards 71–3
feeding method 71, 73
increasing motivation for 190–1
foods, heating 192
'freezing' behaviour 11–12

gag bits 48
gates 34–6
generalization 24, 131–4, 148–9
George 64–5
Ginger 146
girths 43
goals 211–12
grass reins 29
grazing
finding shelter 109
management 62–4
nutritional value 192–3
grooming 39–41
mutual 73
grooming brushes 40–1

habituation 23, 25, 152–61, 175
brain linking process 167
Hackamores 48
hacking 56
see also shying; spooking; traffic
shyness
halters
pressure type 120
rope 49–50, 124–5
halting, led horse 120
Hamish 107–8
'handedness', of horse 193
handling
accidental rewards 68–70
classical conditioning 122–7
foals 155–7, 158
improving techniques 214
inadvertent punishment 34–68
picking up feet 35, 36, 69, 117–18,
176
see also leading horse
'happy' feelings 91
Harry 118, 176, 178

hay-dipping 165–6
headcollars 49–50, 120
rope 49–50, 124–5
health of horse 197–200
hearing 15, 16
herbal calmers 96–7
Highland pony 53, 107–8
hooves, picking up 35, 36, 69, 117–18,
176
Hopes, R 63
hormones 143
'humane' bitting systems 47
'humane' girths 43

Iceland, riding techniques 147
imprinting 155
indoor arena 56
instrumental learning, see operant
conditioning
intelligence, of horse 90, 187
irrelevant stimuli 145–7, 152
isolation anxiety 64–5

Jigsaw 17–19, 143
'join up' 38–9, 111–12
jumping
causes of problems 26, 66–8
coloured fences 157–8
grids 20

knowledge
cultural 161
of trainer 213–14

latent learning 81
lazy horse 107–8
lead ropes 49–50, 144
bungee 164
safety of 124
leading horse 120, 144–5
doorways and gates 34–6
headcollars and halters 49–50,
124–5
method 37–9
use of strings of conditioned stimuli
144–5
learning
ability for/rate of 81, 90–1, 187
restrictions on 91
to learn 212
learning curve 98–9
Libby 44–6
loading 23–4, 61–2, 170
'burling' method 177

'natural horsemanship' methods
    112–13
  safety 170, 172
  shaping 170
  time needed to resolve problems
    79–80
loriner 206–7
lorry 60, 61
lungeing
  equipment 50–1
  use of voice commands 115

magazines, equestrian 209
Maud 204–6
maze performance 194
memory 89–97
  and diet 191–3
  long term 92, 94–5, 100
  short-term 92
men, horse's fear of 133
Mercury 79–80
Miller, Bob 155–6
Minton 159–60
mirrors, riding arena 57
motivation 75–8
  maximizing 33, 190–1
mounted games ponies 119, 213
mouth, pain in 47
move over 122–7
mud fever 83–4

nappy horse 48, 71, 74
'natural horsemanship' methods 29,
    32–3, 112–13, 122, 124–5
negative reinforcement 28
neurotransmitters 92, 93, 95, 97, 143,
    192
nipping 105–7
nosebands, drop/flash 49
novelty, effects of 25–6
nudging 105–6
numnahs 42–3

observational learning 21–2
operant conditioning 29, 101–4, 128
  learning by 104–9
  strings of stimuli 142–4
  training by 109–13
over-learning 96, 100

pain
  back 204–6
  behaviour due to 37
  mouth/teeth 47

'party tricks' 117, 125–7
pasture, *see* grazing
patience 24, 216–17
Pavlov, Ivan 113–14, 143
perceptions
  horses' (of stimuli) 15–19
  of time 91–2
phenothiazine-based drugs 97
physical problems 36–7
physiotherapists 199–200
placebo effect 97
play behaviour 102
Polly 188–9
ponies
  mounted games 119, 213
  riding school 28–9, 115–17, 158–9
positive reinforcement 28
practise 217
Preliminary Teaching Test 207
pressure, relief from 74
progress, measuring 97–9
progressive training 211–12
protein, dietary 192
pulling back 118, 176, 178
  re-training horse 163–4
punishment 28, 29, 32–3
  consequences of 88
  delayed 27
  inadvertent/accidental 33, 34, 57–8,
    129
  use in operant conditioning 111–13

qualifications
  alternative therapists 196–7, 198
  behavioural consultants 201–2,
    203–4

racehorses 11–12, 144
rate of learning 81, 90–1, 187
re-training methods
  brain linking processes 183–5
  counter-conditioning 32, 173–8
  shaping 169–73
  systematic desensitization 178–82
  using new conditioned stimuli 147
rein back 36–7
reinforcement
  negative 28
  positive 28
  schedules of 28, 87–9
repeats, *see* trials
repetition 94–5, 96
'respect' 29
reversal set learning 90

rewards 31
  accidental/inadvertent 68–70, 89,
    104–5
  choice of 76–8
  effectiveness 33, 75
  food 28, 71–3
  increasing motivation for 190–1
  timing of 33, 78
rhabdomyolysis 64–5
rhythms, daily/circadian 84–5
ridden problems
  causes 14, 28–9, 146–7, 163
  and saddle fitting 204–6
  use of consultants 203
rider
  aids, *see* aids of rider
  body/position awareness 14, 57–8
  confidence 66–8
  'feel' 74
riding instructors
  qualifications 203, 207–8
  voice commands 116–17
riding school horses/ponies 28–9
  classical conditioning 115–17
  extinction of responses 163
  habituation to rider's aids 158–9
riding schools, BHS approved 208
riding surfaces 55–7
riding techniques
  accidental reward of horse 69
  improving 214
  inadvertent punishment of horse
    57–8
  rewarding horse 74
  see also aids of rider; rider; schooling
Road Safety training 208
road surfaces 56
road traffic accidents 28, 71–2, 93–4
rodeo riding 161
rope headcollar/halter 49–50, 124–5
Rory 157–8
round pen work 111–12
rubber matting 60
rugs 51–5
  fear of removal 55, 181–2
  need for 54

'sacking out' 160
saddle fitters 204, 206
saddles 42, 204–6
safety 32, 33, 218
  loading 170, 172
  tack and equipment 43, 124–5
sand, as riding surface 55–6

saturation therapy 160
schedules of reinforcement 28, 87–9
  fixed ratio 87, 172
  variable ratio 88–9, 100
schooling 193–5
  and fitness 57, 193–5
  keeping simple 210–11
  maximizing learning 193–5
  methods 58–9
  minimizing distractions 195–6
  surfaces for 55–7
sedative drugs 97
senses, horses' 15–19, 132
serotonin 97, 192
Shadow 133–4, 176
shaping 98, 169–73, 183
shelter, finding 109
Sherry 126
shoeing
  corrective 200
  habituation to 154
  preparation of horse for 82–3
  systematic desensitization 182
  see also farrier
shying 12–13
  systematic desensitization to stimuli
    182
  see also spooking
sight 15, 16–19
Silver 110
Simpson, Heather 33
smell, sense of 16, 132
social dominance-related problems
    38–9, 163, 189
sounds
  perception of horse 1–15, 16
  as stimuli 135–6, 144–5
spooking 12–13, 14, 87–8, 133–4
  as work avoidance 166–7, 177
  see also shying
spurs 14
stable doorway 34
stabling 64–6
'starting' of horse 139
stimuli
  bridging 78, 134–8, 149–50
  conditioned 114, 116–19
  generalization 24, 131–4, 148–9
  irrelevant 145–7, 152
  perceptibility of 15–19
  specificity 10–14
  strings (chains) of conditioned 32,
    78, 138–45, 150–2
  timing 19–20

unconditioned 114
stimulus-response 103–4
stress 95, 196–7
sunlight 54
superstitious learning 145–7, 152
'sweet metal' bits 48–9
systematic desensitization 82, 160–1,
    178–82
  brain linking processes 185–6

tack 41–2, 204–7
  bits 46–9
  girths 43
  headcollars 49–50, 124–5
  lungeing equipment 50–1
  numnahs 42–3
  rugs 51–5
  saddles 42, 204–6
targets 11–12
TEAM TOUCH system 164–5
teeth 47, 198–9
Tellington-Jones, Linda 164–5
thalamus 90, 92
ticklish horse 40–1
time
  perception of 91–2
  for training 79–80
timing
  of antecedents/stimuli 19–20
  of consequences 26–7
  of rewards 33, 78
  rider's aids 19–20
  of training programme 82–5
tongue clicking 136–7
traffic shyness/fear 28, 174, 181
trailer 59–62
  horse panicking in 179–80, 181
  loading problems 23–4, 61–2,
    79–80, 112–13, 170, 172, 177
training programme, planning 81–7,
    95, 100, 214
training sessions
  frequency 81, 85–6, 95
  length 85
  timing 84–5
transitions 140–1
  canter 120–2, 141–2
travelling 59–62
  foal 23–4
  problems during 179–80, 181
  speed of driving 62
  see also loading
treats
  feeding 71, 73

nipping/mugging people for 105–7
  see also rewards
trials (repeats) 27–8, 80–1, 87
  frequency of 96
  number of 85, 89, 96
tricks, training 117, 125–7
triggers 114
tryptophan 97
turn on the forehand 210
tying up (pulling back) 118, 163–4,
    176, 178
'tying-up' (azoturea) 64–5
tyrosine 192

un-learning (extinction) 162–7
urination, straining/'pretending' 107–8

ventilation, stabling 65–6
veterinary surgeon 37, 40, 61, 197–8
  dental work 199
  and farrier 200–1
  fear of 132–3
  qualifications and registration 197
  referrals 198
vision, *see* sight
visualization 142
voice 137
  calming horse 73
  as conditioned stimulus 115,
    116–17
  shouting at horse 159–60

water, drinking 16
weather change, horses' detection of
    142
welfare of horse 32, 33
Western style riding 147
whip, use of 135
whistles 135–6
winter coat 52–4
withers, rubbing 73
wounds
  treatment 39–40
  untreated causing behavioural
    problem 55, 181

Zak 182